Language, Bureaucracy and Social Control

Real Language Series

General Editors:
Jennifer Coates, Roehampton Institute, London
Jenny Cheshire, Universities of Fribourg and Neuchâtel, and
Euan Reid, Institute of Education, University of London

Titles published in the series:

David Lee Competing Discourses: Perspective and Ideology in Language
Norman Fairclough (Editor) Critical Language Awareness
James Milroy and Lesley Milroy (Editors) Real English: The Grammar of English Dialects in the British Isles
Mark Sebba London Jamaican: Language Systems in Interaction
Janet Holmes Women, Men and Politeness
Ben Rampton Crossing: Language and Ethnicity Among Adolescents
Brian V. Street Social Literacies: Critical Approaches to Literacy in Development, Ethnography and Education
Srikant Sarangi and Stefaan Slembrouck Language, Bureaucracy and Social Control

Language, Bureaucracy and Social Control

Srikant Sarangi and Stefaan Slembrouck

LONDON AND NEW YORK

First published 1996 by Addison Wesley Longman Limited

Published 2013 by Routledge
2 Park Square, Milton Park, Abingdon, Oxfordshire OX14 4RN
711 Third Avenue, New York, NY 10017

First issued in hardback 2014

Routledge is an imprint of the Taylor & Francis Group, an informa business

Copyright © 1996, Taylor & Francis.

All rights reserved. No part of this book may be reprinted or reproduced or utilised in any form or by any electronic, mechanical, or other means, now known or hereafter invented, including photocopying and recording, or in any information storage or retrieval system, without permission in writing from the publishers.

Notices
Knowledge and best practice in this field are constantly changing. As new research and experience broaden our understanding, changes in research methods, professional practices, or medical treatment may become necessary.

Practitioners and researchers must always rely on their own experience and knowledge in evaluating and using any information, methods, compounds, or experiments described herein. In using such information or methods they should be mindful of their own safety and the safety of others, including parties for whom they have a professional responsibility.

To the fullest extent of the law, neither the Publisher nor the authors, contributors, or editors, assume any liability for any injury and/or damage to persons or property as a matter of products liability, negligence or otherwise, or from any use or operation of any methods, products, instructions, or ideas contained in the material herein.

ISBN 13: 978-1-138-83603-7 (hbk)
ISBN 13: 978-0-582-08622-7 (pbk)

British Library Cataloguing-in-Publication Data
A catalogue record for this book is
available from the British Library

Library of Congress Cataloging-in-Publication Data
Sarangi, Srikant, 1956–
 Language, bureaucracy, and social control / Srikant Sarangi and Stefaan Slembrouck.
  p. cm. -- (Real language series)
 Includes biliographical references and index.
 ISBN 0-582-08622-1 (pbk.). -- ISBN 0-582-08623-X (cased)
 1. Bureaucracy, 2. Bureaucracy--Language. 3. Conversation analysis. 4. Discourse analysis. 5. Social control.
 I. Slembrouck, Stefaan, 1963– . II. Title. III. Series.
 JF1501.S27 1996
 350--dc20   95-45637
                                                CIP

Set by 7 in 10/12pt Sabon

For our parents
and our parents-in-law

Contents

Foreword	ix
Acknowledgements	xii

1 Language, bureaucracy and social control 1
Bureaucracy 1
Bureaucracy and social control 4
Language and bureaucracy 6
Synopsis 13

2 Bureaucratisation and debureaucratisation in contemporary society 17
Introduction: what discourse practices are construed as bureaucratic? 17
Bureaucratisation and debureaucratisation 19
Changing discourse practices as action and as process 21
The analysis of language use 26
The language-situation dynamic 28
Social control as an area of struggle 31
Conclusion 33

3 The pragmatics of information exchange in bureaucratic discourse 36
Introduction: information exchange as a focus of study 36
Bureaucrats seeking information and clients giving it 38
Interpreting information exchange in pragmatic terms 45
Reversing the roles: clients seeking information and institutions avoiding giving information 53
Conclusion: regulated information exchange and social control 57

viii CONTENTS

4 Role behaviour in discourse 61
Introduction 61
Modes of talk and multiple role behaviour 62
Discourse roles 66
Shifting role relationships and the construction of social
identities 71
Role perception in discourse 80
Conclusion 82

5 The client's perspective: clients as citizens 87
Introduction 87
Challenging the inhuman face of bureaucracy 88
Creating an edge over the institution 91
Talking to bureaucrats in order to maintain
non-clienthood 93
Client's response to institutional failure: the case of
lost mail 95
Conclusion 117

6 The bureaucrat's perspective: citizens as clients 123
Introduction 123
Alarming the client 123
Maintaining bureaucracy through official documents:
forms and leaflets 127
Conclusion 142

**7 The discourse of mediation: bureaucrats' dilemma and
clients' wisdom** 146
Introduction 146
Social workers attempting to redress the imbalance 148
Counselling institutions 153
Institutional monopolies over mediation 169
Conclusion: socio-economic struggles over multi-tier
bureaucracy 177

8 Instead of a conclusion 181

Bibliography 191
Appendices 195
Index 232

Foreword

There are two powerful interlocking tendencies affecting contemporary public discourse in Britain and other similar societies. The first is a tendency to what we might call the 'marketisation' of discourse – the extension of the discursive practices of commodity markets to, for instance, professional and public service domains. An example is the proliferation in these domains of forms of advertising discourse. The second is the 'conversationalisation' of public discourse, the appropriation and simulation in public discourse of features of conversational discourse. These changes in discursive practices are part of wider processes of social change affecting late modern societies – the incorporation of vast new areas of social life into markets, and the colonisation of ordinary life by economic and bureaucratic systems. Social change in advanced capitalist societies is increasingly centred upon cultural change, and cultural change often takes a pre-eminently discursive form. Consequently, analysts of discourse are in a position to make a substantive contribution to understanding the fundamental processes of social restructuring which dominate contemporary life, by investigating tendencies such as the marketisation and conversationalisation of public discourse. This book takes a significant step in that direction in its analysis of the discursive aspect of major current changes in the ways in which bureaucracy works in modern societies.

An apparently paradoxical feature of contemporary public institutions is that while there are many signs of a retreat from traditional forms of bureaucratic practice, there is at the same time ample evidence of major new inroads in bureaucratisation. Take the case of universities. If one looks at the publicity material universities produce to attract students, the bureaucratic apparatus of complex conditions and procedures for entry seems to have been replaced by an approach which entices individuals to sample

x   FOREWORD

the goods on offer. Yet the widespread experience of people working in universities is that processes and relationships are being bureaucratised – what could be achieved by an informal word not long ago now often requires a formal written procedure, and aspects of relations between academic staff and students or academic staff and assistant staff which have long been rooted in practice and experience may now be governed by written codes of practice. Sarangi and Slembrouk centre these contradictory tendencies in their book through an identification of twin processes of bureaucratisation and 'debureaucratisation' (this term is perhaps misleading, because as they point out what appears to be debureaucratisation may be no such thing). The key point is that these are contradictory dimensions of a single process of social change, and not actually at all paradoxical. The marketisation of higher education which pushes universities to sell their wares to potential 'customers' and so 'debureaucratise', also pushes them to implement processes of 'quality control' which entail intensive new forms of bureaucratisation. Whether universities look more or less bureaucratic than they once were depends upon where you are standing within or outside them, and the same is true of other public institutions.

A strength of the book is that Sarangi and Slembrouck take the analysis of bureaucratic language beyond the analysis of texts to the analysis of bureaucratic interactions, specifically inter- actions of information exchange. There is a corresponding emphasis on pragmatic analysis, yet the authors insist upon the limitations of pragmatics and the need to combine it with critical discourse analysis, so that for instance attention to individual processes of face negotiation in specific exchanges does not lead the analyst to ignore social and cultural changes which frame and shape such exchanges and are constituted by them. A limitation of some work in critical discourse analysis is that it has been overly textual and has lacked this interactional focus; the 'social pragmatics' which they are advocating is welcome in highlighting the need for debate about the relationship between critical discourse analysis and analysis of social interaction, including ethnographic analysis.

Exchange relations in contemporary public life are notable for the unsettled, complex and ambivalent nature of the social identities of both institutional agents and members of publics. One focus of attention in the book is the diverse, contradictory and shifting construction of clients in bureaucratic exchanges – as citizens or as consumers; as naive (and amenable) clients, professional (well-informed and demanding) clients, or as 'warrior' clients who seek social reform. A key question for contemporary analysis of relations between institutions and publics is whether the construction of members of the public as consumers and the associated conversationalisation of exchanges (pervasively evident in leaflets, for instance) actually changes the social relations in any substantive way. Sarangi and Slembrouck are quite clear on this issue. They see these changes in discursive practices as manifesting an 'ideology of cooperation'. (See Fairclough 1995 for a slightly different interpretation which emphasizes the ambivalence of these practices.)

The authors foreground differences of perspective on bureaucratic information exchange, devoting separate chapters to the client's perspective and the bureaucrat's perspective, and analysing cases where it is the client that is seeking information (and redress) from the institution (and ways in which the institution avoids giving it), as well as cases where the institution is seeking information from the client. Many readers will welcome the inclusion of extended examples of bureaucratic exchanges in the appendices, and the careful and detailed way in which the authors analyse them.

A measure of the engagement of this book with current debates about public institutions in the social sciences is the chapter on mediation. Recent work on the 'post-traditional' properties of late modern society has highlighted the distinctively late modern recourse of people to 'expert systems' of various types in the negotiation of their social identities and social lives. The book provides an original and valuable analysis of the discursive practices of processes in which the relationship between clients and bureaucratic institutions is mediated by expert organisations. The authors point to the ambivalent nature of these processes, which on the one hand appear to empower clients but on the other hand anchor them more firmly into institutional procedures and rationalities.

This book is to be welcomed as a valuable addition to the growing literature of critical discourse analysis.

Norman Fairclough

Acknowledgements

We are indebted to the following for their permission to reproduce copyright materials:

The Belgian TV-Licence Authority for translated and original standard letters; Ealing Education and Leisure Service for extracts from material used in Chapter 7; the authors, Christopher Hall, Srikant Sarangi and Stefaan Slembrouck for extracts from their paper 'Moral Construction in Social Work Discourse' (to be published by Addison Wesley Longman in *The Construct of Professional Discourse* (ed.) Britt-Louise Gunnarsson, Per Linell and Bengt Nordberg); Lancaster University for material from their current Teaching Profiles guidelines document; Post Office Counters Ltd for an extract from their leaflet *Post Office Counters Code of Practice* booklet (POS 101/94); Pete Sayers for a dialogue extract from his video (example 1 in Chapter 3); HMSO for extracts from the Income Support Claim Form, extracts from the Family Credit Wallet, the hoarding poster, Crown Copyright is reproduced with permission of the Controller of HMSO.

We also gratefully acknowledge the Post Office for their co-operation in the production of some of the materials used in this book.

Authors' Acknowledgements

First of all, we'd like to thank Euan Reid for getting the project off the ground and Jenny Coates and Jenny Cheshire for their encouragement during the early stages. The detailed feedback we received from Euan Reid and Jenny Coates was most helpful in producing the final version of the manuscript. The book has benefited enormously from constructive and critical comments from various colleagues, in particular Greg Myers, who ploughed through the whole manuscript at an early stage. Andrew Littlejohn and David Gardner commented on a number of individual chapters. Barrie Wynn deserves our special thanks for painstakingly proof-reading the manuscript. Thanks also to Norman Fairclough who read the book at the page-proof stage and kindly agreed to write its preface.

We would like to thank those colleagues with whom we discussed ideas in their formative stages, David Gardner especially, and others including Jan Blommaert, Chris Bulcaen, Chris Candlin, Chris Hall, Niels Helsloot, Jim O'Driscoll, Celia Roberts and Jef Verschueren. In addition, we have appreciated the feedback we received from participants at various forums where parts of the book were presented: the International Pragmatics Association's Forum (Antwerp 1992), the Cardiff Language Seminar (Cardiff 1994), the Sociolinguistics Symposium 10 (Lancaster 1994) and the XIX Annual Congress of the Applied Linguistics Association of Australia (Melbourne 1994).

Data is the oxygen of this book. This would not have been possible without the help of various friends, colleagues and willing informants (including several institutional representatives) who provided us with materials, recounted to us their experiences and, quite understandably, wish to remain anonymous. We hope they will recognise the parts where they have played a role, even

xiv AUTHORS' ACKNOWLEDGEMENTS

if they disagree with our analysis (as, for example, in appendix 9b).

We would also like to acknowledge the generous financial help from the Belgian National Fund for Scientific Research and the Centre for Language and Communication (University of Wales, Cardiff) which made it possible for us to dispense with the Internet for a while and truly collaborate in front of a PC. We are particularly grateful to Nik Coupland and Anne-Marie Simon-Vandenbergen for their support in these matters.

The editorial and production teams at Longman have been very helpful in dealing with several casualties and last-minute alterations, and deserve our special appreciation.

Finally, our sincere thanks go out to Usha and Karin for their unfailing encouragement throughout the writing process. They allowed us the space and time to wear our research hats (even when that meant they had to wear their parental hats solo for longer periods of time, looking after Rakesh and Vincent).

1 Language, bureaucracy and social control

This book is about language, bureaucracy and social control. More precisely, it is about the ways in which language, bureaucracy and social control are interconnected. Our focus will be on the role of language use in bureaucracy so that we can understand better what bureaucracy means. We want also to show how, as a form of social practice, it functions as a device for social control in social domains like education, taxation, welfare provisions and banking. One of the main claims in this book is that a focus on language use can throw light on the making and unmaking of bureaucracy and its interaction with other areas of life.

Each of the three terms which appear in the title of the book – 'language', 'bureaucracy' and 'social control' – is a complex notion, and it is beyond the scope of this book to offer an elaborate review of the mass of literature that has been written on all of them. Instead our main task in this introductory chapter will be to try to elucidate these notions by showing how they bear on each other in different configurations. We will start with the notion of bureaucracy and then discuss its relationship with 'social control' and 'language use'. In that way it will become clear why the interrelationships we have in mind are worth examining.

Bureaucracy

What can we take bureaucracy to mean? Starting with Williams's (1976: 49) *keywords* of culture,

the English use of the root word *bureau* as office dates from eC18;

2 LANGUAGE, BUREAUCRACY AND SOCIAL CONTROL

it became more common in American use, especially with reference to foreign branches, the French influence being predominant. The increasing scale of commercial organisation, with a corresponding increase in government intervention and legal controls, and, with the increasing importance of organised and professional central government, produced the political facts to which the new term pointed.

By implication, Williams goes on, the term bureaucracy is more generally used

to indicate, unfavourably, not merely the class of officials but certain types of centralised social order, of a modern organised kind, as distinct not only from older aristocratic societies but from popular democracy.

(p. 49)

What Williams's account points to is that *bureaucracy*, like other keywords of culture, is a term with an unstable meaning, sometimes used neutrally and scientifically, but more often than not it carries clearly evaluative connotations. Although it is possible to list various definitions of the term, we feel that an attempt to define bureaucracy 'objectively' would precisely strip the term of the shifting investments which make up its 'social currency' in a particular context.

The theoretical use of the term is mostly associated with the work of the German sociologist Max Weber. According to Weber (1922, 1930, 1947), bureaucracy is an impersonal, rational and efficient routine. A bureaucratic organisation, with its emphasis on a rational and efficient way of doing things, is seen as having 'technical superiority' over any other form of organisation. Moreover, instrumental rationality is taken to guarantee objective fairness in decision making. In Weber's original theory of 'rationalisation', the origins of capitalist economy and the bureaucratic forms of administration that accompanied it are rooted in a protestant ethic (with the dominant values of regularity, asceticism and calculated self-interest). This ethic became an 'autonomous' and 'universal' system of behaviour to which individuals must adapt in order to survive, thus marking the shift to modern capitalist cultural values.[1]

Of course, we can question whose rationality, whose efficiency

LANGUAGE, BUREAUCRACY AND SOCIAL CONTROL

and what kind of fairness are being talked about here.[2] In many people's diction, bureaucracy is an evaluative word and it is usually applied to a particular type of event or process associated with slow-working institutions, inquisitive cross-examinations and repetitive procedures. In these cases, the term is used negatively to refer to powerful and repressive state institutions which are insensitive to individuals' wishes and heavily constrain their freedom of action. In this meaning, the term is often extended to denote a particular kind of political regime.

In its present-day sense, bureaucracy is mostly synonymous with state institutions' scrutiny of social activities. In recent years the role of state institutions in many societies has increased in nearly every area of social activity. Consider, for instance, the ways in which child-rearing practices are increasingly coming under the microscope of family welfare institutions. However, this does not mean that state institutions have monopolised 'bureaucratic' practices. Bureaucracy is also often said to be found in the administrative departments of non-state organisations (e.g. hospitals, educational institutions, banks, companies). This suggests then that bureaucracy as a concept has also entered the world of local and private business, especially when it is taken to mean 'business methods' and 'office organisation'. In this sense, 'bureaucracy' is the name for a certain mode of institutional practice, in particular the complicated formalities of 'official' procedures of legitimation with its routines of files, tape, wax, seals, etc. – in a nutshell, what people refer to as 'the paper work'.[3]

In this book we adopt the position that bureaucracy is more than concrete government buildings, standardised documents or quasi-mechanical decision making. It is an event, a process which happens to those involved, whether they are clients or bureaucrats. It does not exist as an 'objective' phenomenon outside our daily lives and experiences. The issue of bureaucracy is so intimately tied up with individuals' experiences that an understanding of 'bureaucracy' requires that we pay due attention to both the bureaucrat's and the client's perspectives in our analysis of bureaucratic events.

Think, for instance, what happens when a young person enters a welfare office and becomes a job seeker. She goes through a bureaucratic process, as her story becomes cast in institutional terms, in other words, 'blackboxed', through the use of files, codes and categories. From the bureau's point of view, such 'typing' of individual clients is necessary as it helps the machinery to work efficiently and, on the surface, equitably in the application of eligibility criteria. As the young person's case is being constructed through her contacts with the institution, we can see bureaucracy accomplishing itself. Part of her life now revolves around the use of certain application forms, the importance of on-record declarations, obligations to report to the institution, etc. Continuing with our example, it is clear that bureaucracy does not stop when the young person gets employment. No longer 'a jobseeker', she now becomes 'a tax-payer', 'a single parent', and so on. The labels change and proliferate, but the bureaucratic process continues as participation in the events in one institution leads someone to get caught up in those of another.

Bureaucracy and social control

This brings us to the relationship between bureaucracy and social control. In looking at bureaucratic practices, we are dealing with the scrutiny of the multiple relationships between social subjects and the state institutions which regulate, through decision making and legitimation procedures, the distribution of rights, obligations, and the organisation of social life in various areas of activity.

The French social theorist Michel Foucault sees such massive scale institutional surveillance of public and private life as one of the core techniques of modern power. 'Modern forms of public provision and welfare, Foucault implies, are inseparable from ever-tighter forms of social and psychological control' (Dews 1987: 141). Consider, for instance, the example of a vehicle licence. Getting a licence means that a driver subscribes to a network of relations which controls car traffic and road conduct: who can drive, what kind of vehicle you can drive, sometimes also where and when to drive. But at the same time, this network is what makes traffic with 'regimented' drivers possible – through threat of sanction to lose one's licence, through surveillance by the police, but also through self-discipline. Casting this in

LANGUAGE, BUREAUCRACY AND SOCIAL CONTROL 5

Foucault's terms, 'power produces; it produces realities; it produces domains of objects and rituals of truth' (Foucault 1977: 174).

From a historical point of view, Foucault's main interest has been in the rise of particular modern public institutions (whose introduction coincides with the conversion from the *ancien régime* to modern, capitalist society – in particular, the 'workhouse', the 'clinic', and so forth. A classic case is the birth of the prison (Foucault 1977) which marks the transition from corporal punishment to the 'more humanitarian' detention in prisons, where prisoners are individually monitored, psychologically observed, with 'behavioural profiles' made of 'criminals', followed by programmes of 'attitudinal reform', 'disciplining' and 'rehabilitation'. In *The Birth of the Clinic* (1973), Foucault starts from the assumption that from the very beginnings of capitalism intervention and administrative control have defined the modern state. Even before the French revolution, there were already demands for the surveillance of the nation's health (e.g. in France, a Royal Society of Medicine, was set up as an authority for recording and assessing all medical activity). According to Foucault, it is the rise of such institutions across seventeenth-century Europe which marks a qualitative transformation in the relations between the state and its citizens. Madness, poverty, unemployment and the inability to work, are for the first time perceived as 'social problems' (and attendant disciplines of 'knowing' arise) which fall within the ambit of responsibility of the state.

As Dews concludes, when one follows Foucault, the 'supervision of, and intervention in, the social domain by agencies of welfare and control is a more fundamental characteristic of modern societies than an economy released from directly political relations of domination' (1987: 147). For Foucault, the shift to centralisation and moralisation are essential characteristics of modern power which is orientated towards the production of regimented, isolated, and self-policing subjects. Foucault thus locates the origins of modern state power and its organisations in the same period as Weber does, but he pays much more attention to the emergence of certain key institutions of modern power, rather than an across-the-board transformation of cultural consciousness.[4] In this sense, one could say that Foucault's

LANGUAGE, BUREAUCRACY AND SOCIAL CONTROL

approach is 'institutional domain-based' and 'activity-type specific', whereas the Weberian programme is orientated towards the collective.

Bureaucracy is one form of social control, but not the only one. Bureaucratic control is closely related to political control, and the political domain is where decisions about the introduction and nature of institutional forms of public scrutiny are made. There is also the question of how bureaucracy relates to the commercial world where institutions may seek to resist its scope of activity. Thus, bureaucratic control is something which happens to institutions as well as to individual clients. For instance, although not straightforwardly bureaucratic, a bank may be forced to introduce control measures in its dealings with the public as a result of legislative changes which define its relationships with other institutions such as, say, the tax authorities. Just as legislative changes may curb the power of institutions, the delegation of certain types of decision making to clients also signals a change in the flow of bureaucratisation and attendant forms of social control.

Language and bureaucracy

A basic assumption in this book is that bureaucracy and social control are *constituted* in language. Whether it is institutions relating to clients, or institutions relating to other institutions, we strongly believe that language use is at issue. The relationships within and between institutions are struggled over and communicated using language. Changes in relations may imply changes in the category labels which bring about changed states of affairs, new sets of questions to be answered by clients, new file types, different modes of liaising, and so on. For instance, in Australia and Britain, the label 'unemployment benefit' has recently been changed to 'jobseeker's allowance'. This change may not make much difference in terms of the benefits paid to those out of work, but it does make it possible for eligibility to become even more conditional upon the provision of certified evidence of active job seeking.

Linguistic research into bureaucracy

Let us first very briefly look into some dominant strands of earlier linguistic analyses of bureaucracy before introducing the approach we have in mind. Given the vast amount of research into bureaucracy carried out in sociology and politics, it is surprising that within linguistics such research, characteristically published under headings like 'the language of bureaucracy', is very scarce.[5] The question that immediately comes to mind here is this: What do researchers mean by 'bureaucratic language'? Is it language used in bureaucratic settings? Or, is it language used in a particular way?

In very broad terms, available research into bureaucratic language can be discussed under four headings: the object of study, the data used, the mode of analysis and the recommendations which are made. Let us consider how one of these researchers delineates her object of study:

> Studies of language use in the real world have thus far focused mainly on bilingualism, doctor–patient communication, advertising language and legal language. There is another sublanguage, however, that affects us in one way or another, from the moment we are born. It's called bureaucratic language, and it manifests itself in birth certificates, hospital forms, medicare/medicaid forms, tax forms and booklets, grants applications, regulations, credit agreements, notices and so on.
>
> (Charrow 1982: 173)

When it comes to data analysis, researchers have tended to opt for a discrete itemisation of linguistic features of, say, birth certificates and tax forms. In this type of approach, it is taken for granted that bureaucracy is a stable form of social organisation and that it yields a clearly identifiable set of linguistic features which can be labelled as distinctly bureaucratic.[6] This mode of analysis is essentially descriptive as it pays most attention to measurements of grammatical complexity, the formal identification of jargon, and so forth (see, for instance, frameworks offered by Charrow 1982 and Redish 1983, among others). In contrast, Iedema's (1994) analysis of the language of administration goes one step further in adopting an interpersonal level of analysis. He examines successive steps in how social

LANGUAGE, BUREAUCRACY AND SOCIAL CONTROL

processes are increasingly talked about as if they were impersonal things. This is referred to as 'demodalisation'.[7] However, the problem remains as to how one goes about identifying bureaucratic language. Because in such a research paradigm, any language used by certain institutions could be identified as representative of the language of bureaucracy. Another shortcoming is that these studies almost exclusively deal with written documents rather than spoken interactions, because this is where one would find the properties of 'bureaucratic language' (e.g. in the extremely formal properties of impersonal small print).[8]

Another feature of bureaucratic language research is its orientation towards problem solving. Typically, on the basis of descriptive inventories of officialese and jargon, a number of recommendations are made for more accessible and user-friendly forms of language use. Redish's (1983: 167) suggestions as to 'why should we change the language of the bureaucracy' is a case in point:

- The growth of government does place a paperwork burden on us all.
- Reorganizing and rewriting bureaucratic documents can significantly reduce that burden.
- Reorganizing and rewriting bureaucratic documents can increase compliance with government rules and save the government money.
- Bureaucratic documents can be improved and still be legally accurate and sufficient.

Similarly, Charrow proposes to change the surface features of bureaucratic documents:

> Given the fact that many features of bureaucratese are counter-productive, we can only hope that it will change, and become more like ordinary – well-constructed – discourse. The consumer movement seems to have motivated a move toward 'Plain English' in bureaucratic documents, and many agencies are, in fact, trying to improve their documents and train their staffs to write clearly.
>
> (1982: 187–8)

We may wonder whether it makes much sense to talk about the improvement of, say, the language of application forms if one does not look at the nature of information exchange in bureaucratic encounters and how this affects decision making and the classification of clients into case types. Rather than questioning the Weberian rationality and efficiency conditions associated with bureaucracy, recommendations of the above kind subscribe to making bureaucracy more workable through the simplification of language forms. Taken to its logical conclusion, this means there can be bureaucracy without bureaucratic language.

When using terms like the 'language of bureaucracy' or 'bureaucratic language use', one also runs the risk that the interactive and interpretative dimensions in an individual's experiences of bureaucracy are lost sight of. One question in particular tends to be avoided: What exactly makes an encounter bureaucratic? For us, bureaucracy is a type of event, a particular kind of encounter or contact situation, as this is how it is experienced by social subjects. It is then crucially important to observe how bureaucratic events take shape through language use, thus capturing the interrelationships between language, bureaucracy and social control. This will require that we discuss the question whether bureaucratic language should only be considered to include language used by the institutions or should also include language addressed to the institution. Obviously, it makes more sense to look at an application form for, say, tax reduction, which has actually been filled in by an applicant, to see how that sets in motion the bureaucratic procedure rather than studying only the application form itself as a reflection of bureaucratic practice. For us, a filled in application form or a letter sent to a particular office counts as dialogic and is therefore a better data source for examining bureaucratic events.

One practical consequence of bureaucratic language research is now widely felt in the proliferation of 'new look' leaflets and application forms which claim to be user-friendly. Can we conclude that institutions have indeed become less bureaucratic, or that they have entered into a less hierarchical relationship with the client, or should we see this as further camouflage for introducing new forms of public control? Have clients really become more literate when leaflets invite them to decide beforehand whether they can be entitled to, say, welfare benefits?

10 LANGUAGE, BUREAUCRACY AND SOCIAL CONTROL

While one cannot be quite categorical, one can be a little sceptical at least because the diagnosis focuses on symptoms rather than causes, and surface-level linguistic analysis may have contributed to this trend. Instead, we need an analysis which focuses on the creation of social identities and objects, rather than an analysis which would be aimed only at removing symptoms by, for example, simplifying word choice or explaining the rules. Similarly, pulling down the 'role barriers' between institutional representatives and visiting clients does not necessarily lead to the disappearance of the agonies of bureaucratic encounters. Roles and forms of talk cannot be separated from each other and therefore, in the context of bureaucratic discourse, the relationship between them is an important issue. In short, understanding bureaucratic processes also means understanding the multiplicity of roles of both bureaucrats and clients in situated encounters, while addressing the question of how labelling and role identity are also the outcome of discursive events.

What is called for is something very fundamental: in fact an analysis of changing practices of language use against the background of contemporary social change. For example, it is noticeable how linguistic simplifications are being called for at a political point in time when state-governed welfare is being generally discredited and state resources are being drastically cut. In addition, there is the question of attendant developments in so-called non-bureaucratic institutions, say, banks. We believe it necessary to analyse comprehensively the nature of citizens' identities in contemporary society – whether that involves being a social welfare client, a post office client or bank client. Traditionally, one would hesitate to conflate these three categories, but, looking at recent developments, distinctions seem to disappear in terms of how citizens are talked about in similar fashions by different types of institutions. Consider the following excerpt from the Post Office Counters Code of Practice booklet (POS 101/94):

A POUNC [Post Office Users' National Council, which is defined as a 'statutory watchdog organisation for the Post Office'] report published in September 1989 examined the service given at a wide range of our outlets and compared it with that at a similar number of alternative High Street outlets and organizations. This research found that although some Post Offices did have queuing problems at certain times, the quality of the service generally, measured by the time customers have to wait, was better in the Post Office than it was in banks, building societies and supermarkets and in the majority of cases customers were served within five minutes.

Novel in this 'research report' is the fact that the citizen in the post office is put on a par with the one in the bank and with the customer in the supermarket (waiting time provides the basis of comparison, as an index of quality of service). However, note also how government organisations like the Post Office Counters, who in recent years have become subjected to rigid scrutiny from watchdog bodies, have begun citing instances of reported 'good practice' in their leaflets.

A critical linguistic perspective

A new perspective on the role of language use in bureaucracy should not take for granted the assumption that certain institutions are always bureaucratic and that others never are, or that bureaucratic language can be reduced to the identification of a situationally specified set of formal features. Even if the latter were possible, it is not clear where linguistic research would stand in relation to changing practices as they are happening at the moment. In sum, what is needed is an action-orientated view of bureaucratic encounters which makes it possible to look at how bureaucracy is something which happens in everyday practice and examines the effects of situated language use on the wider development of a society.

One way to draw conclusions about the macro level is to examine micro discourse events. The framework of critical linguistics offers this possibility. In recent years, linguistic analysis has in various ways moved beyond its self-imposed boundaries and looked at what it can contribute to the agendas of other social scientific disciplines. It has moved into different areas of social activity and, with the introduction of a critical linguistic perspective, it has also sought to capture the complex relationships between language use and social practice (e.g. Fairclough 1989, 1992a; Fowler et al. 1979; Kress 1989; Kress and Hodge 1979).[9]

12 LANGUAGE, BUREAUCRACY AND SOCIAL CONTROL

Critical linguistics aims at integrating the contributions which conversational analysis, pragmatics, discourse analysis, genre analysis and sociolinguistics have made to language study, but, in its turn, demands that the analysis aims at explaining language use in relation to macro developments in society. The view that bureaucratic processes are constituted in discourse has a backdrop in social theory. It is based on a dialectic view which sees language as not only reflecting the social, but also as shaping, maintaining and constituting complex social realities.

Central to a critical linguistic approach is the notion of 'discourse' – taking advantage of the various levels at which the term can be used. Discourse can be looked at as text, as processes of text production and interpretation, but also – following Foucault and others – as an ideologically invested vehicle in a societal formation (to be studied in terms of hierarchical orderings of discourses). Ideological investment implies that discursive practices are linked to the interests of particular social groups and that certain practices may occupy a more dominant position than other, alternative, practices – even to the extent that the former appear 'natural' to language users (Gramsci 1971).

Critical linguistics thus pays attention to how language both reflects and gives shape to the social – in short, how linguistic practices not only contribute to a reproduction of society, but also how they may bring about a transformation of social relations. The underlying dichotomy between the situation-creating and the situationally determined aspects of language use can be mapped onto a conceptual tension between two tendencies in social and linguistic theory, namely language as a form of action which brings about a social state of affairs versus language use as a structured means of social reproduction.

Finally, critical linguistics is about social conflict and struggle, since it pays special attention to both stable and changing relations of power through ideology and the role which language use plays in these relationships. For instance, from a critical linguistic perspective, an analysis of bureaucratic language is not a matter of 'jargon' versus 'plain English', or a matter of having to deal with a humane bureaucrat versus an impersonal repertoire of rules and regulations. Such dichotomies may prove of little importance if we do not examine whether the occurrence of one or the other leads to a different distribution of actual power and

LANGUAGE, BUREAUCRACY AND SOCIAL CONTROL 13

challenges naturalised ideologies in the sustenance of state authority.

Synopsis

A summary of the book's contents now shows how each chapter contributes to the multi-dimensional argument we have just sketched out.

In Chapters 2, 3 and 4 we concentrate on an outline of the framework we use for analysing bureaucratic encounters. Chapters 5, 6 and 7 bring into focus particular bureaucratic cases. But each chapter has a number of theoretical and a number of analytical themes. This is because we have adopted a line of argumentation in which the usefulness of theoretical positions is shown through actual analyses of data and where, conversely, the analysis of data informs theoretical positions.

The dynamics of language and situation, which are at the core of the critical linguistic perspective, are the main theme of Chapter 2. Does language use simply reflect situational variables or should it also be seen as a major component in the definition of a situation? This language situation theme is broached by looking at contemporary discursive changes in the ways in which institutions address social subjects. The changes we focus on in Chapter 2 are not restricted to the bureaucratic domain but are particular instances of macro social and discursive changes which have been noted in other work in critical linguistics – thus strengthening the claim that a micro-macro approach is a very fruitful and explanatory one.

At the analytical level, Chapter 3 notes some of the fundamental asymmetries which underlie bureaucratic encounters. To this purpose, we concentrate on issues developed within pragmatics, such as cooperation/confrontation in institutional encounters, assumptions which talkers have about one another, (macro) speech acts like volunteering information or warning someone, information exchange (including tactical insincerity and being economical with the truth), and so on. These issues have been put on the research agenda by linguistic pragmatists, but we feel they should be reassessed in the light of a critical linguistic approach. For us, pragmatics is at a level in between discourse

14 LANGUAGE, BUREAUCRACY AND SOCIAL CONTROL

and text because it emphasises the interpretation of discourse. Interpretation plays a double role in this book and its importance as an issue is an area where the concerns of pragmatics and critical linguistics overlap. There is (i) the interpretation which participants give to moves in the discourse and there is (ii) the assessment of the significance of a particular move. Like Fairclough (1989) we take the view that the analyst's interpretative activity is very much like that of a discourse participant but it is informed by linguistic and social theory.

Chapter 4 continues the theme of language and situation but focuses on 'role behaviour'. How much of social roles is discursively shaped and maintained? How does this relate to earlier pragmatic work on 'discourse role'? What is the relevance of social theoretical work on role (e.g. Foucault's notion of the 'dispersed subject') for our analysis? Can social subjects ever have a roleless identity?

In Chapters 5, 6 and 7, we will follow bureaucratic cases through their various stages and exchanges – application, decision, appeal, and so on. In doing so, we will look at bureaucratic events from the perspectives of clients and institutional representatives. The aim here is to show how the analysis of individual cases can throw light on how institutional members have responded to the asymmetries in bureaucratic encounters.

In Chapter 5, we address the question of the kinds of client behaviour the asymmetries in bureaucratic encounters can give rise to. In particular, we look at cases where clients challenge the practices of institutions and, by following an extended set of written correspondence between one client and three institutions involving a complaint over institutional practices, we seek to throw light on the role which 'face' plays in bureaucratic encounters.

In Chapter 6, we shift our attention to the institution and its representatives. How have they responded to the asymmetries? What sort of client do they principally address and construct? We look at assumptions underlying application forms and the production of information leaflets, a factor which has played a central role in the ways institutions have responded to demands for change, coming from the public but also from the political domain.

Chapter 7 brings into focus (other) institutionalised attempts

LANGUAGE, BUREAUCRACY AND SOCIAL CONTROL 15

to bridge the communicative divide: the role of mediating professions (e.g. social work) and mediating institutions (e.g. the Advisory Centre for Education), which have been brought into being to help clients in the way they approach the institution with an application or an appeal.

In conclusion, Chapter 8 attempts to tie together the key issues which arise from the various analyses, highlighting in particular the complex interplay of notions like 'accountability', 'choice' and 'accessibility' associated with the recent forms of bureaucracy. In a final analysis, we contextualise our findings within contemporary social-theoretical debate about the conditions of late capitalist society.

Notes

1. Weber thus analyses the rise of Western capitalist societies in terms of an unleashing of the autonomous dynamic of means–end logic. This line of argument is still prevalent in Berger and Luckman (1972) who identify the following properties as characteristic of the way bureaucratic institutions function: the habitualisation and routinisation of behaviour (including the use of simplified procedures, the occurrence of objective rules) and the use of sanctions and strictures as the outcomes of bureaucratic decision making.
2. Weber's use of the term 'rationality' coincides with Habermas's notion of 'strategic rationality', as distinct from 'communicative rationality' (which, rather obviously, is *not* a property of institutional encounters).
3. Charles Dickens was one of the first to parody the rationality and efficiency of bureaucratic procedures in his portrayal of the 'Circumlocution Office' (*Little Dorrit* ch. 10):

   > If another Gunpowder Plot had been discovered half an hour before the lighting of the match, nobody would have been justified in saving the parliament until there had been half a score of boards, half a bushel of minutes, several sacks of official memoranda, and a family vault full of ungrammatical correspondence, on the part of the Circumlocution Office.
   >
   > . . .
   >
   > Whatever was required to be done, the Circumlocution Office was beforehand with all the public departments in the art of perceiving – HOW NOT TO DO IT.
   >
   > (1966: 104)

16 LANGUAGE, BUREAUCRACY AND SOCIAL CONTROL

4. Unlike in Marxist theory, the origins of state intervention are not seen (solely) as a response to the crises which are inherent in a capitalist economy. For instance, according to classic Marxist theory, economic liberalism would initially have led to an entirely deregulated, freelance kind of medicine, with the role of the state reduced to maintaining social order. See Dews (1987, especially ch. 5) for a detailed account of the differences.

5. We exclude from this overview two strands of enquiry which have concentrated more on context and belief systems. One strand focuses on how contextualisation cues (Gumperz 1982) or the concept of index (Collins 1987) can be used as parameters to distinguish ordinary conversation from bureaucratic interaction. The second strand is concerned with mismatches arising out of bureaucratic encounters – what Philips (1987) calls insider *versus* outsider knowledge. See also Agar (1985) on the clash between institution and client frames.

6. This is identical to research into professional language as a register (Heath 1979).

7. In the following example (Iedema 1994: 8), the word 'directives' (used as an impersonal abstraction) is construed as governing the way financial reports are written: 'The purpose of the Code is to establish financial reporting directives to govern the form and content of departmental financial reports.'

8. It is worth noting that similar imbalances can be detected where researchers examine language use in 'other' professional contexts. For instance, analysts of doctor–patient interviews have tended to put more emphasis on spoken encounters rather than analyse, say, written medical reports. The same is true of studies focusing on service encounters in institutional settings.

9. Both the social theoretical turn in linguistics and the adoption of a discourse perspective on institutions owe a great deal to Foucault, and have mainly found their shape in the critical linguistic paradigm, a reading of which has been immensely important to the linguistic viewpoint set out in this book.

2 Bureaucratisation and debureaucratisation in contemporary society

Introduction: what discourse practices are construed as bureaucratic?

In Chapter 1, we characterised bureaucracy as an event, as something which happens to people and institutions. In answering the question 'what is bureaucratic?' we have to look at what people perceive it to be. This means that our object of study is not something that can be 'objectively' delineated, but something which is subject to how groups of people in society classify their experiences, and what their stakes are in doing so. By problematising the notion 'bureaucratic' in this way one is equipped with a very flexible working assumption.

What, then, do people label as 'bureaucratic'? A closer look at the meanings typically associated with the term 'bureaucracy' and its various derivations (bureaucratic, bureaucrat, and so on) reveals two salient elements: (i) the extent to which the term is used to refer to the world of government, especially its organisations which process requests from individuals and maintain contact with the general public, and (ii) the extent to which the term 'bureaucratic' often has negative overtones, and hence belongs especially to the dictions of those who undergo the institutionalised routines. It is fairly easy to provide a list of commonly recounted experiences of institutional practices which people label as 'bureaucratic'.

For example:

- Applications must be filled in in writing.

18 LANGUAGE, BUREAUCRACY AND SOCIAL CONTROL

- Information asked for has to be provided, even if the applicant fails to see what it has to do with the entitlement applied for.
- The insensitivity with regard to the provision of the same routine information, such as name, date of birth, to which the institution already has access.
- The application must reach the authority in question before a certain date for it to be valid.
- The requirement of applying through 'validating' intermediaries.
- A fee levied on formal applications.
- The expectation or the occurrence of a pre-set response range (which your case does not fit into) and fixed correlations with decisions.
- The dependence of decisions on procedural criteria; for example whether the form was filled in correctly is more important than whether it reflects the situation dealt with.
- The outcome of the procedure is only communicated in writing at a time deemed appropriate to the institution.
- The occurrence of irrevocable black and white decisions.
- Standard responses from the institution, with little explanatory value.
- Appeal is technically possible, but only through long-winded formal procedures.

In spoken encounters at the service desk, for example:

- Bureaucrats never say 'sorry to keep you waiting'.
- Bureaucrats inform you that the procedure is going to take at least a number of days or weeks, or, that the duration is out of their hands, as it depends on how quickly the other institution processes the application.
- Bureaucrats refer clients to a particular leaflet, rather than respond directly to the contents of a particular query.
- Bureaucrats take for granted that clients are familiar with bureaucratic routines, for example replies like 'you need a ZX20' without saying what ZX20 stands for, what it is used for or how it is different from other ZX forms.
- Bureaucrats never disclose examples of similar cases and their outcomes.
- Bureaucrats tell clients that some information has to be given 'for the record'.

We should not underestimate the extent to which these aspects of bureaucratic practices may go unnoticed as social subjects are routinely bureaucratised. However, if there were a change in these practices or in the domains in which they occur, what would be the intended impact and how would such changes be experienced by those affected? What happens when talk between a civil servant and a client in, say, a tax office is experienced by both interactants as conversational, despite the fact that it takes place in what would be considered a bureaucratic institution and even though the interactants may be talking about the client's tax declaration. The onus on researchers of language use is to map any observable changes – and the ways in which they are experienced – onto wider societal processes.

Bureaucratisation and debureaucratisation

An analytical discussion of the domain of bureaucratic discourse often implicitly assumes the important distinction between the public and the private. Bureaucracy is always located in the public domain and its existence is defined in terms of rationally and efficiently managing the needs and wants emerging from the private domain. Many accounts of this distinction draw on or echo Habermas's (1981) analysis of Western capitalist societies in terms of a world of systems (the private economy and the public administration) and corresponding private and public life- worlds.[1] The focal point in Habermas's analysis is the gradual uncoupling of the lifeworlds by the world of the systems in modern capitalist societies and the increasingly problematic nature of the exchange relationships between the various domains.

This makes it possible to distinguish between two aspects of bureaucracy as a process: bureaucratisation and debureaucratisation. Bureaucratisation implies the gradual adoption of a mode of talk and decision making which is experienced as bureaucratic in areas which are not usually associated with 'bureaucracy'. By a similar token, debureaucratisation means that bureaucratic strongholds strive to appear non-bureaucratic by resorting to certain modes of talk and by inviting clients to participate in the decision making process.

A first glance at the attendant discourse practices suggests that

LANGUAGE, BUREAUCRACY AND SOCIAL CONTROL

bureaucratisation and debureaucratisation are two distinct and opposite processes. We will start our analysis from this assumption. Raising the question of what causes these apparent social changes will lead us to state the importance of the interrelationships between language, bureaucracy and social control. By concentrating on the impact which bureaucratisation and debureaucratisation have it will become possible for us to assess whether debureaucratisation in particular is just a new or transformed type of institutional practice in the Gramscian hegemonic sense, which does not necessarily displace the existing imbalances of power.

Although the definitions of bureaucratisation and debureaucratisation do not exhaust the possibilities, the way we have cast them matches the trends which at the moment can be observed in various Western societies. We can point to a number of things which have happened over the last decade and which indicate that institutionalised bureaucracy is under pressure to change. Certain political groups – whether in power or in opposition – argue for government services to be based on market economy principles, equating a renewed sense of citizenship with a consumer culture, where good service is expected and demanded (cf. the 'Citizens Charters' in Britain). Consider the headline:

> Major revamp of British civil service gets under way – Aim of reform to turn hostile bureaucracy into a well-run corporation.
>
> (*The Straits Times,* 17 April 1993, p. 17)

This headline suggests an opposition between public and private institutions on the basis of, for instance, efficiency, accessibility and profit-making. Dunleavy (1991) observes that unlike profitable corporations, bureaucracies have striven to maximise their own agency and have grown out of proportion, making government and welfare provisions non-transparent. New Right politicians believe that citizens will get a better deal if government institutions are turned into profitable, self-supportive organisations which make fewer demands on public funds and enter into a commercial relationship with citizens. This argument is based on a narrow and economistic conception of what people want and a view of individuals as inherent maximisers (trying to get the best possible deal out of the institution rather than what

BUREAUCRATISATION AND DEBUREAUCRATISATION IN CONTEMPORARY SOCIETY 21

he/she is entitled to). These developments are not restricted to Britain or to places where right-wing governments are in power. In the Belgian context, similar privatisation policies and reforms of the civil service have been initiated by a centre-left government, while the existing right-wing Liberal party renamed itself as the 'Party of the Citizen'.

The above newspaper headline also invites the following questions: Is the opposition between hostile bureaucracies and well-run corporations justified? Is it a matter of compensation for too many rules and too few client rights? Whose perspectives are being adopted here? Is there no bureaucracy in the private economy and other traditionally unbureaucratic institutions?

In order to understand these broader social changes one needs to look at concrete instances of changed discourse practice. Think, for example, of the increasing ways in which governments have turned to television and other forms of mass advertising for their information campaigns, or the important role which the distribution of leaflets has come to play in the process of filling in application forms for passports, social benefits, work permits, and so on. Consider too the increasing ways in which employees in educational institutions are now required to keep work diaries and write 'progress' reports. While analysing a number of cases of (de)bureaucratisation, we will also address the question of how the relationship between language and bureaucracy can best be seen.

Changing discourse practices as action and as process

Let us look at occurrences of change with two pieces of data: a poster from a government body and a personnel profile used in a university. The first example is a poster put up by the British vehicle licensing authority, the DVLA (Driver and Vehicle Licensing Agency), which is responsible for the registration of cars, trucks, and so forth. The poster warns drivers not to forget the annual payment of the road tax.

Example 1

DVLA-poster

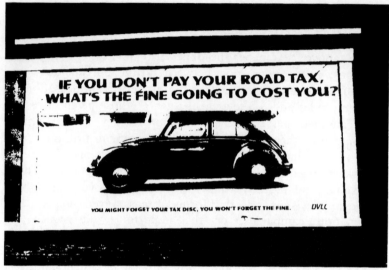

This kind of message is very different from the traditional small print at the bottom of, say, a vehicle licence application form (V10):

Example 2

Keeping or using an unlicensed vehicle on a public road is an offence which could result in a penalty of £1,000 or five times the annual rate of duty, whichever is the greater.

On the face of it, example 1 is an instance of debureaucratisation, if by this term we refer to a shift from a written mode of small print to a visual message with conversational address (cf., for example, the use of direct address 'you', the use of a question, the use of everyday vocabulary). What may have prompted the government to change its practices? The authority which issued the poster must have believed that the use of advertising is a more effective and user-friendly way to get its message across than the resented small print on the payment form.

The use of an advertising poster points to a tendency to make

BUREAUCRATISATION AND DEBUREAUCRATISATION IN CONTEMPORARY SOCIETY   23

messages from authorities to the public appear less bureaucratic. By turning to billboard advertising, the institution becomes apparently less constrained in format and language. The text on bureaucratic forms would have a fixed format and the expectation would be that these would stay the same for every form that is issued over a long period of time. As opposed to this, the use of an advertisement means that the message format, its style or the contents, can in theory change with every new communication, or, that simultaneously a set of different variants of the same message can be launched in a campaign. The poster will also have been seen, on the one hand, as a more effective way of dealing with the 'problem' of people not paying the tax, and on the other, as a cost-effective way of recouping the cost of the advertisement from an increase in tax revenue and fewer expenses in chasing non-payers.

Let us now look at the following example of a teaching profile, whose recent introduction in many educational institutions points to a tendency to make certain areas of academic life 'more accountable'.[2] The accompanying 'Guidance Notes for Staff with Teaching Responsibilities' state that:

Example 3a

The Purposes of the Profile

The Teaching Profile has two principal purposes. Firstly it is a method by which a lecturer may reflect upon their professional practice and evaluate their development through the collection and analysis of a range of information about their teaching.

Secondly, the completed Teaching Profile document can provide evidence to the Promotions Committee on the range and quality of teaching undertaken by a candidate for promotion.

Collection of Material

The various headings under which material may be presented will be given later in these guidelines. It helps to collect material as teaching proceeds. Examination papers, results, handouts, student evaluations, teaching materials, and so on, should be filed as they are produced. As experience grows the process will become refined. Each individual can decide whether or not to include evidence under any heading. Moreover, candidates for promotion can add information on any other aspect of their teaching at the

24 *LANGUAGE, BUREAUCRACY AND SOCIAL CONTROL*

> end of their profile. Where ever possible statements made should
> be substantiated by evidence of colleagues, students, or persons
> from outside the University (e.g. external examiners or colleagues
> from other relevant institutions).
>
> (page 1, paragraphs 3–5)

Here, an elaborate (and compulsory) form of on-the-record written commitment is being introduced which is very likely to have an impact on areas which before were largely the terrain of face-to-face conversation. Earlier, it was up to individual lecturers to decide whether or not to discuss their teaching methodology and practices with anyone else in the department or in the university, and which of its aspects to discuss. Now, the prospect of regularly having to compile a teaching report with added observation reports has turned record keeping and communication in writing about teaching practice a regular feature of any lecturer's activity. Note that, although the instructions for collecting material give applicants a considerable amount of freedom in how to construct their own profile, emphasis is given to an automatic filing habit and the collection of objective evidence in support of statements.

The teaching profile has a fixed set of addressees at various levels in the university:

Example 3b

> The profiles of candidates would be considered first at
> Departmental level and then by the Area Committee, to ensure
> that they are seen by those with experience of the teaching
> contexts described. In effect, these two stages of consideration will
> validate the profiles. The Promotions Committee will then receive
> the profiles of those candidates who are short-listed.
>
> (page 1, paragraph 6)

In explicating the various stages of the promotion process, the profiles contribute to the hierarchically monitored construction of an individual lecturer's role and obligations within a departmental set-up. In this case, the prospect of record keeping, detailed reporting and refereed observation is also likely to give rise to bureaucratisation at the level of personal relationships within university departments.

BUREAUCRATISATION AND DEBUREAUCRATISATION IN CONTEMPORARY SOCIETY   25

There is also bureaucratisation at the level of information processing: on what kind of information will the assessment of teaching be based? Although the profile does not specify a rigid agenda, it does suggest a relatively fixed set of topics, as is clear from the set of headings with suggested entries outlined in the 'Elements of the Profile':

Example 3c

Teaching responsibilities
A statement of the courses taught and the associated teaching loads. Service as a Course Director, Senior Tutor, membership of a Course Committee, or similar post concerned with teaching, should also be mentioned.

Educational Aims and Objectives
A statement or statements showing what you are trying to achieve in different areas of your teaching. This will provide a context for the interpretation of statements about the methods of teaching and assessment, outcomes of student learning, and so on, which will be presented later in the profile.

Teaching Methods
Statements of the way in which you go about your teaching and whether any special methods or materials have been introduced. It is recognised that 'special' is a relative term and what is established practice in one discipline may be highly innovative in another.

Assessment and Evidence of the Outcomes of Teaching
A description of the way in which students are assessed, and how they are given feedback about their work. Information should also be given about what students seem to have achieved and what they have subsequently done. The effectiveness of the assessment methods might be commented upon, in relation to the relevant aims and objectives.

Course Evaluation
Description of course evaluation processes and outcomes, the evidence so obtained, and the light it throws on the teaching which has taken place. Normally teachers should be devising systematic and objective methods of obtaining feedback on courses, at least from students. Such activities should be continuously maintained.

26 LANGUAGE, BUREAUCRACY AND SOCIAL CONTROL

Evidence of the Continued Study of Teaching and Learning
Measures taken to improve your own teaching and that of your discipline and institution. Courses and workshops which have been attended, or offered for the benefit of others, and materials which have been published about teaching and learning.

Teaching References
A statement should be submitted from an appropriate internal or external referee. The statement should include any other appropriate features of your teaching. This teaching reference is in addition to the references for research. There must also be a written assessment from your head of department or experienced colleague of teaching sessions observed.

(pages 2–3)

Again we can ask ourselves what may have prompted the institution to change its practices. In the background is the introduction of market economy logic within educational establishments, which involves a screening activity to guarantee that students will receive 'value-for-money'. Lecturers' career advancement and job preservation are then linked directly to forms of teaching assessment.[3] Part of the thinking behind such measures is that the wide-scale continual monitoring of teaching practices is essential to quality control, and is also a cost-effective manner of looking for ways to re-distribute falling financial and other resources.[4]

The analysis of language use

The institutional measures we have just pointed to essentially affect the ways in which talking or writing within the institution or between the institution and the general public is accomplished. In this section, we want to argue that through a closer analysis of the discourse properties it is possible to gain more insight into the actual significance of the trends. To that purpose, let us first reconsider the DVLA poster.

Although we have characterised the poster as 'advertising', it is not a straightforward advertisement. While it attempts to persuade passers-by to do something, the aim is not to direct consumer behaviour in the sense that the poster makers want to increase their sales figures. There is, in fact, a duality in the

BUREAUCRATISATION AND DEBUREAUCRATISATION IN CONTEMPORARY SOCIETY   27

poster between, on the one hand, the bureaucratic contents of a reminder to pay the licence fee and, on the other hand, the use of advertising as a means of communicating the warning.

The use of a hoarding poster clearly belongs to 'advertising', also suggested by the fact that the message consists of a combination of visual and textual cues, and that to interpret the message one has to rely on a particular way of 'reading'. In order to interpret the poster, passers-by have to work out a particular meaning by making a connection between the written text and the visual cues. They are likely to interpret the poster as saying something to the effect that 'You'd better not forget to pay your annual road tax, as you'll be so hard up having to pay the fine, that you'll have to sell your car'. But this is not the only possible interpretation; nor is it necessarily the most likely interpretation. For instance, one can interpret the sign 'FOR SALE £500' as indicating that the car is being sold or as indicating the amount of the fine. One could also argue that the poster suggests that the authorities can literally force you to sell the car if you fail to pay.

On the basis of this brief – and by no means exhaustive, analysis some conclusions can already be drawn about the impact of the change in discourse practices. Compared to the use of an explicit warning in the small print of an application form or leaflet (such as in example 2 above), changing the textual format also involves switching to a kind of interpretative behaviour which relies heavily on making implicit connections between 'loose' bits of message, with the result that – as is often the case with advertisements – more than one interpretation becomes possible and likely. On the basis of this linguistic analysis, one can thus conclude that in the actual impact of this 'new' kind of public communication, there is a contrast between the assumed 'user-friendliness' and 'accessibility' of the message and the increased vagueness as to what exactly is being communicated. Indeed, it is not unthinkable that a reader may be misled about the exact consequences of failure to pay. From the point of view of the text producers, the vagueness is very efficient in scaring the public by implying a severe penalty but not revealing its extent.

The language-situation dynamic

Taking the analysis of the DVLA poster one step further, we can now make a number of observations about the dynamic relationship between language use and the situation in which it is used. If the poster is representative of the genre of advertising, as analysts we are called upon to look for the ingredients of the advertising genre. In this case, it is easy to classify the poster as an example of the genre. But this does not answer why the genre was selected by the text producers or what effect it has on the relationship with readers.

When turning to the advertising mode, the DVLA borrows from a mode of language use which is constraining its communication potential. But why would it borrow a self-defeating mode? Our analysis above has shown that it concerns a creative use of the advertising mode which pays off for the institution. In the analysis of the DVLA poster we have talked about 'carry-over' effects, that is certain things which the introduction of the advertising mode in public institutions brings along (and which are perhaps unlikely to have been foreseen). The DVLA now has to act under new constraints which allow only a certain leeway. Some kinds of messages cannot be translated into the poster format so some interpretations are ruled out. For instance, as soon as it has been decided to use a poster format, it becomes difficult to continue to use the same text of the small print as in example 2 above. Hence, the advertising component in these 'new' forms of public communication in a sense becomes situation-determining. It functions to construct a particular identity for the institutional client, but one cannot really predict the outcome. For instance, the message is now addressed to everyone passing by (car owners, payers, non-payers, prospective owners, but also cyclists and dedicated pedestrians – who have not been DVLA-addressees before). Unlike the small print warning, the tone is critical as it casts non-payers as irresponsible. However, granted that the real intended addressees are non-payers, how would they receive the message? As streetwise addressees of other advertisements they can easily ignore, refuse to take seriously, become ironic, or disqualify the poster as boring or unaesthetic. But can they afford not to see the hidden but definitive small print warning in the

BUREAUCRATISATION AND DEBUREAUCRATISATION IN CONTEMPORARY SOCIETY 29

poster? Thus, there are limits to how much passers-by can rely on their previous experience of advertising.

This observation leads to the point that, next to the claim that language depends on the situation in which it is being used, the reverse is equally true and equally important. Language use is situation-creating by constructing a particular kind of social relationship between the interactants, in this case, a 'new' type of bureaucratic relationship with effects on the ways in which social subjects relate to government messages and to advertisements per se.

The importance of the situation-creating capacity of language use can also be shown, when one looks at those cases of increasing bureaucracy in traditionally non-bureaucratic domains. If one only considers the dependency of language on situational factors such as setting, participant relation, and so on, it becomes difficult to explain why the introduction of certain institutional measures in institutions in the private economy or educational establishments are experienced by employees or clients as 'bureaucratic'. For instance, why is the introduction of a teaching profile experienced as an increase in the number of formal rules of conduct and procedures which are applied uniformly, and why does it also lead to an atmosphere of distanced, impersonal control over the performance of teaching duties? Why in such a situation should employees suspect career advancements to become dependent on their on-record cooperation with these formal procedures (rather than on their commitment in the classroom)?

Moreover, the introduction of a teaching profile also encourages lecturers to engage in self-promotional discourse, that is a form of language use, which although part of a bureaucratic procedure, is unlikely to have the characteristics traditionally associated with bureaucratic language use. Inherent in a one-sided position of situational dependency is the risk that one only looks for 'bureaucratic language' in traditional bureaucratic strongholds such as tax offices, social welfare authorities and immigration offices.

The recognition of the situation-determining properties of language-in-use harmonises with a view that language use is a stake central to the construction of and struggle over social identities. In the bureaucratic context, governments have tried to

30 LANGUAGE, BUREAUCRACY AND SOCIAL CONTROL

redefine their relationships with citizens.[5] So far we have looked at some of the changes in modes of talk this has brought about. Similar changes are also discernible in the 'speak' of public notices, leaflets and forms.

There are at least two common complaints about the filling in of forms for public authorities: first, people have difficulties with the questions and find it difficult to fit their situation precisely into the pre-set response categories; secondly, there is the occurrence of vital information in the small print (where it is less likely to be noticed and is experienced as 'deceptive').

Against this background let us examine the following leaflet, entitled 'About the Canvass' (see Appendix 2a) which the Lancaster City Council enclosed with the form for 'Community Charge Registration' (see Appendix 2b).[6] The registration form was to be used to establish who was to pay the then 'new' type of local taxation.

On the front page of the leaflet, it says:

Example 4a

THIS LEAFLET IS DESIGNED TO ASSIST IN THE
COMPLETION OF THE ENCLOSED CANVASS FORM.
PLEASE READ IT CAREFULLY. FURTHER ASSISTANCE IS
AVAILABLE BY TELEPHONE.

Here the public authority is taking on the role of 'offering assistance' in filling in the form – a practice which nowadays has become very common – and which shows how authorities have tried to meet the criticisms implied in its routines being called 'bureaucratic'. Note also, for instance, the use of 'please' where imperatives are being used, the offer of individualised assistance in the form of a 'helpline number' and the advice to be cautious about 'unauthorised' canvassers who may appear at the doorstep. Finally, there is also the concluding, conversationally direct, 'thank you for your cooperation' on the last page.

So much for the friendly and helpful tone, which in the registration form is realised in two ways: referring the addressee to a section in the leaflet and providing examples with particular boxes. What is also remarkable about the registration form is the warning in the text immediately underneath the title:

BUREAUCRATISATION AND DEBUREAUCRATISATION IN CONTEMPORARY SOCIETY 31

Example 4b

The PENALTY for failure to supply this information is £50 for the FIRST OFFENCE and £200 for the SECOND AND SUBSEQUENT OFFENCES.

The warning is not given in small print at the end of the document but highlighted on the first page before the categories to be filled in. At the same time, the form is very explicit about the fine that will be incurred (compare with example 2 above).

Social control as an area of struggle

In the Community Charge leaflet and registration form, there is certainly a tension between the polite markers, such as 'please' as in 'Please complete this section if anyone in your household is over 18' and the explicit warning that 'Civil penalties will only be imposed where there is an outright refusal to provide information'. One important factor in the background is undoubtedly that the Community Charge (also known as the 'Poll Tax') was a very sensitive political issue, and various social groups (including some politicians) had already announced they would refuse to register or pay. This contrasts rather starkly with the apparently 'conversational' and, at times, 'friendly' tone of the leaflet which announces itself as 'designed to assist in the completion of the enclosed canvass form'.

Let us further examine two points in the leaflet which strongly suggest a tendency towards 'debureaucratisation'. In part 6 the leaflet reads in capitals:

Example 4c

BEING RESPONSIBLE FOR COMPLETING THIS FORM DOES NOT MEAN YOU WILL HAVE TO PAY A COMMUNITY CHARGE FOR OTHER PERSONS SHOWN IN PART 2[7]

This information, at first sight, functions to pre-empt some of the worries the person filling in the form may have. One element which is often in people's minds when they fill in and sign a form is the extent to which they are committing themselves. In the absence of information about this, worries such as 'Will I now have to . . . ?'

32   LANGUAGE, BUREAUCRACY AND SOCIAL CONTROL

often make the filling in of forms something people dread. But the apparent reassurance in this form also functions in another way here – to make people less reluctant to provide certain kinds of information. The introduction of the Community Charge meant that adult lodgers would be responsible for paying the local tax (whereas before, in the displaced 'rates' system, the local tax was to be paid by the house owner who could incorporate it in the rent). The reassurance, therefore, encourages house owners to declare their lodgers as residents when told that homeowners cannot be made to pay the charge if their lodgers fail to do so.

Looked at from this angle, the reassurance functions as a form of social control: to guarantee the declaration of adult lodgers and to avoid lodger and owner striking a deal between them at the expense of the government department. This is in addition to other indirect reasons for wanting to find out who lives where (e.g. to trace homeowners' undeclared profits from renting out a part of their house). Readers of the form may have seen through this practice, but only if they were aware of the details of the new law on local taxation.

The same is true for the second excerpt we would like to look at in greater detail. The section we have in mind is the paragraph under the heading 'The Canvassers – Your Security' (see Appendix 2a). Although the leaflet may give the impression that registrees will not be bothered more than necessary and seems to offer a routine 'security' warning against impostors, the real fear of the authorities was that anti-Poll Tax campaigners would canvass to try to persuade people not to fill in the form.

The form here turns a political struggle into a legal one. The underlying intention is to stop a political movement from gaining further ground in bringing about actions which will make the implementation of the tax impossible. In short, in addition to assisting individuals by explaining to them the details on the registration form, the leaflet also functions to impose the legitimisation of the Community Charge and its implementation as a fact. The core of all this is social struggle, during which language use may become invested with social values. Although the new type of leaflet may be interpreted as a move towards a more 'open' and 'friendly' type of procedure – and the user may get the impression of being better informed about his/her rights and obligations and may feel more comfortable in using the

BUREAUCRATISATION AND DEBUREAUCRATISATION IN CONTEMPORARY SOCIETY

documents – these moves at the same time leave room for certain, perhaps more subtle, kinds of public control.

Conclusion

Debureaucratisation is symptomatic of bureaucratisation being a problem, but – as we hope to have shown – it does not tackle the causes of bureaucracy. Bureaucratisation and debureaucratisation are both the outcomes of macro social changes, which may transform existing relations in the public sphere in ways which are not immediately transparent to users. While the DVLA poster is a reflection of the marketisation of public life, the introduction of interim reports in universities is a result of increased government control over the budgets and running of universities, inspired by an ideology which wants to make universities accountable to the fee-paying student-consumer, thus giving rise to tightened forms of control over the institution's teaching staff.

Debureaucratisation manifests itself in certain forms – marketisation and the use of promotional discourse and conversationalisation. These forms harmonise with discourse changes in other domains. Fairclough (1992a) points to the inherent ambivalence in what he calls 'conversationalisation', the modelling of public forms of discourse, including written ones, on informal, face-to-face talk. Conversationalisation can be a sign of a more democratic mode of relating, and/or it can be used for the strategic purposes of the more powerful party to simulate equality. What is really important to our analysis is the fundamental ambivalence between these two possibilities, a sign of the extent to which egalitarian discourse forms are a stake in the social struggle. In this respect, it is difficult to conclude whether or not the poll tax leaflet and form we looked at is just a case of genuinely promoting accessibility. We must also remember that it is strategically directing behaviour to fulfil a vested interest related to a specific political project.[8]

Another conclusion to be drawn is that an explanation of these changed discourse practices must include a notion of 'genre' or 'mode of talking' which occurs in some form of institutional ordering. This can be straightforwardly illustrated by looking at the way 'explicitness' is handled in the DVLA poster and the

LANGUAGE, BUREAUCRACY AND SOCIAL CONTROL

Community Charge leaflet. Although both tend to point in the direction of the 'debureaucratisation'-end of discourse routines, they go in opposite directions when it comes to the text being more or less explicit. In as much as the poster is vague about the consequences of late payment, the Poll Tax leaflet is very explicit about the consequences of non-compliance. Clearly, there is no direct correlation in itself between less/more explicit kinds of information provision and debureaucratisation. Therefore, debureaucratisation cannot be reduced to a straightforward set of linguistic features. Instead it is a reflection of current social discoursal tendencies. As we have already pointed out, conversation and advertising are two genres which, in the current institutional orderings, have a capacity to move beyond the institutional domains in which they are traditionally used, and hence they may enter and take over the discourse practices of other domains, with the result that the changed discourse practices are characterised by a mix of 'old' and 'new' conventions and interpretations.[9] These genres are also the ones which institutions perceive as providing effective means for dealing with existing social problems or criticisms.

Notes

1. For introductions to Habermas's explanatory model, see Fraser (1989) and chapters 8 and 9 of Thompson (1984).
2. The teaching profile was first piloted in 1990. It became compulsory in 1994. See Appendix 1 for the full text of the document.
3. Note that in the 'Guidance Notes' it is claimed that the practice of using teaching profiles has been borrowed from other higher education institutions, but the notes do not reveal that those institutions must have borrowed it from private economy models which are performance-based. Cf. also the recent trend to collect 'student feedback' on teaching, again an institutional practice which resembles 'consumer satisfaction' surveys.
4. Value-for-money for the students may not really be a concern to those who institute the profile procedure, but the appeal to consumer values is certainly one way in which they try to sell their new policies.
5. See for instance Gyford (1991) on attempts of local authorities in Britain to get closer to the public by improving access to information about procedures and client rights.
6. At present, the revised council tax replaces the Community Charge

BUREAUCRATISATION AND DEBUREAUCRATISATION IN CONTEMPORARY SOCIETY   35

(commonly referred to as the 'Poll Tax'). Its introduction in 1990 was an event of historical significance.
7. That is, anyone aged 16 or over and living at the address.
8. We will discuss the adoption of a promotional mode by institutions in greater detail in Chapters 6 and 8.
9. See Fairclough 1992a,b for a detailed discussion of 'intertextuality'.

3 The pragmatics of information exchange in bureaucratic discourse

Introduction: information exchange as a focus of study

In this chapter we argue that bureaucratisation and debureaucratisation processes can be studied by focusing on information exchange. In accordance with the position outlined in Chapter 2, we suggest that the basic tenets of bureaucracy – which include hierarchical (unequal) structure of authority, rationality, and so on – are constructed through information exchange and therefore the study of contemporary bureaucratic processes requires an analysis of the discourse practices of information giving and information seeking.

Bureaucracies are seen as performing social tasks in which the processing of information plays an important role. Put very directly, bureaucracy is about processing people on the basis of information they provide, for instance, to decide on an applicant's entitlements to unemployment benefit, a vehicle licence, a passport for travelling, a grant to embark on a course of study.

Bureaucratic procedures usually entail a set of activities (e.g. a telephone enquiry about the procedure, answering questions at the desk when applying, filling in a complaint form). Such procedures suggest that institutions are social orders with a particular activity-structure, associated with which are 'orders of discourse' (Foucault 1971). By these are meant particular orderings of discourse types with overlaps, but also sometimes with rigid boundaries between them, characterised by a single practice (e.g. the same type of circular letter which is used for reminders) or by a mix of conventions (e.g. filling in a form in

THE PRAGMATICS OF INFORMATION EXCHANGE IN BUREAUCRATIC DISCOURSE

the office is sometimes but not always accomplished while interacting with an institutional representative). Also, clients need to know what is allowed in one activity type but not in another. For instance, some information about the decision making cannot be asked for when a client is in the application stage of a procedure but it can be asked for after, say, an entitlement has been denied. In contrast with this, it is possible to enquire about the steps of information provision during almost any of the activities that make up a procedure. In addition, there is also the question who in the discourse context can or cannot afford to transgress the boundaries of an activity. Thus, bureaucratic encounters can be seen as 'language games' in Wittgenstein's (1958) sense, with attendant language practices which conform to particular norms and conventions (Levinson 1979). However, bureaucracy is also seen as a game in a different sense: following received client wisdom, bureaucracy is all about 'playing the game'. But, as will become clear in this chapter, knowledge of the rules is unequally divided over social groups – not everyone is equally good at this game.

In the processes of information exchange, bureaucrats function as gatekeepers of a social order. Gatekeeping, however, is largely accomplished through discourse processes. Often bureaucracies are described as administrative 'machines', but bureaucrats are not 'passive agents', as their decisions can have lasting effects on the way life-chances are created or denied. When someone is entitled, say, to a driving licence, she/he becomes a member of the category of 'licensed drivers', which entails a number of things he/she is allowed to do, and a number of things which he/she cannot do. In other words, the outcomes of bureaucratic procedures have a crucial impact on subjects' social identities, including the regulation of social dos and don'ts in particular areas of their daily life. Obviously, it is institutional members who make decisions about entitlements. This happens on the basis of the information provided by the applicant, which is received and processed by staff at various levels in the office hierarchy. Hence, it is important to examine the nature of information exchange in the bureaucratic context.

This is the point of departure for both linguistic studies of bureaucracy, which pay little attention to how language use informs bureaucratic practices, and for sociological studies, which

38 LANGUAGE, BUREAUCRACY AND SOCIAL CONTROL

have recently looked at the changing forms of bureaucracy without paying enough attention to the role which language plays in these social transformations.

As a starting point, we shall concentrate on questions such as: When do clients and bureaucrats think they should seek information from one another and in what mode? For instance, clients need to decide whether to speak to an institutional representative over the telephone or to write to them. Likewise, bureaucrats have to decide whether to advertise or volunteer information without being asked to or to give information only on request and whether that information should be given in writing or not and who in the institutional hierarchy should respond to clients' requests for information (no matter who the letters are addressed to). This will also include situations where institutions ignore requests, where they blatantly refuse to give information and how in certain societies, the letters are addressed to husbands, although the initial request was made by their spouse. In other words, we concentrate here on a number of assumptions which underlie discourse in institutions and how they contribute to the construction of a particular kind of social identity, that of clienthood.

The focus of this chapter is on two aspects of information exchange: 'seeking' and 'giving' information. We will discuss both the bureaucrat and the client in these positions, thus drawing attention to how clients and bureaucrats in various situation types respond to given information or request for information. It will appear that bureaucrats function mainly in a 'seeking' frame and clients in a 'giving' frame. Only in a marginal way are the roles of supplier and receiver reversed. This, we argue, is linked up with the ways in which institutions maintain social control, as information exchange is instrumental in drawing certain divisions between clients and institutions.

Bureaucrats seeking information and clients giving it

Whatever their functions, it is obvious that bureaucratic institutions follow set procedures, which nearly always begin with a stage of gathering information. Procedures and sub-procedures have recognised beginnings and ends and usually a number of

THE PRAGMATICS OF INFORMATION EXCHANGE IN BUREAUCRATIC DISCOURSE   39

steps in between. These stages are taken through irrespective of the amount of effort this requires and irrespective of the quality of the information provided by the client. We will approach this issue of information through a comparison with conversational practice and police interrogations.

Let us consider a few turns of a bureaucratic encounter in a British social security context. The client came in with the purpose of asking about the restrictions on savings when someone is on family income supplement. Without allowing the client to state his problem, the bureaucrat (CS) imposes a routine procedure leading to a redefinition of the client's query, which now becomes whether or not Abdul (AL) is receiving the correct amount of social security money. At this point in the interaction, the age of the children is established through what may appear to be routine questioning about the client's personal details. The interaction then moves on to the topic of the client's rent.

Example 1

CS: How many children have you got mister Abdul?
AL: Five.
CS: Five children. Erm how old are they?
AL: Who?
CS: Your children?
AL: Erm.
CS: What ages?
AL: Twelve as twelve and a half.
CS: Twelve and a half that's one.
AL: Erm first one ehm nineteen seventy four second one nineteen.
CS: Nineteen seventy four nine.
AL: Nineteen seventy four.
CS: Born in nineteen seventy four.
AL: Yeah.
CS: And the third child?
AL: Nine year nine years.
CS: Nine years yes.
AL: Eh seventy six.
CS: Seventy six.
AL: Ehm seven year.
CS: Alright.
AL: Right. Eighty.
CS: Eighty. So that's three.

40   LANGUAGE, BUREAUCRACY AND SOCIAL CONTROL

AL: Eighty.
CS: No?
AL: Ehm another eighty two.
CS: Eighty two.
AL: Last.
CS: Erm do you pay rent?
AL: Yeah.
CS: Or do you have money to buy house? Rent?
AL: Rent, yeah.
CS: Rent. How much did you rent?
AL: Twenty pounds.
CS: Twenty pounds.
AL: Yeah.
CS: Do you get your money from for your rent from the council? Do you fill a form in?
AL: Yeah.
CS: And money sent to you from the council?
AL: Yes I sending but not finding now.

The following general point can be made about information seeking in this example. It applies to many bureaucratic encounters which are initiated by the client. There is some sort of focusing in on what the bureaucrat thinks the outcome will be based on, something which the client may not see as related to his/her query. This shows how bureaucratic encounters are fairly routine events. It also shows that information seeking becomes the core of the activity independent of the client's story. Thus, one is tempted therefore to characterise a bureaucratic encounter not so much in terms of the nature of the query (e.g. taxation and family income supplement) but in terms of information seeking itself. Let us now look at some further aspects of this information seeking process.

Putting a name to a face

Bureaucratic procedures almost invariably begin with establishing details of identity, even though the information may already be known to the institution. Clearly, institutions see this sort of low-level information gathering as relevant to the procedure, but often clients see this as time-wasting, trivial, a cross-examination and a form of harassment. This part of the information gathering is the most routine aspect, even to the extent that often clients introduce themselves with a near-complete account of personal

THE PRAGMATICS OF INFORMATION EXCHANGE IN BUREAUCRATIC DISCOURSE   41

details, as Akhtar Rashid (AR) does in the following interaction
with a civil servant (CS).

Example 2

CS: Can I have your name please?
AR: Yeah, my name is Akhtar Rashid.
CS: Akhtar Rashid
AR: I live in . . . Akhtar Rashid [pause] I live in [unclear]
    Bradford seven. [pause] I have some [pause] problem about
    general rate and supplement supplement ment
CS: Supplementary benefit.
AR: Supplement benefit. That's it.

This example shows how clients pre-empt the institution's
information seeking routines. AR provides full details about
where he lives and what the purpose of his visit is even before the
CS asks.

Matching sub-categories

In the bureaucratic encounter, bureaucrats take clients through
the procedure step by step. Each layer of information has to be
self-contained and the order of topical progress is fixed by a set
agenda which must enable the labelling process. In example 1,
the age of the client's children is established early on in the
encounter although it is not apparently clear what functional
purpose this information may serve. The children again enter the
discourse at a later point when their health and education details
are discussed. Such a discussion of the children's background
suggests that the institutional sub-categories take priority over the
development of a narrative account about the children.

The topical units in a spoken encounter match the boxes on an
application form, and, indeed, in many cases, the spoken
information gathering goes on together with the filling in of a
written form. As a result, the interaction is driven by sub-goals
and clients are discouraged from prematurely completing the
picture and drawing global conclusions. The overall labelling will
be based on the outcome of the sub-labelling process, and
bureaucracies work under the assumption that clients' answers to
sub-questions should not be informed by any predictions they

42 LANGUAGE, BUREAUCRACY AND SOCIAL CONTROL

make about the impact of their answers on the procedural outcome. As clients are taken through the procedure step by step, they are prevented from developing a long-term outlook on the procedure. The scope of topics is restricted to visible and discrete steps in the procedure. In the case above, although it is obvious that the number and age of the children have a bearing on an application for family income supplement, the exact relationship is not made explicit. Clients at the desk are also often left in the dark about the next step in the procedure.

In police interrogations, there is even more secrecy about the relevance of seemingly factual questions to the procedure or the allegation. Suspects are first asked to provide details in such a way that it is difficult for them to know how the details relate to the charge. Again, this serves to avoid the adoption of tactical response strategies. Only after a suspect has been subjected to the detailed interrogation, is she/he told about the charge. Such an examination of details is also characteristic of bureaucratic situations, where decisions about entitlements are made on the basis of seemingly unrelated bits of information sought of the applicant.

Confirming emerging labels

Notions of fairness and rationality in bureaucracy dictate that all clients are taken through the same step-by-step process before a decision can be reached. Therefore, further probing may be necessary within a sub-routine until the client gives a satisfactory answer. Compare this with written application forms, where a form may be returned to the applicant because it lacks certain bits of information or because the information is deemed to be inadequate. Until the information gathering stage is carried out satisfactorily, it is not possible to move on to the next stage in the procedure. Let us look at a university employee's holiday leave form. Although the leave in question is called 'holiday leave', the university not only expects staff members to give an 'acceptable' reason (something which the staff member may perceive as intrusive), but the institution also refuses to process the application until the information is provided. A staff member may resort to a vague answer (e.g. 'personal reasons') but this may not count as a satisfactory answer; in fact it may work against the staff member's case, as such an answer is likely to be

THE PRAGMATICS OF INFORMATION EXCHANGE IN BUREAUCRATIC DISCOURSE   43

met with suspicion. Note, however, how this contrasts with the university seeking seemingly redundant information.[1] Compare also the following warning from the Australian High Commission attached to a letter asking for further information before a visa can be processed.

Example 3

If the requested documentation is not lodged within 30 days of date of this letter, your application will be determined on the basis of the information available (i.e. your application will be rejected). If then you want additional prescribed information considered, you will be required to lodge a new application (Form 47) accompanied by the fee.

In this case, failure to provide information by a certain deadline will automatically lead to a rejection of the application and the procedure has to be re-initiated from the start. It is presupposed that incomplete information automatically leads to a summary rejection, that is an invalid application, although the wording 'will be determined on the basis of information available' at first suggests that incomplete information need not necessarily lead to an unfavourable outcome. This semantic twist is quite revealing, but may be indicative of the difference between how institutions actually deal with cases as opposed to what they lead clients to believe about the institutional procedure.

Bureaupretation

The information gathering stage we talk about here coincides with what Agar identifies as the diagnostic stage of institutional discourse: it is the process 'through which the institutional representative fits the client frame to the institutional frame' (1985: 149). This is what we would like to refer to as *bureaupretation*: the bureaucrat's interpretation of the client's state of affairs as communicated to the institution.

Turns and contributions receive interpretations which are different from 'standard' conversational practice (cf. police interrogation: 'Earlier you did say x, how can you now say y'; 'Why didn't you say so?'). How rigid is this departure from conversational practice, that is how conversational can bureau-

44 LANGUAGE, BUREAUCRACY AND SOCIAL CONTROL

cratic encounters and police interrogations be? The amount of variation can be studied in order to understand the degree of bureaucracy – and probably a departure from conversational practice goes together with an increased resemblance to police interrogations. For instance, in an informal conversation between strangers, personal details may also be exchanged in an evaluative way often leading to extended side sequences. A bureaucrat, on the other hand, may be unlikely to comment on the area where a client lives as a good or bad location, but such comments do sometimes occur in bureaucratic encounters – and they may give the encounter a conversational feel. In a police interrogation, however, such comments are ruled out. Similarly, the pressure to repeat a sub-procedure until it leads to a satisfactory outcome is low in a conversation but high in a police interrogation. In a bureaucratic encounter, failure to comply with a request for information may lead to a freeze in the procedure – quite often at the expense of the client, while holding clients responsible for the freeze in the procedure. Hence, there may be less pressure to repeat the procedure than in police interrogations.

It is normal for clients to initiate conversational divergences, as they are often in the dark about what exactly is relevant to the institutional agenda. Clients may tell conversational stories, but bureaucrats interpret them differently. The bureaucrat is likely to interpret whatever is said in direct relation to the institutional agenda. Clients may therefore be seen as deliberately 'opting out' of the institutional routine, and hence worthy of suspicion. This also explains why bureaucrats often ignore some client moves. What makes information exchange in bureaucratic contexts non-conversational is perhaps not that divergences from the procedural agenda do not occur in bureaucratic encounters, but that, when they do occur, institutional representatives try to 'steer' the direction. This, of course, involves the imposition of judgements of relevance.

In bureaucratic procedures, responses also receive an interpretation which is different from 'conversational practice'. For instance an admission of not having complied with some part of the procedure can be used as grounds for not granting a particular entitlement. As interpretative assumptions are not made available to clients, this is often disadvantageous to them (cf. 'anything you say can be used as evidence' in police interrogations). In other words, details carry a potential of evidentiality in them, even when clients reveal them as part of a story they are trying to get across.

In our earlier discussion we showed that bureaucrats expect clients to go through the entire routine procedure and provide any additional information asked for. An extreme case of such routine control over the supply of information occurs when clients are actually denied the opportunity to express their lived experiences. Also, whatever information clients volunteer is not interpreted in terms of its expressive contents load, but only in terms of the procedural routines. You cannot rely on letting your utterance speak, because the information contained in the utterance itself is subservient to the procedures. Implied meanings which do not bear on the procedure are likely to be ignored by the institutional representative.

This raises the fundamental asymmetry which underlies information exchange in bureaucratic encounters. However chatty the bureaucrat may become, the procedure is what will go on-record and the procedure can never disappear completely from the interaction.

Interpreting information exchange in pragmatic terms

Pragmatics is well equipped to allow us to study the processes of information exchange, but, as we will argue in the remainder of this chapter, for that purpose one needs to situate pragmatics within critical linguistics.

Pragmatics' concern with language as social action has perhaps found its strongest manifestation in the concept of speech acts (Austin 1962), which highlights the sense in which moves in an exchange can be interpreted as 'things done with words', namely 'promises', 'requests for action', 'threats', 'congratulations'. Although information exchange and speech acts analysis have to some extent developed as separate domains of pragmatic enquiry, our analyses throughout this chapter are informed by a view of complementarity.

As Fairclough (1992b) argues, pragmatic analysis is not really text analysis in the more traditional sense, but it is much closer to an analysis of discourse as a social event, entailing the potential –

46   LANGUAGE, BUREAUCRACY AND SOCIAL CONTROL

not always realised in practice – to examine the impact of talk in a particular situation on the longer term development of a society. In short, one central concern of pragmatic analysis is its preoccupation with the way in which moves in an exchange are interpreted by participants and the assumptions they have of one another. This concern harmonises with our aim, which is to examine the role which information exchange plays in the institutionalisation of social life.

In Chapter 2 we argued for a notion of language use as a form of social practice. This concern is shared with pragmatic theory, which equally views language use as a form of social action. The fundamental asymmetry underlying information exchange which we have begun to lay bare, can be examined further with a few pragmatic notions. We shall be referring to notions like cooperation, directness and indirectness, face and politeness in relation to principles of information exchange. Their application has dominated pragmatic analyses of various discourse contexts, particularly conversational ones.

Grice (1975) has been the first to attempt to put cooperation and its bearing on information exchange and indirect communication on the agenda of linguistics. His model is applied to institutional discourse in, for example, Heath (1979) where it is used to highlight the ways in which medical interviews divert from the mode of information exchange which Grice claimed to be characteristic of conversation. Our own work (Sarangi and Slembrouck 1992) focuses on the theoretical implications of applying these 'conversational' notions to institutional discourse. For us, pragmatic notions such as (non)-cooperation and (in)directness can be fruitfully used in a linguistic analysis which aims at offering social explanations, but their theoretical underpinnings must be reassessed in the light of a critical linguistic approach. Like Mey (1987), we argue that the way principles of information exchange apply in context requires a social explanation (including an examination of how relations of power and ideology bear on the practices of information exchange).[2]

Bureaucrats on duty: 'We shall continue until we get to the truth'

Let us first concentrate on the assumptions which interlocutors have about the quality and nature of one another's information

THE PRAGMATICS OF INFORMATION EXCHANGE IN BUREAUCRATIC DISCOURSE   47

exchange. Bureaucratic encounters take place with the assumption that the information provided by the client cannot be accepted at face value. As opposed to this, whatever speech act the bureaucrat performs comes with a guarantee of sincerity. Bureaucrats are supposed to be cooperative, but it is not possible for that cooperation to become an object of scrutiny. It is taken for granted that they will not lose valuable documents and it is assumed that promises to do something will be carried out.

Expressed in Gricean terms, institutions work under the assumption that applicants do not necessarily enter interactions as 'cooperative' talkers. The assumption that they will speak sincerely and provide all relevant information is open to scrutiny and often subjected to on-record declarations of intent. In contrast, institutions make no provisions for a similar guarantee on their side. Their 'cooperative' behaviour is supposed to be beyond question, which, of course, does not mean that applicants take it for granted.

Let us now look at an actual example of someone applying for a visa for travelling to a European country. The applicant provides the required proofs (including his passport and plane ticket). Both documents are quite valuable to him. It is not enough that the officer on duty has seen the ticket. Instead it is retained so that anyone else in the office can inspect it. At this point in the conversation, the client seeks some sort of reassurance that the documents will eventually be returned to him.

Example 4

Applicant: Will it be alright if my wife came and collected the
             passport and ticket for me?
Officer: Yes. As long as she comes between two and four.

The client's question is met with a response which answers the 'literal' question. The officer clearly ignores the assurance seeking request, or, perhaps it is more likely that he fails to interpret it as a request for reassurance. The key point here is that the bureaucrat is to be taken as trustworthy in what he or she says and as conscientious in what he or she does. The client should not have such fears of bureaucratic betrayal or negligence.[3]

One may wonder why the client did not insist or put his

48 LANGUAGE, BUREAUCRACY AND SOCIAL CONTROL

request more directly. He may have felt this could jeopardise his case, as such a request would come with an implicit accusation of inefficiency. Embassies are fairly intimidating institutions partly because the criteria for issuing visas are not transparent and the rules of conduct which apply in 'home' institutions do not apply in 'foreign' embassies. What we see is that clients are reluctant to ask in a direct way what they perceive as their right because it could turn out to be face-threatening, and bureaucrats can afford not to pick up the implied request. What is more, bureaucrats can rightfully treat with suspicion any information the client provides, whereas the clients are expected to take for granted the truthfulness of what the bureaucrat says. Each of these observations underscores the asymmetry in the assumptions they make about one another. This is essentially linked to an ideology about the stability of states and state organisations (whereas, by contrast, it is assumed that clients may disappear without warning).

Information gathering in a bureaucratic procedure is geared towards establishing institutionally defined truths. In this process, suspicion provides a basis for client construction. This is not only reflected in the discursive moves which bureaucrats make. Clients are also threatened with sanctions if they provide 'false' details. For instance, they are often required to sign forms with truthfulness declarations and produce various kinds of proof, certificates, and so on for facts already communicated in some other form. For instance, an instruction such as 'Photocopies of the following documents which must be certified by a notary public are to be submitted together with your application'. From the signed declaration, 'I declare that the information I have provided is complete and true to the best of my knowledge', it follows that clients are assumed to be likely to withhold information or indulge in lying. Furthermore, by asking clients for further proof (e.g. a legal endorsement of a certificate), their truthfulness declarations are often in themselves treated as unreliable.

Clients as duty-bound: 'Lost or stolen? Probably lost'

In the previous section, we saw that the assumptions about sincerity hold differently for bureaucrats and clients. In this

THE PRAGMATICS OF INFORMATION EXCHANGE IN BUREAUCRATIC DISCOURSE   49

section, we will focus on another asymmetry. Unlike bureaucrats, clients do not usually see themselves as withholding information but as cooperating with the bureaucrat in his/her search for the true state of affairs. For instance, when a woman reported a missing item to the police, the officer on duty asked her whether the item in question was 'lost' or 'stolen'. Uncertain about what had really happened, she replied with a non-committal 'probably lost', trying to cooperate as well as she could. Little did the woman know what procedural implications her answer would have.

Although direct questions are often asked which, at first sight, appear to enquire into fairly 'matter of fact' details, clients are often 'lost' about how their answers are linked to the procedures. In the following case, an apparently straightforward 'factual' question is responded to cautiously:

Example 5

Customs officer: Where do you live?
Arriving traveller: I work in Singapore but I have a flat in the UK
                 [address of place]

In the client's mind, 'Where do you live?' is a question which is far from always associated with customs procedure. But, from the customs point of view, a declaration of residence has consequences for the payment of import duties. The categories in play here are those of a British citizen who returns after work abroad versus a British citizen who is still working abroad but re-enters Britain as a temporary visitor. These categories have implications for the goods that can be brought into the country. But does the formulation of the question give away anything about the implications which a particular response will have?[4]

Consider also the following similar situation at Heathrow airport, where an Indian passenger who arrived from Pakistan on Pakistan International Airlines was called back by the customs officer and asked first, 'Were you on the Karachi flight?' Then a series of questions followed: 'What is the purpose of your visit? How long are you going to stay in Britain? Can I see your ticket? Is your friend going to pick you up?' The passenger was not asked to open his bag and the officer concluded the exchange

50 LANGUAGE, BUREAUCRACY AND SOCIAL CONTROL

with 'Have a nice time, sir'. In this case, the customs officer was asking questions in order to save the arriving passenger from a more thorough examination of his luggage. In that sense, the questions were relevant, although on the surface the client would not expect these questions to be asked by a customs officer (but perhaps by an immigration officer).

The fact that these two institutions can appropriate each other's questions suggests that this is a situation where a client is faced with a phenomenon rather than a particular person. Customs officers may thus be more interested in establishing the activities you will be engaged in than the goods you are carrying. Similarly, in another customs clearance situation in Britain where a traveller was on his way to his viva at a British university, the customs officer, as expected, did open the bag but, to the traveller's surprise, showed much more interest in the doctoral thesis than in the laptop computer which he was carrying (despite the fact that only the latter could become subject to excise duty). Again, enquiries into the purpose of the visit were used to decide whether a further examination of luggage would be in order. In ordinary experience, clients may perceive such situations as confusing, and they may wonder about authorisation, but the fact is that, in most cases, they answer such questions without further ado. This shows that clients occupy the position of truthful information providers. Whoever asks and whatever is asked may not matter so much to them, as their only role is that of an answerer.

In the following customs interrogation at a British port of entry, a seemingly irrelevant but persistent interrogation (about where the driver [DR] and passenger live and whom they would visit) leads to just one question about the actual subject of customs inquiry (scrutinising goods, here: the car).

Example 6

CO: How long are you staying in Britain?
DR: For the week.
CO: Where are you going?
DR: Lancaster.
CO: Where are you staying?
DR: With friends.
CO: Are they English?

THE PRAGMATICS OF INFORMATION EXCHANGE IN BUREAUCRATIC DISCOURSE   51

DR: Yes.
CO: How did you meet them?
DR: We lived in Lancaster for 3 years.
CO: What do you do in Belgium?
DR: I teach at Gent University.
CO: Kent University?
DR: No. No. Gent University. In Belgium.
CO: How long have you owned this car?
DR: Not that long. Two months now, is it?
CO: OK. Cheers.

The officer's (CO) final question about the car was clearly tokenistic: asking a real customs question while the 'green signal' had already been decided upon. As the driver explained to us later, his hesitation when answering the question about the car was caused by memory failure. 'Is it?' reflects that he was turning to the passenger for help.[5] Quite interestingly, this hesitation could have been a reason for the officer to become suspicious. The fact that he did not probe further and the contrast with the persistent probing into the identity of the travellers and their destination and hosts underscores the extent to which the final question about the car was tokenistic in the procedure. However, from a client's point of view, the situation is nevertheless puzzling in that the immigration-type questions appear to be far more important than the real customs-type questions. In this case too the customs have appropriated the immigration routine, thus threatening the client face at the opening stages of the encounter, but there is a restoring of face towards the end by making the encounter close conversationally.

From the client's point of view, the car question was ambivalent. The client could not know at this point whether it was tokenistic or the beginning of the real scrutiny, especially if he assumed that the customs-type questions matter more than the immigration-type ones. Only when the next turn came, could the client infer the interactional significance. Because of this ambivalence, the customs officer remains in control as he has the option to scrutinise further or to voice a closing signal. This interaction also shows that a shift towards a more conversational stance is the institutional representative's prerogative. Clients are not allowed to go conversational, but customs officers can decide

52 LANGUAGE, BUREAUCRACY AND SOCIAL CONTROL

whether and when to turn conversational. The occurrence of a conversationalised ending is symptomatic of a debureaucratisation process, but, as this example shows, interactional asymmetricalities are nevertheless sustained.[6]

From the institution's point of view, a question asked by the bureaucrat has relevance to the procedure, but this relevance may not be apparent to the client. Still, the client is asked to provide a relevant response – even though the ultimate decision about relevance rests with the bureaucrat. Clients may be uncertain about the relevance of questions, but their answer can nevertheless trigger off one course of action rather than another and thus bring about an altogether different outcome. For instance, in the following case, a woman rang a town police station to report and enquire about her wallet, which had disappeared while she was out shopping in town. She was asked whether the wallet had been 'lost or stolen'. Uncertain about what had really happened, she replied with a non-committal 'probably lost'. Without further questioning, she was connected to the lost goods department where she now was asked about the wallet's colour, brand, and so on, and advised to ring back a couple of days later to see if anything had been brought in. In this case the question 'lost or stolen' was functionally linked to two mutually exclusive categories which trigger two distinct police routines. But this procedural 'dilemma' was not visible to the client (although she could have inferred its importance from the question).[7]

A similar subservience to the procedure applies when applicants are filling in forms issued by the bureau. For instance, a traveller who re-entered Singapore from Johor Bahru in Malaysia, reported to us on the uncertainties which arose out of the ambiguity of one of the questions on the immigration form at the border control.

Example 7

Is this your first visit to Singapore?   Yes/No

Strictly speaking, this was his second visit to the country in question, but in a different sense, it was still part of his first visit as he had gone across the border just for the afternoon. Part of

THE PRAGMATICS OF INFORMATION EXCHANGE IN BUREAUCRATIC DISCOURSE   53

his anxiety stemmed from his uncertainty about the consequences that could follow from his answer. In the case of 'lost' versus 'stolen', the client did not realise that her reply would have categorical consequences in terms of police procedures. Not surprisingly, some clients perceive information-giving as a risky undertaking, because of the inherent uncertainty about the links between any response which is given and the next procedural step.

Reversing the roles: clients seeking information and institutions avoiding giving information

Some clients do not want to be kept in the dark, because too much may be at stake. They decide to ask for information. In this section we want to focus on such cases of apparent role reversal to make the point that the procedures are unlikely to be revealed (whether or not it involves general information, additional or specific information). We saw in the earlier examples that clients cannot ask questions about the bureaucrats' questions. Now we see that clients are not even expected to ask questions of the bureaucrats, although some of them do so in certain circumstances.

Asking for general information may appear a straightforward move on the part of clients. If an applicant knows what 'matters' in a procedure (what information is relevant), he/she can be more efficient and cooperative in providing the needed information. But as the following case reveals, the client's cooperative stance is not necessarily matched by the bureau. A woman who had just moved into Belgium wrote to the TV licensing authorities for information about TV licences. She did not have a set but was planning to borrow one from her sister-in-law. No information was provided by the institution. Instead, the following letter arrived:

54 *LANGUAGE, BUREAUCRACY AND SOCIAL CONTROL*

Example 8

[Name]
[Address]

YOUR LETTER OF   YOUR REF   OUR REF (1)   APPENDICES
                              [reference]
                              Cite please

Concerning: Identification of your registration of a car radio
            and/or television set.
                Your registration number: -----

~~Madam~~, Sir,

It has been noted that your first name is missing from your
registration with my department.

To avoid any confusion which could arise from this, I ask you
to return this letter in a stamped envelope within 10 days, after
you have filled in your first name and date of birth in the box
below.

Yours sincerely,

FOR THE DIRECTOR GENERAL
THE HEAD OF THE ADMINISTRATIVE DEPARTMENT

[name]

| First name of the holder: |
| Date of birth of the holder: |

----

(1) Please mention our reference as well as your registration
number(s) consisting of 8-digits (see part B of your payment slip)
on all letters or payments to the Department of Television and
Listening Tax.
        (Translated from the Dutch. See Appendix 3a for original.)

The letter, which is addressed to the woman's (assumed)
husband, is asking for the man's first name and his date of birth.
Not only did the institution routinely misinterpret the request for
information, thereby failing to supply the information or

THE PRAGMATICS OF INFORMATION EXCHANGE IN BUREAUCRATIC DISCOURSE   55

acknowledge the request, it also turned a citizen into a client (cf. 'It has been noted that your first name is missing from your registration with my department'). The man's personal details having been given in a dutiful way – despite the seeming absurdity of these details – next came a payment slip for a colour TV licence.[8] In short, a general request for information about the procedure was not replied to but responded to by setting the actual procedure in motion.[9]

From this example, it is clear that bureaucrats are reluctant to concede to applicants' requests for information about procedures. Institutions process clients on the assumption that they will provide the information required, but also on the assumption that the institution can withhold any information that is not in a narrowly defined and practical way related to whatever the procedure requires. The reason is that the institution will not provide any information that could be used to the client's advantage (or put institutional interests at risk). This is also clearly revealed in the following exchange, where a Commonwealth citizen rings the local British High Commission to sort out a few problems about his visa for Britain.

The visa which he had received in 1991 from a British High Commission in Singapore was one for multiple visits. It read:

Example 9

valid for presentation at a United Kingdom port/within six months from date of issue/within the validity of this passport.

It was taken up for the first time shortly after that for a work-related trip. Later in the year (June 1991) he planned another work-related trip to the UK in September but planned to come back after the visa for entry had expired. He also foresaw that he would be making more trips to the UK after that, and decided to contact the High Commission to gather more information. Below is a reconstruction of the telephone conversation between the client (CL) and the diplomat (DI):

Example 10

CL: I am just calling you to find out if you could help me with some information I have got a visa for multiple visits which erm

LANGUAGE, BUREAUCRACY AND SOCIAL CONTROL

> expires on the 18th of September 1991 and erm I will be erm I'll
> be erm arriving in London on the 15th so that will be just 3 days
> before it expires I shall only be returning after 18th what I need
> to know is do I need an extension of my visa before I set off
> DI: yes erm as long as you present the visa before the expiry date
> you can return after it has expired
> CL: so I don't need to apply for an extension
> DI: no the visa is valid if you can manage to enter before the date
> stamped on your visa
> CL: could I just ask another thing because I keep going to the UK
> rather frequently mostly in connection with some academic work
> you have struck out 'within the validity of this passport' as a
> duration for visa so could you please tell me what these two
> things mean within six months from the date of issue and within
> the validity of this passport I would like to know if I could get a
> visa which is valid until the expiry date of the passport
> DI: oh no you can only get into Britain before 18th of September
> the other option is not for you
> CL: yes but could you please tell me on what grounds do you
> consider offering such an extended visa
> DI: I don't think we tell these things but this has something to do
> with indefinite visa
> CL: thank you for your help
> DI: you're welcome
> CL: bye
> DI: bye

Two salient points emerge from the conversation: (i) The institution does provide some information, but only in as far as this is related to the dos and don'ts of the present visa entitlement. (ii) Any question which deals directly with the procedure is replied to in an evasive manner. This is a straightforward case of a client who – strategically – tries to extract some information which is regarded as 'secret' and the bureaucrat avoids disclosing it.[10]

Clients may especially seek information at the beginning of a (follow-up) procedure as in the cases we have just looked at. Another information-seeking occasion typically occurs at the end of a procedure when an applicant wants to find out why a particular entitlement was not granted. For instance, a woman who had applied for an extension of a work permit was at the counter to collect her passport with the necessary endorsements.

THE PRAGMATICS OF INFORMATION EXCHANGE IN BUREAUCRATIC DISCOURSE   57

At that point she discovered that an extension had been refused. She asked, 'Why?'. The reply was: 'Officers don't give reasons.' Why was she denied an explanation? Not only is the discretion of the bureau invoked, there may also be a face-redressive aspect here, namely officers at the desk may not necessarily know reasons. Similarly, a university employee wrote to the personnel department to ask directly why he had been denied conference leave and had instead been granted holiday leave.

Example 11

I shall be very grateful if you would let me know the circumstances under which conference leave has been denied in this instance. This will clarify, in general, the regulations concerning approval of conference leave (with or without financial assistance).

Clearly the purpose here was to find out more about how decisions are arrived at. A direct request of this kind was met with an equally direct refusal to reveal anything. The personnel office wrote back:

Example 12

I refer to your recent letter on the grant to you of holiday leave instead of conference leave for the [name] seminar.

The grant of conference leave is entirely at the discretion of the University, depending on the merits of the case. The University had considered your application and had resolved not to grant you conference leave for the seminar.

A reason is given together with a reassurance that the decision was arrived at in a fair way, but the client is not any better informed about the decision process. The reference to individual treatment is one way in which the institution tries to clear itself of any suspicions of unfair treatment.

Conclusion: regulated information exchange and social control

One may conclude from these examples that in most bureaucratic encounters the client is cast in a supplier role, while the bureaucrat is in a demander role. Bureaucratic procedures reveal the limits bureaucratisation can stretch itself to. Although – as we have observed in Chapter 2 – institutions nowadays appear to go out of their way to become more informative, and it is even fashionable to assure clients that individualised treatment is available, it is clear that clients' participatory rights remain constrained. There is a point beyond which bureaucratic communication ceases to become reciprocal. For instance, institutions like the Home Office may – anticipating future discursive moves – take away your speaker rights on a particular topic by stating in their letters that 'no further communication will be entertained' or an exchange initiated by a citizen may simply not be responded to by the institution.

The line which is drawn between social subjects and the institutions they deal with also has a dimension of client obligations. There is a point beyond which a client cannot refrain from participation as reflected in warnings of the type, 'Civil penalties will only be imposed where there is an outright refusal to provide information' (from the Community Charge leaflet discussed in Chapter 2). Or, in a weaker sense, a client is directed to follow a particular path when filling in a form (and failure to do so would be very 'costly' to the client as he/she may be asked to do the procedure all over again). In this chapter we have aimed at a qualitative specification of some patterns of information exchange in the bureaucratic context. In particular, our interest has been to look at where and why clients and bureaucrats seek information, provide information or withhold information. These issues will be taken up later in Chapters 5 and 6.

Our analysis has focused on various asymmetries which underlie information exchange in bureaucratic encounters. Explanations for these asymmetries have to be sought at the level of socio-economic stakes and interest relationships. Foucault's pre-occupation with technologies and techniques of power in the modern era has directed researchers to investigate technologies of discipline. Interviews and cross-examinations are core techniques in these technologies. This is also true for bureaucracy. Applying for eligibility entails both (i) the examination of whether someone qualifies (for which various discursive events are staged, namely filling in forms, asking for further details, interviews, and so on),

THE PRAGMATICS OF INFORMATION EXCHANGE IN BUREAUCRATIC DISCOURSE   59

and (ii) entitlement which always comes with a batch of 'dos and don'ts'. Hence, there is also a strong, implicit disciplinary dimension to bureaucratic procedures and their outcomes. In these processes, information exchange plays a very important role and basically follows the path of an examination with an examinee supplying information to an examiner, who, in his/her turn, is also mandated to doubt, challenge and probe into any aspects of the applicant's life that he/she may deem relevant to the procedure. This reiterates our point that 'institutions process people' – as in, for example, education (exams), police (interrogation), bureaucracy (application forms).

Our analysis in this chapter also has implications for pragmatic theory. As we also argue in detail elsewhere (Sarangi and Slembrouck 1992), the Gricean notion of 'cooperation' cannot be used as an archetype for interaction. Instead, it must be replaced by a view of complex, multi-level types of socio-economic interest relationships at a personal and at an organisational level which are conventionally (and strategically) linked to adopted principles or maxims of information exchange. It follows from this observation that information – seeking/giving – are different things for the client and bureaucrat. For the former there is the relation with the life world which enters the encounter, for the latter there are the relationships within the institution. Therefore, it is important to single out the two participants, as it were, and to look at the roles which client and bureaucrat perform. This is the central concern of the next chapter.

Notes

1. Although the form and procedure are called 'holiday leave', the application form has a slot for the 'purpose of leave'.
2. Most problematic in Grice's scheme is the archetypical status of conversational behaviour (see also Fairclough 1985 and Pratt 1981).
3. One of the most important controversies in pragmatics has been over the status of speech act labels. In our view, speech labels are words. In short, they are *interpretations* of actions performed through words. Verbal actions are interpreted as speech acts with a particular intentional load and a particular social relational value (cf. Leech 1983 for a review of some aspects of this controversy). Later in this chapter we talk about the distribution of rights and

60 LANGUAGE, BUREAUCRACY AND SOCIAL CONTROL

obligations to perform certain speech acts and the assumptions which talkers have about one another's motivations for performing such acts.

4. The traveller's response (perhaps informed by prior experience) may have been a tactical one, making it more difficult for the customs officer to categorise him on the basis of place of residence.

5. He turned to his spouse for confirmation, because he had been out of the country for a month or so on a business trip.

6. It is worth referring here to Tolson's (1991) analysis of 'chat' as a genre, defined as a temporary, conversational dispensing of the central activity in question. Tolson identifies three defining features of chat, which need not operate simultaneously: (i) there is often a topical shift towards the 'personal' (as opposed to the institutional), or towards the 'private' (as opposed to the public). (ii) This shift may be accompanied by displays of wit or humour. (iii) In any context 'chat' always works by opening up the possibility of transgression. 'Chat does not simply reproduce norms and conventions, rather it flirts with them, for instance, it opens up the possibility of the interviewee putting questions to the interviewer' (p. 181). Similarly, chat opens up the possibility for the applicant to ask personal questions of the bureaucrat (and do so strategically, to get to know more about how the institution works!).

7. This example is discussed at length in Sarangi and Slembrouck (1992).

8. Later on we learnt that in Belgium the dates for licence payment are spread over the various calendar months on the basis of holders' initials and year of birth.

9. There is, of course, the possibility that the clerk *did* read the request as a request for information, but, as this would have involved a break of standard procedure, he did not bother to respond to it.

10. A Canadian diplomat revealed (off-the-record) that the main purpose of interviewing visa applicants is to discourage people from entering the country. The point made here is that discoursal non-cooperation is often just the tip of the iceberg: often there is a deeper level at which non-cooperation is an established truth, which also ties in with the suspicions which institutions, as a general rule, harbour against clients.

4 *Role behaviour in discourse*

Introduction

In this chapter, we focus on role behaviour in discourse. But first, a few notes on why we selected this theme. We concluded the previous chapter by arguing that fundamental asymmetries which characterise bureaucratic encounters can be uncovered through the analysis of participants' perceptions of the encounter. At the root of these asymmetries are power differences which derive from social role relationships.

Our starting point for the discussion of role relationships is observable shifts in talk. Consider again the example at the British High Commission (see Chapter 3). The client's question about the use of the current visa is met with a cooperative response, explaining that the expiry date does not affect one's stay once a visitor has entered the country. The client's second question, which is about a long-term visa, addresses an eligibility matter and therefore the criteria are not given away by the bureaucrat. What we see here is a shift in talk initiated by the client – from talking about the use of one type of visa (multiple entry during a specified period of time) to talking about eligibility for an indefinite visa. This shift is matched by a corresponding shift in the bureaucrat's response. One can interpret the client's first question as a leading question, preparing the ground for the second question. However, is this the way the bureaucrat would see things? Would she not see this as a client who is entering an altogether different institutional scenario, where clients' rights to institutional knowledge are perceived as very different?

The shift in this example is perhaps a fairly subtle one, and one can easily think of situations where speakers shift, say, from a professional mode of talk into a conversational one. From an

LANGUAGE, BUREAUCRACY AND SOCIAL CONTROL

analyst's point of view, shifts in talk are very important because they lead one to examine the multiplicity of role configurations which may occur in a stretch of discourse. Shifts in talk are also important because relational asymmetries become visible through them and at such points one can often see social control happening. Additionally, from a participant's point of view, can one see such shifts in talk as strategically employed devices to establish or transform particular role identities?

In this chapter we will examine in greater detail how the participant fits into a social pragmatic model of language use which focuses on the wider societal context of utterance production and interpretation. Our analysis will also enable us to take up a position in relation to previous work on role behaviour.[1]

As in earlier chapters quite a substantial part of the text is taken up by analyses of authentic bureaucratic data, this time taken from the context of banking and social work. In the previous chapters we have mainly taken data from clearly bureaucratic settings. Our choice here of the less straightforwardly bureaucratic contexts of banking and social work is motivated by our wish to develop the notion of bureaucratisation as a process.

Modes of talk and multiple role behaviour

To start our discussion of shifts in modes of talk in institutional discourse, let us look at the following reconstructed interaction from the banking context. In this case, Ms S calls into her account holding branch to request a change of address for monthly statements. At the enquiries desk, Mr L, the bank representative, writes down the new postal address on the individual forms for her current account and higher deposit account. As he was doing this, the interaction developed more or less as below:

Example 1

L: Have you bought this property recently?
S: No, we rent it.
L: Are you thinking of buying a property then? Are you thinking of a mortgage?

ROLE BEHAVIOUR IN DISCOURSE   63

S: Not at the moment. The interest rates are so alarming.
L: I couldn't agree more. Perhaps it's better to wait.
S: Uhum.
L: Have you given any thoughts about any sort of investment then? For instance, buying shares in the market?
S: Not really.
L: In that case would you like an experienced bank rep to talk to you about the ways in which we can help? Obviously your money would grow faster because you get high interest now on all sorts of savings.
[*Ms S welcomed this move. Next, Mr L booked an appointment for a bank employee to visit the S family.*]

Mr L's query about home ownership is prompted by the topic of change of address. His question and Ms S's response 'we rent it' can initially be classified as 'social chat' in the banking context. As the talk then shifts to bank talk – about mortgages and investment – the initial social talk demands to be relabelled.

During the event, the purpose of the customer's encounter – to report and register a change of address – is successfully extended by the bank representative through the use of different modes of talk (from 'administrative talk' to the 'mortgage talk' and then to 'investment talk'). Obviously Ms S achieved her initial purpose of reporting a change of address, but Mr L clearly saw the occasion as an opportunity to sell, which may or may not have been in the interest of Ms S. He saw part of his job as explaining some of the facilities the bank offers even if this meant extending the immediate administrative position he was occupying. For him, Ms S is a potential investment client because of her 'standing' (she holds a higher rate deposit account).

A first shift in talk is accomplished when Mr L asks 'Have you bought this property recently?' Although it may sound like conversational small talk while doing an administrative job (and Ms S may well at first have thought it was) the question is indirectly functional as a subtle pre-move to broaching the topic of a mortgage. The second shift to 'investment talk' is a more direct one. It is initiated by 'Have you given any thoughts about investments then?'. These shifts are not mere shifts in topic, in fact, they are shifts in 'modes of talk'. For instance, the administrative talk (which we have omitted from the dialogue) linguistically required mainly information gathering: Mr L asking

64 LANGUAGE, BUREAUCRACY AND SOCIAL CONTROL

factual questions about the new address, old address, telephone number, account numbers, and so on. The mortgage talk, on the other hand, is more directive. Here the apparent information-seeking questions serve to set up the client to function in a selling script. Thus, the question, 'Have you bought this property recently?', means something different in the banking context than it would in, for example, a chat between colleagues or in the context of Inland Revenue. The same linguistic structure may mean different things in different institutional contexts and may thus affect the talk in different ways depending on the mode of talk it is embedded in.

In addition to the point that different functions can be ascribed to the same mode of talk in different situational contexts, it is also clear that a social subject, like the bank employee, can shift between various roles during one stretch of situated discourse. This is evident from the shifts in talk which occur. Should one analyse this as a straightforward matter of adopting a different mode of talk? Or should one also consider the role bearer's attitude towards the mode of talk he/she is adopting? In the following excerpt, a social worker is being interviewed by a researcher about the circumstances of a particular case of child care proceedings. The case involves a young mother, her cohabitant and a baby aged 10 months. It is worth considering which discourse features can be identified as belonging to different modes of talk and thinking about the reasons for their occurrence. The data below was recorded as part of an internal review and the excerpt comes from the beginning of the interview where the social worker (SW) sketches the circumstances of the case.[2]

Example 2

SW: when the baby was about five months old ehm taken to the GP who was very concerned about the child feeling that the child was underweight ehm was not developing as it should and the referral was made to St Hugo College Hospital it would appear retrospectively that there was a breakdown in communication between the GP and the hospital the hospital perhaps not quite realising the erm the priority that this eh situation should have so it turned out that was a further four weeks before the child was taken to the hospital for an

appointment on being taken there ehm the hospital felt that this was
a clear picture of a failure to thrive the child was as I recall off the
top of my head I think it was two and a half kilos underweight was
very dehydrated and in fact had the situation been left further longer
the child would have died

[. . .]

when I took on the case I took it on with a clear objective in
mind and that was one of assessment (. . .) now unfortunately
the child had been placed with a foster parent and again the
mother was hostile the foster parent found it impossible to work
with her and this was actually in fear of having this mother come
to her home and she in fact was so frightened that she asked for
the child to be transferred (. . .) when the child was transferred
again we were in some difficulty because we felt that we couldn't
arrange access in in the foster home as we normally would so
what happened was that access had to be arranged in area office
which was a horrendous task (. . .) to overcome this and to
enable me to assess this family's ability to care for this child we
involved the family welfare association in B and we involved them
with two erm objectives one was that they would assist in the
assessment of the parenting skills of these parents and secondly
that they would they would provide a venue where access to the
child could could happen (. . .) erm cutting a long story short
the assessment went very well and I managed to develop a
relationship with the mother in particular the father unfortunately
was in a detention centre at that time.

As is clear from the account, the social work intervention takes
place after a medical diagnosis ('when I took on the case I took it
on with a clear objective in mind and that was one of
assessment'). For instance, the social worker's use of terminology
like 'dehydrated' and 'underweight' indicates the importance of
medical diagnosis in the process of labelling of a case of 'failure to
thrive'. Another voice emerges when the social worker mentions
the lack of 'parenting skills' as a cause of 'child neglect', indicative
of his frequent liaising with family counselling institutions. In
such contexts, the social work practice cannot afford to
disqualify or ignore the medical labelling (it has not got the
powers to do so), but nevertheless the social worker here seems
to want to justify his profession's own space for independent
evaluation. Correspondingly we find at the linguistic level that

66 LANGUAGE, BUREAUCRACY AND SOCIAL CONTROL

the social worker only reports the medical proceedings, but when it comes to outlining the social work intervention, the distancing from what is being presented as factual makes room for clear expressions of commitment. Compare for instance the distancing in 'the hospital felt that this was a clear picture of failure to thrive . . . ' (first paragraph) with the commitment implied in 'to enable me to assess this family's ability to care for this child we involved the family welfare association in B and we involved them with two erm objectives' (second paragraph). The social worker's attitude is an important dimension of his role behaviour. This can be captured through the notion of 'discourse role'.

Discourse roles

The distinction in expressing commitment/distancing to propositions/ actions can be understood with the help of the notion of discourse role, which Thomas (1986) defines as specifying the relationship between speaker and message. Examples of such discourse roles are 'spokesperson', 'mouthpiece', 'reporter', 'overhearer', 'bystander' etc. To use Thomas's categories, the social worker in example 2 acts as a 'reporter' for the medical practitioners (thus he is not identified with the medical sources). On the other hand, the social worker acts as a 'spokesperson' for the social work profession, because he is a member of it and can act on its behalf.

Thomas's discussion of various discourse role categories is in keeping with Pratt's (1981: 8) critique of an undiversified speaker concept in pragmatics:

One superficial but revealing consequence of the stress on individual beliefs, desires, intentions, and responsibilities is that speech situations in which speakers speak for or through other people look like marked or abnormal cases. These would include such examples as a person passing on a message, reporting on a meeting, newscasting, representing a client, being a spokesperson for a group, and many others. In fact, it might strictly include speaking in any institutionalized or ritual role that exists apart from the person who occupies it, because for any such role the intentions, beliefs, etc. behind the speech act attach to the office and not the particular speakers.

Questions emerging from this are: Is it always possible to distinguish one discourse role category from another? And are discourse roles the same across situation types? Thomas has already pointed at the possible overlaps between categories. She has further suggested that for each discourse role there is a prototypical form of behaviour. Actual instances of role behaviour may then to a greater or lesser degree conform to this prototype. There are two issues here we would like to elaborate upon in the next section. First, we would like to warn against an undiversified use of discourse role categories such as mouthpiece or spokesperson (and social role categories, e.g. social worker and police officer). Secondly, we feel that discourse role is perhaps better thought of as inevitably linked to social role.

Mapping discourse roles on to social roles

First, in order to clarify why we argue against an undiversified use of discourse role categories, let us return to our bank and social work examples.

We could start by saying that Mr L in example 1 is a bank 'representative' and Ms S is a bank 'customer'. Terms such as 'representative' or 'customer' refer to role categories occupied by the individual participants in the interaction. Having looked at the shifts in talk during the interaction, it is rather difficult to grasp the bank employee's activities through the single category of 'representative', as more subtle distinctions are called for. As we know, the person at the enquiry desk also deals with other aspects of banking, as bank employees rotate between various roles, only some involving contact with the public, others being more purely administrative. In the interaction, we see Mr L acting out some of the different roles the banking profession allows for, those of 'administrator', 'financial advisor', 'receptionist', and so forth. Similarly, in the second example, the social worker occupies the role categories of a 'key worker' who coordinates the actions between the various agencies, a counsellor to the family, a protector of the child, and an assessor with police authority.

Both the social worker and the bank employee can be labelled as 'institutional representatives'. However, when one uses the term 'representative' one may easily be led to believe that all

LANGUAGE, BUREAUCRACY AND SOCIAL CONTROL

would occupy the same role. But institutions like banking and social work are socially located differently and also function differently. Unlike social work, the bank as an institution falls under the private economy. So although Mr L in example 1 appears to take on an advisory role the use of 'counsellor' as a role category label would be unusual in this case (but not in the case of the social worker).

With particular reference to the social worker, we find that the notion of 'discourse role', although helpful on its own in drawing certain analytical distinctions, cannot alone answer the question why in specific bureaucratic contexts certain discourse roles occur at all. The social worker here is a reporter for the medical profession, but the reason why he occupies that discourse role has to be sought in the wider context of social relations. We know that social work involves a multi-agency network in which the social worker very often occupies the least powerful position. In cases of child neglect, the medical profession – not the social worker – decides what is a child abuse case. As far as the medical side is concerned, the social worker's verbal actions are thus restricted to the discourse role of reporting the medical diagnosis. This dependence of discourse role on social mandates is one reason why we prefer an approach in which social roles and discourse roles are seen as very closely interconnected.[3] The same investment talk could be dismissed in a conversation between friends by one party on the grounds of lack of expertise, whereas in the bank context the same would happen on the basis of alleged selling. As we discuss in more detail later, the perception of the interlocutor's membership of a particular role-category and of what that category entails acts as an important cue for how discourse is interpreted.

A second reason becomes clear when one examines whether what counts as the same discourse role category is the same in all social situation types. Let us take here the discourse role category of 'mouthpiece', which Thomas defines as having the prototypical core characteristic of 'neutrally relaying the message the mouthpiece is not the author of'. In the following reconstructed interaction (example 3a) which took place in a Belgian city, Mr D is called to the door by a police constable who personally hands him an 'invitation for interrogation' (example 3b). As is clear from the text of the document the invitation does not

ROLE BEHAVIOUR IN DISCOURSE 69

specify what the interrogation will be about (although the client could easily guess the circumstances that led to it):

Example 3a

D: What is it for?
PC: I don't know. They didn't tell me.
D: I think it is rather impolite to tell us to come for an interrogation if we're not told what it is about.
PC: Are you accusing me of impoliteness?
D: No. I am accusing the person who wrote it.
PC: It's about your house.
        (Translated from the Dutch. For original, see Appendix 4a.)

Example 3b

CITY OF [NAME]   P. 23

POLICE   INVITATION

                  To [name] + [name]
                  [address]

Please report on *Thurs* day *9 August* at *2 pm*, between _____ and _____ or _____ and _____ at the abovementioned police station for *interrogation and providing information* – <u>Both persons must be present.</u>

                  [place], 08/08/90
                  ~~The Officer of Police~~
                  The Police Constable
                  [name]

Please bring this invitation along

                  The name of the authoriser
                  must be in capital letters.

        (Translated from the Dutch. *Note:* The words in italics were hand-written in the original. 'Both persons must be present' was written in red ink and had double underlining.)

70 LANGUAGE, BUREAUCRACY AND SOCIAL CONTROL

Interestingly, the police officer here at first claims to be only a messenger/courier, in Thomas's terms a 'mouthpiece' for the illocutionary act of invitation (a role prepared for by the social role which the PC has to assume). However, as the interaction develops it turns out that he knows very well what the interrogation would be about, (although he remained vague about the topic – see our earlier discussion in Chapter 3). In fact, the next day when the client reported at the police station, it turned out that the same police constable was the only person on the case and took down the client's statement.

The occurrence of a mouthpiece role in this case is strategically functional. The person to be interrogated cannot as a rule be told in advance what the interrogation will be about. This explains why the written invitation does not specify the circumstances. But partly because the mouthpiece here is a police constable, the client (who had a knowledge of these restrictions) expected the constable to be able to elaborate on the message beyond what he was supposed to relay. Let us now compare this with a situation where a departmental secretary acts as a mouthpiece when communicating a departmental head's disciplinary measures. The memo reads as follows:

Example 4

MEMO

From: [name] Date: 15 Jan 1993
To: [name]
Ref: [reference]

I shall be grateful if you will take note that practicals should
finish 10 minutes before the hour, in order for changeovers to
take place. I do not expect to have to wait until after the hour to
get into the astro-physics lab.

Here the secretary is the mouthpiece, as reflected in the 'reference' section of the memorandum. Unlike the police constable, it is less likely that she can expand on the message. These restrictions follow from limitations in social mandate and how they are perceived: the police constable is first a police constable and then a mouthpiece; for that reason he can be expected to shift to being a 'spokesperson'. As opposed to that, it is much more difficult for a secretary to take up a position independent from that of acting out the boss's instructions.

This brings us to question the usefulness of wanting a single definition for the discourse role categories. In Thomas's sense, for instance, the secretary would be more of a so-called prototypical mouthpiece. But, for us, this is one among other mouthpiece types, one who stands in a hierarchical relationship with the authorising body and for whom there are constraints on the extent to which she/he can expand, comment on or recast what has been handed down to him or her. By contrast, our police constable example makes the point that a mouthpiece can be of the same professional rank as the author of the message, with the result of a different potential in the realisation of discourse role. Our retreat into the underlying social categories and interactional contexts reveals precisely that.

Concluding this section, we have argued in favour of giving a social context to discourse role, thus treating discourse role as a subsidiary of social role. In our next section we discuss the relationship between shifts in talk and the construction of social identity through role assignments.

Shifting role relationships and the construction of social identities

Role categories not only call for subtle sub-specifications like the ones we have already drawn attention to: much depends also on the institutional context. One must also be aware that the use of role category labels involves social acts of classification. This leads us to suggest how two types of shift – in roles and relationships – are accomplished through shifts in modes of talk. Clients and institutional representatives not only occupy different sub-roles and shift between modes of talk. The speech acts which they perform – for example complaining, acknowledging – are at the core of changing social relationships.[4]

Let us now look at the clients' role behaviour in two different institutional contexts (banking and taxation). In both cases, the client has written a letter of complaint.

In example 5a, the same bank customer as in example 1

72 *LANGUAGE, BUREAUCRACY AND SOCIAL CONTROL*

complains to her branch about a returned bank cheque. First she receives a letter from the bank.

Example 5a

[Name of bank]	Sorting Code: [code]
[Address]	
Mrs [name]	Your ref:
[Address]	Our Ref: [reference]
	Ext. No.
	Date 21.3.90

We advise that the undermentioned item has not been paid.

☑ CHEQUE	❑ STANDING ORDER	❑ DIRECT DEBIT
RETURNED UNPAID	NOT PAID	RETURNED UNPAID

PAYEE/BENEFICIARY/ORIGINATOR:	DATED/DATE DUE:
[Name]	1.3.90

AMOUNT:	ANSWER GIVEN ON CHEQUE/DIRECT DEBIT:
£200	REFER TO DRAWER

Your account has been debited with the sum of £15 to cover the handling charge involved in the non-payment of this item. Please ensure that in future, sufficient funds are available to meet any cheques issued and/or standing order/direct debit payments due. In the absence of available funds, such items will not be paid and, in the case of a standing order/direct debit the authority will be cancelled. Your account will be debited with our standard charge on each occasion.

THIS ADVICE DOES NOT REQUIRE SIGNATURE

Ms S lodges a handwritten complaint:

ROLE BEHAVIOUR IN DISCOURSE 73

Example 5b

11 April 1990

The Manager
[Bank]
[Address]

Dear Sir/Madam

I would be greatly obliged if you could look into the following queries.

I received an unsigned 'advice letter' from your branch regarding a cheque of mine returned and letting me know that £15 has been debited from my account. This came as a surprise to me. Just a few days before, I had received my statement and it showed a balance of £175 in my account.

Firstly, I'd like to know why should you return a cheque when my account gets a regular sum of money coming in. I had written this cheque in the beginning of the month when I ~~had~~ was sure I had more than enough money and expecting the regular amount from the DHSS.

Secondly, couldn't you have cleared the cheque and charged me for an overdraw instead? I felt quite embarrassed about the whole affair but luckily I could alert the respective authorities beforehand.
I find the whole incident quite strange especially when I have other accounts in your branch. I would be pleased if you could clarify these questions for me PLEASE.

Thank you,
Yours sincerely,
[signature]

Finally the bank responds in a further letter.

74 *LANGUAGE, BUREAUCRACY AND SOCIAL CONTROL*

Example 5c

Mrs [name]
[Address]

Your ref:
Our Ref: [reference]
Ext. No.

12th April 1990

Dear Mrs [name],

Thank you for your letter dated the 11th April 1990, concerning the cheque which was returned unpaid on your account on the 20th March 1990.

Unfortunately, an error has been made by us as the funds on your savings account were not taken into consideration when the cheque was returned unpaid. Your two savings accounts were not connected to your current account and therefore the mistake was made.

Please accept my apologies for this error and if you require us to write to the [name of institution] to confirm your creditworthyness [sic], please let me know and I will be more than happy to write such a letter.

I have now ensured that your savings accounts have been connected to your current account to ensure that in future this error does not happen again.

I notice that we have already refunded the unpaid fee of £15 to your account.

Yours sincerely,

Personal Lending Officer

Note that in her letter, Ms S not only asks for a clarification of the bank's action, she also challenges the bank's characterisation of the situation and suggests an alternative course of action that could have been taken. What is significant here is that the bank acknowledges the client's role behaviour. In its response, it admits to making an error, reimburses the financial penalty and, further, offers to repair the face damage. Let us now compare this with how in example 6, the TV licensing authorities respond (or rather fail to respond) to Mr V's letter of complaint. The first paragraph of Mr V's letter recounts the circumstances as he saw

ROLE BEHAVIOUR IN DISCOURSE 75

them (see also Chapter 3, for an account of what had gone on before).

Example 6a

To [name] 13 June 1990
  Head of the Administrative Department
  Department of Radio and Television Licences
  [address]

Dear Sir/Madam,

Enclosed I return the giro form which you sent us a few days ago. I cannot make use of it because we do not own a colour television and nowhere on this form it is stated how much radio and television tax we have to pay for the portable black and white set which is currently on loan to us.

What's more, I ask myself a number of questions about the way your department operates. A quick summary of events. Early March my wife wrote a letter to your department enquiring about the regulations for radio and TV licences. This information we still haven't received. Instead I received a letter in which you ask me for my first name and my date of birth (RT 1307 NL). I have given you this information and now you are sending a payment slip which says that we owe radio and television tax for a colour set (which we do not own) and that we have been using this set already since March 7 (something you cannot possibly be sure of). That the payment slip is useless comes as no surprise to me, as no one in your department has taken the trouble to find out what kind of set we have and since when we have had it. When somebody asks for more information about radio and TV licences, this does not automatically mean that he or she actually owns a set. Moreover, I really wonder where the department of radio and tv-licences gets the right from to decide on its own what people (do not) own and since when they have owned something. And, most irritating of all is that in reply to a letter sent by my spouse, it is decided that I am to be registered with your department. If this is not discrimination against women!

Yours sincerely,

[name]
[address]
      (Translated from the Dutch. See Appendix 3b for original.)

76 *LANGUAGE, BUREAUCRACY AND SOCIAL CONTROL*

Example 6b

[name]
[address]

YOUR LETTER OF   YOUR REF   OUR REF (1)APPENDICES
[reference]
Cite please

Concerning: legal and statutory regulations of television and radio
tax.
Your registration number: [number]

Sir,
~~Madam,~~

I would be grateful if you took notice of the information in the
following rubric(s) number(s): *7 and 12 (see reverse)*

1. Radio and television tax is due for periods of twelve consecutive
   months. The starting date of the periods is determined by the first
   letter of the name of the holder. Each year the payment forms are
   sent out during the first half of the first month of the period to
   which the holder belongs depending on the first letter of his name.
   Your period of 12 months begins each year in _____
   because your licence is in the name of _____with the number
   _____.

   I draw your attention to the fact that television and radio tax
   must be paid using the payment forms sent out by the department
   of radio and tv-licences.

   If exceptionally you would not have received an invitation for
   payment within one month of your period then you immediately
   have to ask the department of radio and tv-licences for a payment
   form.

   If you find that the details on the pre-printed payment form are
   incorrect, please notify my department in a separate letter.
2. As standing orders with a financial institution are not accepted for
   the settlement of radio and television tax, you are requested to
   pay the amount due only by using the payment forms sent to you
   by the department of radio and television licences.
3. The registration numbered _____ for _____ is now

being cancelled. The licence for _____ is from now onwards registered under the number _____ in the name of _____.

4. The registration numbered _____ in the name of _____ (which expires on _____) will from now on be registered under the number _____ in the name of _____ and will, as a result, expire on _____.
The effect of this alteration is that additional payments are due for the period from _____ to _____, that is _____ months.
Before long, a payment form for _____ BF will be sent to you.

5. It has been recorded that you no longer have a _____ (fixed or portable).
As a result, your registration has been cancelled for the following expired set (that is, from _____ onwards). Tax remains due/has been paid for the running period, which is from _____ to _____.

6. As the payment forms have already been sent out, you are requested to pay television tax for your colour television with the form for a black and white television that was sent to you earlier. A pre-printed payment form for the colour supplement will be sent out to you as soon as possible.
In any case, do not make use of another form.

7. The payment form(s) in your possession (nr. *[number]* for *a colour television*) may now be destroyed.

8. Please only pay using the forms that have been or will be sent to you.

9. The necessary arrangements are being made to refund the amount of _____ BF paid in excess (the postal charge will be deducted, if the refund is by postal draft).
Reason for refund:

10. Cable television.
As the television tax is not included in the annual connection fee for the television cable network, subscribers must meet their legal obligations regarding the payment of the amount of television tax due for owning one of their television sets to the department of radio and television licences.

11. From our investigations, it appears that on _____ you have indeed paid tax for _____ for the period from _____ to _____ and that you are now registered under the number _____.
The payment form for _____ may now be destroyed.

LANGUAGE, BUREAUCRACY AND SOCIAL CONTROL

12. *In the course of July you will be sent a payment form to settle the licence for a black and white television.*

Yours sincerely,

FOR THE DIRECTOR-GENERAL
THE HEAD OF THE ADMINISTRATIVE DEPARTMENT

[name]

(Translated from the Dutch. The text in italics was handwritten in the original letter. See Appendix 3c for original.)

What is striking in example 6b is that the TV licensing authorities do not acknowledge the client's role behaviour in the same way as the bank does in example 5c. There is no explanation. There is no acknowledgement of having received the accusation of sexist practice and rash classification. Instead, the response is restricted to the correction of the error. This difference in treatment we feel is the result of a difference in how the institutions construct the identity of clients. Unlike the TV licensing authorities, the bank sees the client as a customer who can pull out from business if he/she feels a complaint is not satisfactorily responded to. The TV licensing authorities on the other hand act under the assumption that a client cannot opt out. On the contrary, clients can be prosecuted should they refuse to deal any further with the institution.

An even more extreme case in point is the role relationship between police and interrogated. For instance, the police in Belgium can summon anyone for an interrogation without giving a reason. Furthermore, when a statement is concluded the client is not allowed to read it; instead it is read out to the client and this is the only form of access for a discussion of changes or for additions to be made.

Such differences in the client's rights and obligations justify our claim that we are here dealing with different kinds of client, the citizen-client in public administration as different from the consumer-client in the context of business. Although at this point it may be tempting to claim one-sidedly that the bank is not a bureaucratic institution, an analysis of the exchange suggests that at least in part it functions like one. The bank's concluding sentence 'This advice does not require signature' does not only

ROLE BEHAVIOUR IN DISCOURSE 79

sound very bureaucratic as a 'final word' in the matter, it also carries overtones of routine measures being taken indiscriminately and unconditionally for any client in such a situation. Of course, afterwards the bank communicates its decision to take into consideration the client's personal situation. It is the way in which the discourse moves of reprimand, complaint and acknowledgement follow one another that is responsible for the shift away from a bureaucratic mode of talk in this particular exchange.

In both cases clients were trying to negotiate their relationship with the institution. In the case of the TV licence the complaint stemmed also from Mr V's resentment about having been turned into a client without asking for it. But one important question now is how precisely role assignment in discourse and social identity are linked to one another. We take the view that language use is instrumental in inscribing social identity, including the construction of role relationships. For instance, in the first banking case (example 1), the employee at the counter by shifting between modes of talk also constructs the client as an 'investor', a 'potential house owner', and so on. It is up to the bank customer whether or not to accept or attempt to modify these identities, but, as the TV licence case shows, identities are often imposed one-sidedly and clients' attempts to resist a role or, in their turn, define the institution's role, rebound.

Similarly, in the social work example (example 2), the worker's account is not just a mixture of various modes of talking, but each bit also contributes to the construction of a particular social identity for the mother in the case. A particular kind of 'motherhood' is being constructed that goes together with cases of child abuse and neglect. It is constructed at the intersection of various kinds of talk of various institutions which here merge in the social worker's account. But this type of motherhood (obviously) also formed the basis for the interaction with the mother. The mother here is identified as:

- uncooperative (with social worker, hospital staff, foster parents)
- hostile and potentially violent to foster parents ('was afraid . . . ')
- irregular in keeping appointments
- careless and indifferent to the child's well-being ('had the situation been left').

LANGUAGE, BUREAUCRACY AND SOCIAL CONTROL

What we observe here is the construction of a 'non-mother' (uncooperative and uncaring before and during social work intervention). This picture of motherhood (created against the unspoken background of what would be an 'ideal mother') has significant consequences for both child and mother (and is more powerful than any alternative characterisation, for instance, the mother as resenting everyone laying their hands on her child and wanting to control and assess her motherhood).

The attribution of identities to individuals in cases of crises is important, as it is very consequential for these particular individuals. In a more fundamental vein, it also holds that our social identities are constantly modified both through our own talk and that of others. Discourse is thus identity-inscribing, to an extent which escapes the conscious attention of social subjects. It is difficult for the social worker to talk outside the multiple modes of talking he is adopting (as his institutional survival is essentially linked to it).

Within social theory, Foucault (1972) has brought to the forefront the role-creating capacities of discourse formations. His reversal of the subject-statement relationship (the statement appropriates the subject) harmonises with our earlier expressed view that language has a situation-creating capacity (e.g. participation as a situational parameter). Furthermore, Foucault's notion of 'dispersed' social identity undermines the essentialist idea of a unified social subject – a role-less true self. When subjects 'speak for themselves', they do not speak from outside a role (cf. Pratt 1981). Moreover, with this view, it is perfectly possible that, as a result of the compartmentalisation of social life in relatively distinct domains, social subjects take up incompatible role positions without being aware of this. From this point of view, role slippage is largely an inevitable and accidental by-product of the dispersion of the social subject rather than something which necessarily lies within their conscious control.[5]

Role perception in discourse

There is another important aspect to role behaviour, that of role perception. Social subjects bring to discourse situations particular expectations about each other's role. Let us now look at a

ROLE BEHAVIOUR IN DISCOURSE 81

situation where a British government official (GO) is interviewed about his work as an advisor to the Technical and Vocational Education Institutes (funded by the previous Manpower Services Commission). Consider in particular how the civil servant and the interviewer (IN) in the course of their talk together construct the interviewee's professional identity. The extract below begins with the GO outlining how he sees his role.

Example 7

GO: I would like to see myself visiting a school as one of a partnership as between the authority and the commission and in most cases where I think we have a good relationship that's probably what it is

IN: where would your job differ from that of an HMI

GO: erm in a sense I am empowered to make suggestions to them erm I have to ask questions about what they are doing and I suppose the the other difference is that I have a more executive function in the sense that I'm reporting back erm to a budget holder

IN: even some people might regard your job as being like that of a policeman what do you think of that

GO: I I should really hate that erm to some extent er we have an audit responsibility because the commission has that responsibility and to that extent we are but I I don't know how much I kid myself more as visiting colleagues doing the same job from a different standpoint

IN: do you have any sanctions you can use

GO: yes we do erm in the sense that almost unique to the TVEI is the fact that this enterprise is based on a contract erm should that contract be seen to be in breach then of course the contract might be terminated now that's a very drastic sanction and I doubt if it's one we would ever employ I have never come to that point or anything like it yet

What is striking is that the interviewer and the official start delineating the former's role from oppositional ends. The interviewer's questions look for overlap and contrast with the role categories of 'policeman' and 'inspector'. As opposed to this, the GO tries to construct his role in terms of his mediating responsibilities (cf. 'between the authority and the commission', 'reporting back to a budget holder', to honour 'a contract'). The

GO's professional identity comes out as many-faceted, but it is also characterised by internal contradictions (cf. 'I have to ask questions about what they are doing' versus 'I see myself more as visiting colleagues doing the same job from a different standpoint').

Because perceptions are asymmetrical, it should be noted that it is virtually impossible (in analytical terms) to define the contents of a particular role category without creating the false impression of an existing consensus over its contents. The theoretical assumption of a 'common ground among all participants' is characteristic for a consensus-model of language use. As opposed to this, our suggestion to consider for each participant how they see the self/other and the self's/other's role harmonises with the need for a conflict model of discourse. This also has a bearing on how one conceptualises 'role behaviour'.

From the interview in example 7, it is clear that conflicting interests at the social level make it possible for the advisor's role to be cast in the negative terms of police work by those who are inspected. This reveals an underlying power struggle, which makes the advisor's image of a 'partnership' unreal for those under his supervision.

Conclusion

Our main claim in this chapter is that role behaviour provides a link between participants, social identity and discourse practice. Rather than arguing that it is possible to do a 'straightforward' analysis of interactional data, we suggest that one focuses first on each participant's perceptions of their own and the others' role behaviours in relation to what can be inferred from observing the discourse data.

Let us finish the first part of the book with the following piece of data, part of which was already discussed as example 4. Here it is presented in the way it came to us. In our analysis, we will try to tie together our argumentation from the first four chapters.

ROLE BEHAVIOUR IN DISCOURSE   83

Example 8

*Here's a memo I have just got from our HoD, which I thought
you might like for your bureaucracy book (made anonymous, of
course). I almost handed in my resignation when I got it – the
bloody cheek of the man talking down to me in such a
patronising manner!*

MEMO

From: [name]   Date: 15 Jan 1993
To: [name]
Ref: [reference]

I shall be grateful if you will take note that practicals should
finish 10 minutes before the hour, in order for changeovers to
take place. I do not expect to have to wait until after the hour
to get into the astro-physics lab.

Would he talk like that to other members of staff, I ask myself . . .

So far, we have talked about what it is that makes an
exchange of information bureaucratic. We have said that one
must pay attention to the situation of use as well as discourse
processes. We have also suggested that one has to take into
account the perception of interactants, particularly the recipient
of a message, because bureaucracy is as much 'perceiving' as it is
'doing'.

Relevant to this is an analysis of actions and consequences.
What prompts a bureaucratic act and what effects does such an
action seem to have on those who are at the receiving end?
Compare the insensitiveness of bureaucrats with the
over-sensitiveness of clients. In this case, the departmental head is
unlikely to have harboured the idea that the lecturer on receiving
the note would think of 'resignation' as a form of reaction or that
he would feel discriminated against. It is worth noting here that,
although the first sentence of the memo could have been
addressed to all staff members without offending anyone, the
second sentence invokes a hierarchy which the text receiver may
interpret as personal. The contrast between the first and second

84 LANGUAGE, BUREAUCRACY AND SOCIAL CONTROL

sentence is interesting: the message is conveyed entirely in the first sentence (i.e. the principle of finishing at ten minutes to the hour). The 'I' of this sentence is HoD (head of department). The 'I' of sentence 2, however, is an offended individual testily pointing out the bad practice of the addressee. But will the addressee see the two interpretations of 'I'? It is also worth noting that the HoD opted for an individual addressee, but nevertheless kept the complaint at a general level.

The HoD's rationale could be that 'effectiveness' of the system is better guarded by resorting to memos of this kind, because, from his institutional perspective, the other alternative – a verbal reminder – would fall short of the seriousness implied in a 'formal' written memo which contains an on-record speech act of warning. But there is another side to this situation: the HoD resorts to a form of bureaucratic action which denies the receiver any speaker rights. Had he instead opted for a verbal exchange, it could potentially have developed into a confrontational dialogue.

This perhaps explains why the HoD resorted to a 'bureaucratic' mode to remind a colleague about a routine aspect of academic life. The reference – a combination of the HoD and the secretary's initials – marks the on-record status of the memo. It indicates that the memo was produced through the institutional channels and that a copy of it has been filed by the administration. It is also worth noting the mismatch between the triviality of the 'contents' of the message and the serious tone of the 'medium' in which the message is conveyed. This suggests that when one talks about bureaucratisation, one is referring to 'modes of practice', not just degrees of seriousness of 'content'. The fact that the memo presents the problem as 'habitual' is interesting, because this presupposes that a 'serious' form of action is in place (i.e. turn to a typed memorandum).

Let us now shift our attention to the lecturer's perceptions. As a reader, he took the whole memo to reflect the addresser's personal attitude and choice of wording. Even though the secretary may, in part, be responsible for the actual formulation – using phrases she standardly associates with the memo-format – still the receiver is likely to read the memo as expressing the HoD's personal message. This is linked to our discussion of discourse role in the sense that HoDs rely on secretaries to be their mouthpieces, but secretaries draw on impersonal HoD-styles for this. Another aspect has to do with the routinisation of the office. On assuming a new role, an HoD probably starts using fairly routine administrative channels for semi-personal and personal communications, too. This raises the possibility that the HoD did not treat the matter so seriously, but relied on his administrative staff to produce the memo, a small matter to be dealt with along with so many other 'smaller' administrative tasks.

This, of course, does not necessarily mean that he did not pre-formulate (part of) the memo. Memo style is best seen as something which writers slip into. Bureaucratisation can then mean that institutional members gradually fail to deal with sensitive matters (how a fellow lecturer organises and runs a practical) at a personal level – here clearly an area where their interpretation of their role has become unacceptable to others.

The HoD also used his role as HoD, not as colleague, to deal with the issue, although changeovers between practicals could just as well have been seen as a matter between lecturers of equal status. Certainly, if he had not been the HoD at the time, and the problem of access to the laboratory had arisen, he would have used neither the memo format nor this kind of language to bring the matter to the lecturer's attention. This makes the point about where and why people adopt different positions of 'speaking'. Note the recipient's covering note where he says 'a memo I have just got from our HoD'. In other words, the lecturer would have been further surprised if such a memo had originated from a colleague who cannot assume the role of head.[6] The lecturer's perception of the HoD 'talking down' to him shows that he interprets it as a move which he would not make with other colleagues in the department.

This suggested diversification in analytical perspectives gives us the backbone to the structure of the remainder of the book: Chapter 5 examines bureaucratic language from the viewpoint of the client, Chapter 6 from that of the bureaucrat. But perhaps most important of all is that we devote proper attention to the multi-directional social relations in which social subjects are daily involved. For the chapters which follow this means that participation in discourse is best seen as entailing planes of social relations, to which are attached particular combinations of role behaviour which are in complex ways interwoven with one another.

86 LANGUAGE, BUREAUCRACY AND SOCIAL CONTROL

Notes

1. Earlier work on role behaviour in institutional contexts includes Berger and Luckmann (1972), Hymes (1977) and Goffman (1981), which precede the introduction of the study of discourse roles into pragmatic research (Levinson 1981 and Thomas 1985).
2. For a fuller discussion of this case, see Hall *et al.* forthcoming.
3. Our view of discourse roles as 'social roles in discourse' resembles Halliday's (1978) concept of social role relationships which are tied to certain 'registers' (i.e. genres or modes of talk).
4. The notion of 'modes of talk' can usefully be applied at various levels, namely, at the level of 'discourse moves' with speech act value and at the level of discourse type (e.g. investment talk versus mortgage talk). What is important is how the levels interact to bring about changing role relationships.
5. Habermas (1974: 4, quoted in McCarthy 1984: 335) makes the point that conventional role theory 'surreptitiously stylises the case of total institutions into the normal case' – a criticism which can also be applied to Foucault's 'totalitarianism' of discourse formations. In this respect, Habermas's (1968, 1970) three theses on role behaviour provide a complementary view. As social subjects inhabit a world divided against itself, it is highly unlikely that subjects would altogether fail to see the many contradictions between competing and conflicting interpretations of one particular role. However, this does not mean that the essentialist subject can be restored.
6. We learned from the addressee of this memo that the head of department is a rotating post.

5 The client's perspective: clients as citizens

Introduction

In the previous chapters we gained some insight into how information exchange is regulated in bureaucratic encounters and how clients and bureaucrats occupy certain roles and responsibilities, although in practice these role relationships are in a state of constant flux. We looked at cases from various settings, some less straightforwardly bureaucratic, to show how certain modes of relating become recognisable as bureaucratic (discursive) practice. In order to come to grips with the notion of fluctuating role relationships, we shall in this chapter focus on instances where institutions are under threat – as their practices and procedures are being challenged by clients. Our main objective is to provide a broader explanation for the occurrence of different client types, their practices and perceptions, and the specific ways in which they do or do not cooperate with the institution.

In Chapter 3 we discussed a number of instances where clients cooperate with the institution, providing all requested information (even if they fail to see the relevance of some of it). We looked at this cooperation in terms of the assumptions which clients make about the institution and how they perceive their own role. Client perceptions, looked at from this perspective, give an indication of how the bureaucratic process accomplishes itself. In this chapter we will shift our attention to clients who challenge the institutional framework in some form or other, as they bring different assumptions to the institutional processes, and, in doing so, lay bare some of the hidden bureaucratic processes. We will pay particular attention to the role of 'face' in such confrontational circumstances. Let us here briefly introduce the notion of face.

88   LANGUAGE, BUREAUCRACY AND SOCIAL CONTROL

For linguists (at least), the most widely known theory of face and politeness in language is Brown and Levinson (1978, 1987), who draw a basic distinction between a speaker's 'positive face' wants (roughly, the social desire to be appreciated) and a speaker's 'negative face' wants (roughly, the desire not to be imposed upon). When speakers perform linguistic acts which are face-threatening they rely on the use of (face-redressive) politeness strategies (see also Leech 1983). Our use of the term 'face' in this chapter goes further than Brown and Levinson's concept of positive and negative face wants, and this means bringing to the fore Goffman's (1955) original emhasis on 'face' in the socio-cultural space. Goffman (1955: 213) defines 'face' as 'the positive social value a person effectively claims for himself' – an image bestowed on a person by society in accordance with culture-specific values. To quote Goffman (1955: 215) again:

> While his [sic] social face can be his most personal possession and the center of his security and pleasure, it is only on loan to him from society; it will be withdrawn unless he conducts himself in a way that is worthy of it.

This will harmonise with our practice in this chapter of interpreting entities such as 'customer credibility', 'liability to financial compensation' or 'being a reliable payee' as lying within the domain of 'face'. What is important therefore is, for instance, the way in which institutions construct clienthood by leaving clients with no 'face' at all.[1] In addition, one also needs to talk about the face of third parties involved in a certain encounter, which is typical of bureaucratic settings.

Challenging the inhuman face of bureaucracy

Clients can and do challenge the legitimacy and real-life credibility of mismatches between their needs and institutional provisions. By implication, a client may be regarded as just ineligible for the services in question, until of course he/she restates the facts to match the institutional criteria. Let us consider two concrete cases where this is at stake. Both are encounters of clients (CL) with a housing officer (HO) in Britain.

THE CLIENT'S PERSPECTIVE: CLIENTS AS CITIZENS 89

Example 1

CL: What are the points?
HO: The points reflect your housing needs. You gain points for the fact, for instance, you are just using one room. The only other way you're going to get an increase in points is through a change in circumstances basically through your accommodation getting worse or something like that.
CL: What is worse? How can I make it worse? Bring the two children in one room and me and my wife all of us in one room. Will that make it worse? No if that is you know the points you need I can get that done today. If all sleep on the floor in one room is that how you increase the points?

The client's first move can be considered both as an information-seeking question as well as a challenge – that the points system, however he has understood it, is hopeless when dealing with his situation. The officer's response shows that he is responding to the information-seeking aspect of the client's question as he provides more information on how to increase 'points', and hence, 'eligibility' for housing entitlement. There is an implicit suggestion here for the client to act 'institutionally' (i.e. to come back with changed circumstances). However, by reacting verbally in his second move, the client is challenging the institutional norms which, to him, appear inhuman.

Why do clients decide to challenge the institutional norms and the basis on which institutions operate? What is their perception of the individual bureaucrat they are dealing with? It is very unlikely that the institution will bend its rules under pressure from individual clients and the bureaucrat in example 1 is certainly not the 'author' who is responsible for introducing the points system. As a representative of the institution he has to safeguard the institution he is representing.

How do clients react to an unsuccessful outcome, which may or may not be caused by a challenge? Bureaucrats, as a matter of principle, are required to distance themselves from clients (as human beings) whereas clients often regard bureaucrats as inhuman beings, who forget that there is an institution which constrains bureaucratic actions. Let us look at the next example in this light:

90   LANGUAGE, BUREAUCRACY AND SOCIAL CONTROL

Example 2

CL: Obviously she [mother] is homeless but not in such a way, you know.

HO: Erm, we can take the threat of homelessness seriously if we have more evidence that you asked her to leave. For example you asked her to leave.

CL: Surely you wouldn't ask your mum to leave would you?

Here again, a 'helping' face is peeping from under the cloak of institutional authority, when the housing officer suggests that by simply performing a speech act ('asking the mother to leave the house'), in whatever (im)polite terms and in whatever language, the client can prove his grandmother's housing entitlement. Why does the client not do what is suggested and resolve the matter? Why does he throw the question back and ask the bureaucrat to consider what the latter would do when faced with such a suggestion? Is the client 'naive' here, as he fails to read the implicit, hidden message in what the HO says and, moreover, questions the housing officer's moral disposition rather than the housing institution's 'inhuman' rules? Perhaps clients demand that bureaucrats, even if they fail to grant an entitlement, recognise that the client's lifeworld experience is more valuable than the institutional frame of reference.

It is worth noting that in both examples the client not only challenges the credibility of the institutional rules, but also attempts, interactionally, to reverse some of the asymmetricalities inherent in bureaucratic forms of information exchange. Note that here it is the client who asks questions, demanding a clarification, in a situation centred on information gathering, in which the bureaucrat is in the asking role and the client in an answering role. Not all clients faced with a potentially losing situation decide to challenge the institutional criteria. In relation to example 2, consider a similar instance involving another client. Although M wanted to move his 'homeless' aunt temporarily into his flat, he finally decided against this because such action would mean that his aunt would no longer qualify as 'homeless'. M here played his role the institutional way, which meant that his aunt had to stay in 'bed and breakfast' accommodation for a while.

THE CLIENT'S PERSPECTIVE: CLIENTS AS CITIZENS   91

Creating an edge over the institution

Client challenges are not always as overt as the above examples suggest. Sometimes institutions are put on the spot without the client intending this. For instance, when clients genuinely ask for information, this can hardly be seen as a challenge. But in some cases such requests can be interpreted as challenges.

Let us re-examine the case where a Belgian citizen was summoned for interrogation (cf. Chapter 4, page 69).[2] The client's insistence on knowing what the interrogation would be about is, in a way, a challenge to police practice. The result was that the constable gave away the topic of the interrogation, which he would normally have revealed only at a later stage. In a sense, we see here a client hopping the procedural steps in trying to find out what information is useful/relevant before undergoing the procedure.

Let us take this exchange, which took place at the client's door, bit by bit. As required by the procedure, the PC personally hands over to the client (D) the slip which states the time and place of the interrogation.

Example 3

D: What is it for?
PC: I don't know. They didn't tell me.

These first two turns are recognisable. The client seeks information about the purpose of the procedure, and the bureaucrat responds by claiming he has not got the information. Later on it became clear that he did know, as he conducted the interrogation. Why then did he not say: 'I can't tell you' instead of 'I don't know'? He was probably assuming he was dealing with a client who was acting strategically. 'I can't tell you' would have presupposed he knew. 'They didn't tell me' reveals that the PC was assuming the client was trying to turn his messenger role into one of spokesperson. As the client reported to us, this was not his intention. This is also clear from the next turn.

92 LANGUAGE, BUREAUCRACY AND SOCIAL CONTROL

Example 3b

CL: I think it is rather impolite to tell us to come for an
    interrogation if we are not told what it is about.
PC: Are you accusing me of impoliteness?

Believing what the PC had said, the client makes a general
comment about police practice. In his response, the PC partly
gives himself away (he is indeed in the know) and the client could
now have become even more cheeky and named the PC as the
'author' of the message (but, as the client reported afterwards, he
did not make this link). Instead the client aimed at countering the
accusation, after which the PC revealed the topic of the
interrogation.

Example 3c

CL: No I am accusing the person who wrote it.
PC: It's about your house.

From an interactional point of view, it is clear that the client's
specification makes the challenge even harsher. Although it
diverts the accusation away from the PC, it re-emphasises the
resentment at the procedure. The PC, in his turn, responds by
providing the information initially asked for. He was probably
lost for an answer or wanted to close off the topic to prevent
further challenges. In short, the answer ('It is about your house')
to the request for information ('What is it for?') is only given
after the PC's face is threatened. This meant that the client had to
interrogate the PC, whose 'side-stepping' was both a concession
and a recognition that the client had scored. Side-stepping has to
be legitimised in some way or other for it to become possible – as
institutional representatives cannot afford for it to be seen as a
straightforward, unproblematic deviation from institutional
norms.

In this example, it is the client's face-threatening behaviour
which makes 'side-stepping' possible. The accusation of
'impoliteness' does the trick, as it invokes personalised face rather
than an on-record challenge of the procedures (cf. example 2
above). 'Impolite' is more about persons than it is about
procedures, 'ridiculous' or 'unjust' would have had a different

THE CLIENT'S PERSPECTIVE: CLIENTS AS CITIZENS   93

effect as it would imply stronger accusations which question the validity of the procedures. The PC picked up on this personalised aspect in his next turn (thereby ignoring the implicit underlying challenge of the procedure). At that point, the PC dissociates himself from the institution, as it were. His own personal face is now at stake.[3]

Talking to bureaucrats in order to maintain non-clienthood

The client's face too may be at stake when the institution makes unwarranted assumptions about clienthood or about a person being a client at all. The irony here is that one can only refute the client status by addressing the institution as a client. In this section, we will illustrate this point with two examples.

In the first case, which is the TV licence case introduced in Chapter 4, a hitherto non-client was assigned clienthood in the course of an exchange which was initiated by an information-seeking request by the client's spouse. Forced to respond, the client used the occasion to challenge the institution's practices, although he realised he could not escape clienthood. In his letter of complaint, Mr V challenged the institutions on four counts: the assumption that a request for information meant that he owned a TV set; the assumption that it had to be a colour TV; the assumption that the institution did not have to respond to the request for information; and finally that the institution could reply to a request from a woman by writing back to her husband. The institution replied through a standard format with 12 possible responses and ticked off two as relevant: the payment slip for a colour TV set could be destroyed; a new one will be sent for a black and white set in due time. In short, only one of the four complaints was responded to, namely the one that provided the information which had a direct bearing on the payment of tax itself.

The second example (example 4) is also about assumptions in the ways institutions address citizens. Upset about a reminder from an urban development corporation about mosquito precautions, a recipient communicates his resentment about being addressed as an irresponsible citizen. In his letter he wrote that he felt unjustly reminded of the precautions.

94 LANGUAGE, BUREAUCRACY AND SOCIAL CONTROL

Example 4

10th June 1991

Dear Mr [name],

I am writing in reply to your letter of 31st May regarding the Ministry of the Environment's complaints about mosquito breeding in this area.

As a resident of [name] Road, regularly bitten by mosquitoes, I am the last person who needs to be reminded of basic housekeeping practices. I pay for the grass within the house compound to be cut every month; in accordance with the Ministry's recommendations, no water is allowed to remain in plant pot saucers. With regard to the possibility of stagnant water in the drains immediately in the vicinity of the house, I drew your attention to the fact that these drains may be sunken when I wrote last August requesting other repairs to be carried out.

Not wishing to contract malaria or dengue fever during my stay in [country], I am as anxious as you are to ensure that mosquito breeding is reduced as far as possible in this area.

Yours sincerely,

Two aspects of the letter stand out. First, the client disclaims neglect because he does exactly what is recommended and therefore he does not need a reminder. A second challenge is even more directly about rights and obligation: the urban development corporation has no right to accuse him of neglect, while the organisation itself has failed in its role as 'public watchdog'. Both aspects are face-related. The citizen has to save his own face by showing he is responsible (this way refuting the threat to it from the corporation), in the same way as the corporation wanted to save its face with the Ministry by distributing the circular referred to in the letter of complaint.[4]

As in the TV case (Chapter 4, example 6), where the challenges were not responded to beyond the narrow demands of the procedure, the letter of complaint to the development corporation was met by silence from the authorities. In both cases, the client is pointing out 'loopholes' in the system, but the institution fails to apologise, explain or even acknowledge receipt.

From the point of view of the institution, one individual case cannot necessitate a review of institutional policies and

THE CLIENT'S PERSPECTIVE: CLIENTS AS CITIZENS   95

procedures. Institutions work in a collective way (sending out information to all people). Institutions address 'all' (or address individuals through standard letters), but people read and interpret 'individually'. There are forms, leaflets and letters which make addressees feel neglectful (cf. also the DVLA poster analysed in Chapter 2 as another example where an institution takes on a reminder role with indiscriminate address). A collective address often prompts an individual response, which, in its turn, often fails to elicit an individualised response from the institution.

So far we have discussed clients who take offence at certain practices of information exchange and raise a voice of protest. One way of looking at this is to examine how certain client types partly break away from the passive roles which the institutions maintain for them. Another situation in which clients take up a critical position is when institutions are responsible for damage to the client. However, in such cases, clients must call upon the institution to achieve repair. Hence, their discursive behaviour has to be finely balanced between criticism which is mild enough to secure institutional goodwill but also strong enough to guarantee a repairing response. In the remainder of this chapter we shall follow one case of extended correspondence to examine how a client goes through the process of claiming damage repair for something which happened in a network of institutions. We will pay particular attention to the ways in which complex role relationships are appropriated, modified and challenged and struggled over in discourse.

Client's response to institutional failure: the case of lost mail

In November 1992, Roy received a notice from his overseas bank about an overdraft. He phoned his bank to find out the cause of this, and learnt that a draft he had sent earlier had not been credited to his account, but the standing order for mortgage payment had been honoured. It turned out that the bank had not received the letter with the draft which he had sent in October. The letter was registered, but appeared to have gone missing.[5]

How and where did the letter go missing? Can Roy in his client role find out? Does he have to act in a particular way to deal with this? We have seen, in Chapter 3, how bureaucrats can

LANGUAGE, BUREAUCRACY AND SOCIAL CONTROL

be characterised as investigating officers in search of the 'true' state of affairs. They not only have the situational power to address citizens indiscriminately, they also have the discourse power to persist with their truth-finding mission (they can ask any number of questions and continue the interrogation for any length of time), and they have the authority to declare their finding as 'the truth'. A client may embark on a similar truth-seeking mission (especially when material loss is involved). It is in such circumstances that bureaucrats come under pressure. Here the parties involved are: the client who had sent a bank draft in a registered envelope, the addressee of the letter (the London bank), the carriers of the letter (the postal agencies of both countries, who between them are responsible for delivering the letter). Because the case involves more than one institution, our analysis will focus on the role of 'face' in client-institution and institution-institution relationships.

When things go wrong

Let us start with the bank notice about the overdraft.

Example 5a

5 November 1992

I am writing to advise you that your account is overdrawn by £181.00 against the agreed limit of £100.

I felt it best to bring this matter to your attention as soon as possible as I am sure you will want to make arrangements to rectify the position.

Please remember, operating your account in this way does incur additional charges in accordance with our published tariff. This is in addition to the £12 which has been charged to your account in respect of this letter.

I am sure you will wish to try and avoid these charges in the future and, if you would find it helpful, I would be happy to discuss matters with you.

Please do not hesitate to contact me.

(Account Manager)

THE CLIENT'S PERSPECTIVE: CLIENTS AS CITIZENS 97

We see here the account manager adopting various discourse roles, which are face-related: a counsellor who offers Roy help out of financial difficulties, but also an authority who reminds the client of the punitive measures the bank will take when dealing with an untoward situation (and charges the client £12 for this reminder). Finally, as a spokesperson for the bank, the account manager also comments on what is (in)appropriate client behaviour. Note that, although this overdraft situation is a one-off thing as far as Roy is concerned, the wording of the letter suggests that Roy has been a regular offender (especially the offer of help in the fourth paragraph, which seems to suggest Roy's case can be cast in pathological terms). This letter is almost certainly in a standard format, with only the personal details being changed each time it is used. But, of course, clients read such letters as individualised addresses (cf. our discussion on page 95 above) and this impression may be heightened by the manager's adoption of a counselling role. However, note that in this case the impression of individualised address is heightened with the result that addressees may altogether fail to see that such reminders are 'standard format'. In short, the letter is more face-threatening and clients may interpret such moves as patronising.

It is also worth noting that the bank, in its letter, did not refer to Roy's routine practice of sending them a draft every month to fulfil a standing order commitment. This way the bank did not inform the client about the cause of the overdraft, even though this information would have helped the client. However, from the bank's point of view, it would be quite odd if the accounts manager were to make a reference to the sort of transactions which Roy makes. It would be seen as an intrusion into the client's privacy. Clearly, the accounts manager saw her role as restricted to pointing out that an overdraft had been incurred, but not as telling the client what had caused it.

However, note that the bank, by allowing the overdraft, had saved Roy's face with the payee of the standing order – a service for which he is charged. Compare the bank's action with the similar situation discussed in Chapter 4, where another UK bank charged a client, Ms S, for issuing a cheque which would result in an overdraft but refused to honour the cheque. The differences in the banks' actions reflect not only a difference in the importance

LANGUAGE, BUREAUCRACY AND SOCIAL CONTROL

which these institutions attach to the client's face in relation to the bank and to third parties, but also a difference as to the point at which face-saving actions enter the procedure. In the case involving Ms S, the charge was withdrawn as soon as the client contacted the bank to sort the matter out and the bank offered further face-repair in the form of a letter addressed to the payee of the cheque to restore the client's credibility with the payee. It was clear that the bank's imposition of a fine was only a temporary suspension of face-wants, aimed primarily at instigating prompt action. As unfolding events will show, it took a great deal more effort before Roy could get the bank to reimburse the fine and recognise his face wants.

On receiving the letter, Roy first telephoned his bank and spoke to the accounts manager. The manager confirmed that the letter which Roy had sent in October had not been received by the bank. At this point Roy also requested a transfer of funds from his reserve account to get out of the overdraft situation, thus minimising the penalty.

Being in the dark

Roy believed the bank's explanation that it did not receive the letter. Therefore one of the two postal agencies must have been at fault. Roy decided to find out and initiated a search action at the source. We will refer to this as the overseas postal agency (OPA).

The letter that went missing had been sent as registered post, for which Roy had received a 'Registered Article Posting Receipt' with a registration number and the addressee on it. In fact the small print of the receipt included the following:

Example 5b

Note: The registration fee does not cover the fee chargeable for any enquiry concerning the registered article.

After depositing an inquiry request with the OPA, Roy faxed the following details to his bank:

THE CLIENT'S PERSPECTIVE: CLIENTS AS CITIZENS 99

Example 5c

For the attention of the Accounts Manager

11.11.92

Dear Ms [name]

Re – Account no [number]

I am writing following your letter of 5.11.92 and our telephone conversation of yesterday.

(1) Regarding the demand draft for £550 which I sent to [bank] on 16.10.92, I have contacted [OPA], who claim the letter containing this draft was despatched by them on 16.10.92. I have initiated an enquiry which should establish where my letter to you now is and who is responsible for its delay/loss. In the meantime, if you consider it appropriate, you may like to contact the Post Office in London and inquire about the fate of the letter. The registration number is: 1935. It was despatched by air from [country], air despatch number 290, on the Special List no. 1, item 12. The letter was addressed to the Manager, [bank], and bore the full address of the [branch]. I would be very grateful if you could do this.

(2) Could you please transfer a further £200 from my Reserve account. This is in addition to the £555 which was transferred by your colleague on 10.11.92. The money should be transferred into my current account [number].

(3) Incidentally, your letter of 5.11.92 arrived within a week although it was franked with 24p (inland 1st class) only, not airmail. It was obviously sent by air, but only through an oversight of the Post Office. I would be grateful if any further urgent communications could be sent by air.

I look forward to hearing from you.

Yours sincerely

This letter functions as a face-restoring device. The client needs to restore his own credibility as a customer. While claiming solidarity with the bank, he also tries to involve them actively in tracing the lost postal item. Let us look in more detail how Roy goes about this in his letter.

In the first paragraph, Roy responds to the implicit accusations

100   *LANGUAGE, BUREAUCRACY AND SOCIAL CONTROL*

from the accounts manager by enlisting his correspondence with the OPA to prove to the bank that he is not a forgetful customer who indulges in overdrafts. By giving precise details of delivery, he wants to come across as a conscientious customer, while making sure the bank has access to the details of the correspondence. Similarly, his reference to further precautions against going into the red in the second paragraph is also a way of showing his conscientiousness in dealing with money matters.

Roy also requests the bank to initiate an enquiry on his behalf with the Post Office, as, going by the information from the OPA, the matter now has to be sorted out at the London end. There is an implicit show of solidarity. Both Roy and the bank are clients of the postal agency and both, in their own ways, have experienced loss and/or delay of an important communication. Both Roy and the bank share the assumption between them that the letter left the source country but did not arrive at the bank. It is implied that the Post Office is responsible for the loss/delay, although the client is stressing the Post Office's 'over-efficiency' when he criticises the bank in the next paragraph.

The third paragraph, in particular, reveals conflicting face demands. While establishing solidarity with the bank, Roy also takes the opportunity to point to 'bad banking practice' (as, were it not for the 'oversight' of the Post Office the notice would have arrived much later). As a valued customer, he asks the bank to send important communications by air mail in future. This part of the letter is face-threatening to the bank but forms part of an act to restore the customer's face.

The matter is now in our hands

Meanwhile, following the lodging of an enquiry with the OPA, Roy received the following letter from them:

Example 5d

14 Nov 1992

Dear Mr [name]

Registered Article no. KTR 01935 posted on 16 Oct 92.

Addressed to [bank], London UK

THE CLIENT'S PERSPECTIVE: CLIENTS AS CITIZENS   101

We refer to your enquiry dated 12 Nov 1992.

2. Our investigation showed that the article had been duly despatched to Gt Britain on 16 Oct 92. We have made an enquiry with the Gt Britain postal administration on this matter. It will normally take them some time to investigate and reply to us.

3. We will advise you immediately when we are informed of the outcome and will keep you informed of its status in a month's time if the outcome is still not made known to us.

4. Meanwhile, please let us know by quoting the above reference, if the article is returned to you, or if you know that the Addressee has subsequently received the article.

5. Please call us at telephone number [number] if you need any clarifications.

Thank you and best regards.

Yours sincerely.

[name]
for Department Manager
Sorting Centre

Why does the OPA go beyond confirming that the letter had been despatched? The enquiry fee requires them to do this. But this is also a situation where, more than locating the letter, credibility and efficiency are at stake, and, coupled with that, inter-institutional face. The OPA can only ward off a potential face-threatening situation by taking the investigation procedure further. The underlying message here is that the case is now in their hands. Institutions rarely ask clients to take charge of some aspects of an enquiry procedure.

But why should it take a month to conduct a simple investigation about the procedure of delivery? Why did not the OPA, after confirming the despatch of the article from the country on 16.10.92, ask Roy to contact the Post Office directly for the pursuance of the missing letter? Enquiries have to follow 'traceable' paths, for instance, by instituting an enquiry in writing.[6] In this way the institutions can always claim afterwards to have taken the actions prescribed in a particular situation (even when the outcome is unsuccessful). This is partly why they

102 LANGUAGE, BUREAUCRACY AND SOCIAL CONTROL

cannot ask a client to conduct part of the investigation since they have contracted to deliver the article.

As it is Roy's credibility with the bank which is ultimately at stake, and since the OPA has confirmed the letter's despatch, Roy's main concern is now to find out about the delivery of the letter. This may explain why, for the second time, he takes an initiative which the institutions would discourage (cf. his request to the bank to contact the Post Office in the fax). He decides to write the following letter to the Post Office, enclosing a copy of the letter above while waiting to hear from the OPA about the outcome of their action. Clearly, some clients perceive it as necessary to go beyond the institutional 'guidelines' when material loss and face loss have been incurred.

Example 5e

21 November 1992

Dear Sir,

Missing registered article [number] from [country].

I am writing in connection with a registered letter which I sent from [country] to London. The letter, containing a cheque, was posted by me on 16 October 1992 addressed to my bank manager in London. However, it had not been received by 12 November 1992. As a consequence, my account was overdrawn and I have been charged excess overdraft fees and interest.

I have confirmed with the bank in [country] which issued the cheque that it has not been drawn (the cheque was a/c payee, non-negotiable). I have also initiated an enquiry via [OPA]. You might already have received a request for an investigation. I understand from the acknowledgement I have received from [OPA] that the enquiry could take some time (copy enclosed). In view of what this delay has already cost me, I would appreciate it if you could investigate and settle this matter as soon as possible.

The details of the despatch are as follows:

Air Despatch: No. [number] to London
Date: 16th October 1992
Special List: No.1, 12.
Registered Article: [reference]
Addressee: The Manager,

THE CLIENT'S PERSPECTIVE: CLIENTS AS CITIZENS 103

[bank]
[address]
London [postal code]
(UK)

I look forward to hearing from you at your earliest convenience.

Roy's knowledge about how institutions respond evasively may have informed his decision to try a number of routes at the same time. One evasive strategy which institutions sometimes resort to is that of holding other institutions responsible. In this case, it looks already that the OPA will blame the Post Office. By working at various fronts at the same time, a client can collect information which allows him to check when an institution is acting evasively and information got from one institution can be played off against another.

After a month, the OPA wrote back to Roy to inform him that, although they had not traced the letter yet, the case was in hand. The OPA, in this instance, kept to its promise: to let Roy know of the outcome of their contact with the Post Office, even if the Post Office remained indifferent to it.

Example 5f

Please refer to our letter dated 14 Nov 92.

2. We are sorry to inform you that we have not received any reply from the Postal Administration of Gt Britain concerning the outcome of their investigation on the above registered article. A reminder has been sent to request them to expedite their investigation and advise us on the outcome in another month's time.

3. We appreciate your patience in this case and we are doing our best to expedite the conclusive outcome. Please give us a call at telephone number [number] if you have any additional information that may help to expedite the investigation.

Thank you.
Yours sincerely,

[name]
for Department Manager
Sorting Centre

104   LANGUAGE, BUREAUCRACY AND SOCIAL CONTROL

Clients are requested to pass on whatever additional information they may have. This reassurance allows the institution to be seen as actively pursuing the matter. The invitation directed at the client to provide additional information can be interpreted as attending to the client's face. Note also that the letter makes no allegation about the Post Office's indifference or inefficiency; it only says that the investigation process is continuing actively. The OPA also tries to show how it is on Roy's side by sending a reminder to 'expedite' the process of investigation. In either case, however, the OPA does not forward a copy of their letter and reminder to Roy. It is clear that some sort of solidarity between the two postal agencies must be respected.

A few days later, OPA writes again to Roy, with the news that the Post Office at last has replied:

Example 5g

Dear Sir,

We refer to your letter dated 12 November 92 concerning the disposal of the above registered articles.

2. We are pleased to inform you that the article has been duly delivered on 19 Oct 92.

Thank you.

The brevity of this letter is striking (in terms of its length and detail of information). The letter functions only as an answer to the inquiry procedure. Hence it also ignores the OPA's more recent, intermediate report to Roy (cf. 'We refer to your letter dated 12 November 92'). The letter also leaves out any references to the parties involved, i.e. the bank and the Post Office. Why did it not say 'the article has been duly delivered to the BANK by Post Office . . .'? The letter emphasises the factual details which require proof ('duly delivered on 19 Oct 92'), but, like the bank in its notice (see page 96), it fails to mention the details of the transaction – even though that would have been more helpful to Roy. Clearly, Roy's face is not the main concern for the OPA and, tactically, the OPA also refrains from making any on-record suggestions about the involvement of other institutions.

Getting hold of the evidence

For Roy, it now becomes clear who must be responsible. The cheque was received by the London bank, but apparently they have been denying this all along (to the extent that the fax which he sent was not responded to). Roy also infers from the letter that the OPA persistence with the Post Office London has finally paid off, although his own letter to the Post Office has not been replied to.

The Post Office has obviously confirmed delivery of the article to the addressee, but this is not explicitly stated in the letter from the OPA. In order for Roy to be able to hold the bank responsible, he requires a confirmation in writing, as it is likely that the bank will ignore any communication received by Roy from the OPA. Next, Roy writes to the OPA, asking for a copy of the correspondence between the two postal agencies. This is obviously an important point in the story. Now that one procedural cycle has come to an end and suspicions about 'who is responsible' are given shape, clients have to make up their mind about 'what is left to be salvaged?'

For Roy, this means his face loss with the bank can be repaired only when he is adequately armed with concrete evidence. So, he requests the OPA to forward to him a copy of the correspondence from the Post Office:

Example 5h

6 January 1993

Department Manager,
Sorting Centre,
[OPA]

Dear Sir,

Thank you for your letter of 24th December 1992 regarding Registered Article No [reference].

You inform me that this article was delivered on 19th October 1992. I assume that this is the information you have received from the Postal Administration of Great Britain. Unfortunately, the Addressee (my bank in London) still claims not to have received the item. Would you be kind enough to let me have a copy of the document sent to you from Britain alleging that the

106 LANGUAGE, BUREAUCRACY AND SOCIAL CONTROL

article was delivered? I will then be able to take up the case with my bank.

Thank you for your understanding in this matter.

Yours faithfully

Note that Roy now decides to address the letter to the Department Manager in the hope that his request will be attended to (and the reply comes from the Operations Manager, see Example 5m). At the same time, he decides to write back to his bank in London:

Example 5i

6th January 1993.

The Manager,
[bank]
[address]
London [postal code],
UK.

Dear Sir,

Missing Registered Letter [reference] from [country].

I refer to my letter of 11th November 1992, addressed to Ms [addressee of fax], regarding, among other things, the letter I sent you enclosing a draft for 550 pounds.

I have at last received from [OPA] a statement that my letter to you was duly delivered on 19th October, a copy of which I enclose. This is a claim made on the basis of information received from the Post Office.

In the light of this, I would be grateful if you could once more check your records to see whether the letter was entered in your record of registered articles received. If you claim that the letter was not, in fact, received by you, would you please confirm this in writing so that I can take the matter further.

I am sure you will appreciate that this matter has caused a lot of worry and involved me in considerable expense. I would appreciate it if you could look into this and reply as soon as possible.

Yours faithfully

THE CLIENT'S PERSPECTIVE: CLIENTS AS CITIZENS 107

At this point it is apparent that somebody is lying somewhere, but it is still not clear where exactly things have gone wrong. The suspicion however gathers around the bank, as the OPA would be unlikely to cover up the Post Office's responsibility. However, the OPA does not take things beyond this point. Note that the OPA wrote to Roy after receiving some sort of confirmation from the Post Office (cf. Roy's reading of the situation in example 5i above: 'This is a claim made on the basis of information received from the Post Office').[7] While giving the bank the benefit of doubt, however, Roy perceives his position as one in which he can afford to demand certain information in a specific mode. He realises that his credibility is no longer at stake: it must be one of the institutions which is at fault.

Roy's suspicions are confirmed when he receives the following information from OPA:

Example 5j

8 Jan 93

Dear Sir

ENQUIRY ON REGISTERED ARTICLE NO. [reference]
POSTED ON 16 OCT 92 ADDRESSED TO [bank], LONDON, UK

Please refer to your letter dated 6 Jan 93.

2. We forward a copy of the delivery receipt in respect of the abovementioned registered article for your retention.

Thank you.

Yours faithfully

[name]
for Department Manager
Sorting Centre

The enclosed receipt (which the OPA had received from the Post Office) has the following information on it:

108   *LANGUAGE, BUREAUCRACY AND SOCIAL CONTROL*

Example 5k

Registered postal packet 397 Office and date of delivery
Office of Posting Registration number

[town + postal code]

Addressed

[bank] STAMP (LONDON SEO)
[address] 19 OCT 92

[name]

Received by: [printed name] [signature]

Roy was relieved to receive this confirmation, because until now the bank had not acted or even responded to any of his correspondence. This proof with evidence is the final device to repair the client's face, and all the correspondence so far can be seen as working towards this moment. Not surprisingly, Roy experienced the bank's neglect of the previous correspondence as very face-threatening.

He was rather surprised that the OPA had complied with his request, despite his initial suspicion that correspondence between institutions is not normally made accessible to clients when they are third parties. This raises the question why the OPA had not sent the receipt in the first place? Roy also now realised that the Post Office had certainly not acted on his earlier request for action. Which raises a second question: as the Post Office *did* produce the evidence at the OPA's request, why did it not respond to Roy's earlier query? The final question of course is why had the bank been lying – even though not in writing – about receiving the registered article? We shall take up the first two questions here and return to the final question later.

As far as the first question is concerned, institutions can be expected to safeguard the face of other institutions ahead of clients. Bureaucratic institutions do not easily give away anything more than the necessary minimum. This is especially so in

THE CLIENT'S PERSPECTIVE: CLIENTS AS CITIZENS   109

'critical' situations where its credibility or that of a sister institution is at stake. This may explain why the OPA did not enclose the receipt in their correspondence dated 24 December 1992. Roy is prepared to take risks as far as the OPA and the Post Office are concerned, because this will help to restore his face with the bank. As the situation develops, the OPA and the Post Office become channels (rather than targets) instrumental in his relationship with the bank. A second explanation is that institutions do not adopt a client perspective in running their day-to-day activities. In this case the OPA could not see the usefulness of forwarding this receipt as they were not aware of Roy's actions and reactions so far, or what Roy wanted to establish with the help of the receipt. Extending this line of argument, we can conclude that institutions offer information previously withheld when clients ask for it on record – as Roy now says 'I will then be able to take up the case with my bank'. A third explanation could be that institutions feel that clients should treat the 'reporting' activity of institutions as 'truthful' and not look for further evidence (cf chapter 3). When the OPA reports that the Post Office has confirmed the delivery to the bank, it should be accepted at face value. If clients undertake to establish the truth by asking institutions to produce adequate evidence, then there is the danger of clients turning 'bureaucratic' (which is different from turning 'professional') – a threat to the existence and power of institutions.[8]

Concerning the second question, that is the Post Office's indifference to Roy's earlier request, institutions do have certain guidelines for what constitutes a legitimate complaint and whether they can be held accountable for attending to it or not. Roy is not a legitimate complainant in this situation. The complaint here is about the missing letter, whether it is lodged by the sender (Roy) or by the OPA. But the Post Office attends to the correspondence from the OPA only, although its credibility would have been enhanced if they had responded to Roy's letter.[9] This is very similar to the kind of warnings you see in public buildings or car parks: 'The public authorities cannot be held responsible for any damage to cars or loss of individual property kept in the vehicle.' Institutions cover their backs in advance against potential liabilities. Likewise, the Post Office will only take action about postal items that were registered with them, or

LANGUAGE, BUREAUCRACY AND SOCIAL CONTROL

when requested to do so through the usual channels by another postal agency.

Let us return here briefly to Roy's fax in which he asked the bank to contact the Post Office about the 'fate of the letter'. It seems the bank did not take up Roy's request. The most likely explanation is that the bank saw such an action as outside the scope of its 'customer services'.

Playing the trump card

The story so far has only four characters, but a very complex plot in terms of actions and role relationships. At various points in the story we see solidarity between parties being created and maintained until such time as these relationships demand redefinition and re-alliance. We saw at the beginning how Roy and the bank formed a 'bond' and treated the Post Office and the OPA as 'the other'. In fact, as we have pointed out, Roy and the bank are both clients of the postal agency. This bond is created and maintained through one-sided discourse. It is obvious that the OPA and the Post Office stand together, although one can see a bond developing between Roy and the OPA which in the end pays off for Roy. The Post Office's and the bank's failure to extend the enquiry at the client's request has the effect that the Post Office is protective of the bank (by not responding to Roy's complaint), in the same way as the bank is protective of itself and of the Post Office (by not taking up Roy's request to contact the Post Office). In terms of reciprocation, there is only dialogue between Roy and the OPA on the one hand, and the OPA and the Post Office on the other. Roy's attempts to enter into a dialogue with the Post Office and the bank have failed up to this point. Clients can try, but often do not succeed in getting round the inter-institutional channels which institutions have agreed on. In situations where face damage is at issue, clients may try to bypass certain channels so as to settle the matter quickly, but institutions resist such attempts – partly for face reasons.

The story goes on: following official confirmation of delivery, Roy immediately writes to his bank.

THE CLIENT'S PERSPECTIVE: CLIENTS AS CITIZENS   111

Example 51

13th January 1993

The Manager,
[bank],
[address],
London,
[postal code],
UK.

Dear Sir,

MISSING REGISTERED LETTER FROM [country]

Further to my letter of 6th January, I am enclosing a copy of the registration receipt number 1935, signed by your [name], which I received on 12th January 1993 via [OPA]. It is therefore clear that my letter, containing the draft for GBP550, was delivered to the [branch] of [bank] on 19th October 1992, contrary to what I was told by [name] on the phone on 10th November 1992. Would you please check through your records and let me know immediately what action you propose to take.

May I remind you that I have received no reply to my fax of 10th November 1992 to [name] nor to my letter to you of 6th January 1993. If I do not hear from you by return of post, I shall contact the Customer Services at Head Office.

Yours faithfully

Roy

Encl.

What we find here is that clients are ready to maximise their efforts when they are sure the institution is at fault and there is evidence to suggest this. The institution, on the other hand, is prepared to get involved in a long-winded discourse when the client can no longer be ignored: Roy now has evidence and demands that certain investigations be carried out. As is clear from the explicitness of Roy's letter – for instance, his references to previous correspondence – the client makes use of everything he has. He also issues a threat (appeal to higher authorities). This threat is highly calculated, given the non-compliance of the bank so far in responding to any of Roy's previous communications. As reported to us, his main worry was that the bank might try to

112 LANGUAGE, BUREAUCRACY AND SOCIAL CONTROL

cover up by claiming that his claim to a draft in the letter was false.

He receives the following reply from the bank:

Example 5m

Our Ref: [reference]

20th January 1993

Dear Mr [name],

I refer to your letter of the 6th January from which I was disappointed to learn of the problems you have recently encountered concerning a Registered Letter sent to this office in October last year.

With the benefit of the copy receipt enclosed with your letter, I have looked back through our records and quite frankly, I am at a loss to explain the fate of this particular item as I can trace neither any record of the letter having been entered in our books nor that we have processed a cheque for the amount in question at that time. This gives me great cause for concern as our internal regulations covering such items are clear and should be strictly adhered to – this particular instance is one which I shall be pursuing internally with the individuals concerned.

Clearly, the Bank is at fault in so far as we have acknowledged receipt of an item which has not then be processed. In order to resolve this situation, it would be helpful if you could approach the issuer of the draft in order to obtain a duplicate. I am sorry to have to ask you to do this and if it does involve you in any out-of-pocket expenses, then I would be more than pleased to reimburse you in due course. In the meantime, I have arranged for your account to be credited with the sum of £550 from one of our internal Suspense Accounts in order that you do not suffer through lack of funds.

I do, of course, ask you to accept my sincere apologies for the recent unfortunate sequence of events. In my experience, such problems are not typical and I thank you for bringing the matter to my attention.

I trust the above is in order and look forward to hearing from you further in this matter in due course.

THE CLIENT'S PERSPECTIVE: CLIENTS AS CITIZENS 113

Yours sincerely,

[name]
Operations Manager

The bank implicitly acknowledges Roy's identification of individuals. As expected, the bank admits fault ('with the benefit of the copy receipt'); it offers face-redressive action by apologising to Roy and by assuring him that disciplinary action will be taken against the individuals concerned. The implicit suggestion is that Roy should not take matters any further! Like the OPA, the bank now takes charge of subsequent action.

The letter comes from the Operations Manager, whom Roy has not been in touch with at all. This may explain (in part) why it does not address all the points which Roy raised. For instance, there is no apology about not responding to his earlier letters. But can it be assumed that one person in the bank has access to the complete 'file' (cf. the division of labour between various departments)? Clients have a complete picture of their case and how it has built up, but institutional representatives are not necessarily equally familiar with all the details of a case, even though clients often expect them to be.

The resolution which follows this acknowledgement of fault is two-fold: what Roy should do (obtain a duplicate draft) and what the bank has done (credit from internal Suspense Account). Notice that the bank's crediting action comes too late for Roy, as he has already taken steps to transfer money after the telephone contact with the Accounts Manager. In the meantime, Roy's account has been credited with another draft over the counter via his friend, but there is no mention of these transactions in this letter. The offer of credit suggests, misleadingly, that Roy has not taken any action about getting out of the 'red' and the expression 'in order that you should not suffer through lack of funds' can be seen as patronising the client. In other words, the bank casts Roy as a fairly naive client, so that its generosity will be in place. Moreover, the bank offers to reimburse any 'out-of-pocket expenses' (note the expression!) in getting the duplicate draft, but it does not mention the overdraft charges (cf. letter of 5 November). The other assumption is that this loss of post has not involved any other expenses, although Roy in his previous correspondence said things to the contrary.

114 *LANGUAGE, BUREAUCRACY AND SOCIAL CONTROL*

The receipt from the Post Office counts as eligibility evidence, so the repair procedure can now be set in motion. As in other situations, when procedures are initiated, the institutional representative starts by gathering information from the client (here, asking for a duplicate copy of the draft).

Clearly, an apology has followed the resolution of the case. But is it typical of institutions to offer an apology? Here the apology is mitigated by face-saving devices (e.g. 'such problems are not typical'; 'an unfortunate sequence of events'). At this point, the bank's credibility is at stake: institutions do not admit faults in the system itself, but allow only for one-off failures. The bank now recognises the client's face, and there is a temporary shift of power, as the outcome now depends on Roy's goodwill. Compare its use of 'we look forward to hearing from you' (the underlying message being that Roy would cooperate by responding) with the counselling gesture in the initial overdraft notice ('If you would find it helpful I would be happy to discuss matters with you. Please do not hesitate to contact me.').

The story ends

The bank obviously feels that its apology will be satisfactory, but Roy decides to put forward all his expenses for reimbursement. In his next letter he details his expenses for reimbursement and asks for an *ex gratia* payment which would be acceptable as compensation. But from our point of view what is also interesting is his persistent anger about bad banking practice. He asks in writing that such an error will not occur again in the future:

Example 5n
[. . .]
I shall in the future wish to continue to credit my account with sums transferred while I am abroad. What guarantee can the bank offer to ensure that a similar mishap does not recur and that a similar cycle of costly, aggravating and embarrassing events is prevented? Can the bank undertake, for instance, to acknowledge such letters and the transactions made?

He is offered a reimbursement and a set amount in compensation, subject to his acceptance. In relation to Roy's

THE CLIENT'S PERSPECTIVE: CLIENTS AS CITIZENS 115

point about a written assurance, the bank writes:

Example 5o

With regard to your final comment, I would assure you that I
have tightened up on our procedures covering such items so as to
prevent any recurrence in the future. Notwithstanding this I
would be more than happy to arrange for any similar transactions
to be acknowledged but would ask that a request to do so is
contained within each transaction as our normal practice is that
items are only acknowledged when requested.

The bank is reluctant to change its routine practice, when it
involves just one complaint which can be easily brushed aside as
atypical.

Roy felt insulted at the meagre offer of the compensation
payment and wrote back, asking for a bigger amount:

Example 5p

Regarding the amount of compensation you proposed, the figure
of £40, I am sorry to have to say that I do not consider it
adequate, given the circumstances; I feel that a sum in the region
of £105 would be more appropriate.

In the next letter, the bank asks for a detailed breakdown of how
Roy arrived at the amount:

Example 5q

With regard to the question of compensation, I note that you feel
a sum of £105.00 would be more acceptable and, in order that I
may give the matter full consideration, I would appreciate your
comments regarding the breakdown of this sum.
I look forward to hearing from you in due course.

In return, Roy refuses to comply with this request, but asks the
bank to produce the breakdown of its figure:

Example 5r

Thank you for your letter of 24th March regarding a 'breakdown'
of the sum claimed for compensation.

LANGUAGE, BUREAUCRACY AND SOCIAL CONTROL

I have already referred in my letter of 3rd February 1993 (page three, first paragraph) to the time and energy I spent trying to find out the whereabouts of the draft and eventually establishing who was responsible for this whole mishap. This time and energy (letter-writing, visits to the Bank and Post Office), and the attendant anxiety and inconvenience while waiting for the matter to be resolved, are reflected in the sum I mentioned by way of a guideline in my letter of 11th March.

By the way, may I in turn ask whether the sum of forty pounds that you offered in your letter of 16th February represents your assessment of acceptable compensation?

I look forward to hearing your comments.

The discourse of complaint and defence has now turned into a discourse of bargaining. It is interesting that each side is bidding a price without making it apparent how they justify it. Of course, Roy has read, perhaps correctly, the bank's previous letter as an invitation to negotiate the compensation money, and if the bank now offers what Roy asks for, that reading will be confirmed. At the next stage, the bank succumbs to Roy's compensation claim, even though Roy did not comply with their request for a detailed breakdown of expenses:

Example 5s

Dear Mr [name]

Having considered the matter further, I would advise you that I am prepared to meet your claim in the sum of £105 and that a payment in this sum will be applied to your account in the course of the next few days.

I trust that you will find this acceptable and hope that this unfortunate episode can now be considered to be satisfactorily resolved.

[. . .]

The final stages of the case begin with Roy being on the winning side, as the bank is forced into a position where it can only make face-redressive moves. By contrast, Roy is non-cooperative. In cases where participants protect each other's face,

THE CLIENT'S PERSPECTIVE: CLIENTS AS CITIZENS 117

face-redressive action is reciprocated. Here the offer of reserve funds is taken to be an insult. What is more, the topic shifts from reimbursement to *ex gratia* payment. Clearly, once Roy is on the winning side, he maximises his efforts. But there are limits to which the bank is willing to go to offer face-redressive action. It shifts back into a face-threatening and non-cooperative stance in an attempt at minimising its financial costs, until, finally, it gives way and pays up. Figure 1 details this development.

From this point of view, it becomes clear that the capacity to attend to face is crucially important in the realisation and sustenance of social and/or economic interests. For instance, the bank's tactics of first threatening a client's face, but then restoring it immediately as soon as the client is brought back, into line, is one good illustration of this. We can see the ways in which clients have to employ dual face-related strategies to make sure that a complaints procedure does not get stranded by being strong enough in one's criticism to make sure something is done, but also being mild enough to ensure the institution's cooperation). As we conclude in this chapter, 'professional' clients are very sensitive to face in interaction.

Conclusion

In Roy we can see a professional client. In the course of experience, clients learn about the institutional frames of reference – as different from their own – and they may become 'professional'. A professional client can manipulate the organisation through the institutional representative with an ability to read and manoeuvre the style and discourse devices used by the professionals. He/she tries to anticipate procedures or, when in doubt, indirectly seeks information about the nature of the procedures and decision making before setting the procedure in motion. This kind of client is after maximal personal gain and minimal personal loss, and hence uses his/her expertise and knowledge about the system not to demand or bring about change in any broad way but to bring about favourable personal outcomes. Mutual face and victory over the institution are important to a professional client.

118 LANGUAGE, BUREAUCRACY AND SOCIAL CONTROL

ROY	BANK	CULPABILITY
	- - - - - - - - - - - - - - → FACE-THREATENING statement of responsibility demand for an explanation threat to take things further	
	← - - - - - - - - - - - - - - FACE-REDRESSSIVE admission of guilt reassure client announcement of internal enquiry offer of reserve funds (unspecified) offer to reimburse expense	
	- - - - - - - - - - - - - - → FACE-THREATENING demand for *ex gratia* payment statement of full expense request for guarantee re future transactions	
	← - - - - - - - - - - - - - - FACE-REDRESSIVE specified offer for compensation assurance that necessary measures taken	
	- - - - - - - - - - - - - - → FACE-THREATENING (specific) offer declined claim for bigger amount	
	← - - - - - - - - - - - - - - FACE-THREATENING request for evidence of expense	
	- - - - - - - - - - - - - - → FACE-THREATENING statement that evidence already furnished (in turn) request for evidence of offer	
		BARGAINING

Figure 1

THE CLIENT'S PERSPECTIVE: CLIENTS AS CITIZENS   119

Roy is a paradigm-case of a 'professional client'. For instance, he anticipates that he will not be able to claim anything from the bank unless he has a copy of the letter which the Post Office sent to the OPA in which the Post Office states that the letter was delivered. He also seeks indirect information when asking the bank to check with the Post Office. Surely part of the reasoning here must have been that any information obtained this way can be used, should the OPA not respond satisfactorily. The strategies adopted by Roy are also clearly face-sensitive. Criticisms are implied, and most of the letters request information or request routine forms of action. Threats stay out of the picture, until suspicion about the bank's careless procedures is confirmed and evidence can be supplied for it. There is also the strategic use of discourse devices to get the institution to do what he wants them to do (cf. great care in providing all the details of letters and postings).

But, the case also clearly illustrates how a client's professionalism is based on 'trial-and-error' methods. For instance, one aspect of Roy's 'professionalism' is revealed when we see him as a client who knows that there are loose ends to inter-institutional paths. Hence, his basic strategy is working at the end of each institution which is involved to increase the chances that the lines will connect (apart from also making sure the same does not happen again in the future and trying to recover his loss). However, in spite of being armed with these insights, it turned out to have been unrealistic to expect that the bank would enquire with the Post Office about the missing letter, or that the Post Office would respond to a query which did not follow the usual channels. If there is a next time (we hope there will not be!), Roy will follow a different course of action.

A professional client is different from a 'warrior' client, who wants the bureaucrat to come out and fight over moral and social principles and who is willing to sacrifice procedural outcomes. Moral victory is more important than personal gain; as bureaucrats are unlikely to come out and lose their face, moral victory is almost always theirs. This is the client who demands social reform. Although keen to attack the bureaucrat's face, this kind of client is worried about his/her own face. In Chapter 7, we will look more closely at a case where a warrior client turns to an intermediary institution to engage with a local education

120 LANGUAGE, BUREAUCRACY AND SOCIAL CONTROL

authority. Our focus will be on how intermediary institutions channel clients' warrior efforts towards tactical cooperation rather than towards resolving face matters.

The professional client can also be contrasted with the 'naive client', who acts in a 'Gricean' way, observing principles of maximal sincerity and completeness (cf. Sarangi and Slembrouck 1992). A naive client lays everything in the hands of the bureaucrat and attempts to cooperate maximally with whatever is asked (and is not asked). For instance, when not able to decide immediately what will be directly relevant to an exchange, some clients just tell everything they think could be relevant and let the bureaucrat decide. This kind of client can succeed in forcing bureaucrats to make explicit their procedures. This kind of client is perhaps not very aware of face, but this does not mean that they always lose out.

This characterisation of discreet client types is in itself insufficient to account for how clients deal with institutional reality. Most social subjects fall into one category or another at times, and much may depend on the institution they are dealing with. A client may shift between these categories, intentionally or unintentionally, in the course of one case. This is where the analysis of perceptions becomes very important. For instance, subjects may 'go professional' for a number of reasons: frustration in warriorship for a 'more open' and 'fairer' kind of bureaucracy; cynical exploitation of the system; the realisation that legitimate needs can only be fulfilled by conforming to institutional realities, even when this happens at the expense of one's own perceptions of the needs situation (cf. Fraser 1989).

In each of these cases one ends up discussing a gap between perceived needs and their satisfaction (cf. Habermas 1968), something which makes role-distancing inevitable. The link with 'role' can be made as follows. In Chapter 4, we say that role bears crucially on social identity and role relationships are discursively created, maintained and transformed. So, role conformity and distancing can be situated at the level of a dialogue of empirical subjects with available subject positions in bureaucratic discourse (i.e. how a 'speaking individual' interacts with what is presupposed about a client in a bureaucratic context).

THE CLIENT'S PERSPECTIVE: CLIENTS AS CITIZENS   121

Notes

1. As our analysis of leaflets, standard letter formats, and so on, in Chapter 6 reveals, a wider concept of 'face' invites one to research the gap between, on the one hand, a self-image which clients project for themselves when dealing with institutions and, on the other hand, the denial of the role of such a self-image in the ways in which institutions construct clienthood.

2. Note that this interaction is not a police interrogation, but an administrative step which leads to an interrogation at the station. It should also be clear that citizens' perceptions of public institutions are also constructed through such encounters.

3. How much in this interaction was really intentional and carefully calculated strategic moves? The interaction just went in a particular direction. Participants often realise only later what causes somebody to 'score' in an interaction. Here 'impolite' was the key item for scoring, but its use was probably triggered more by the client's irritation at the PC's use of the doorbell than by a careful choice of wording. The PC had rung the bell three times with great urgency. Likewise, the client reported that with his turn ('I am accusing the person who wrote it') he acted on the information that the PC did not know. Hence, he may not have realized how efficient this turn was in reinforcing his challenge of the procedure.

4. The Ministry cannot write directly to tenants as the houses are owned by the urban development corporation. In all likelihood, the Ministry complained to the corporation and the latter passed the responsibility for action to the tenants.

5. We have been able to know more about this case of lost post from Roy (see his gloss of events in Appendix 9a). Roy has also provided a postscript in which he reacts to our analysis (see Appendix 9b). However, it is important to point out that the latter postscript has not affected our analysis in any way.

6. Roy was asked over the telephone to submit a request for inquiry in writing with the OPA using the prescribed form. The OPA may have also used a similar format to forward their enquiry to the Post Office, and so on.

7. The OPA's investigation did not involve the bank and, of course, as far as the postal agencies are concerned the investigation is paying off. There is a result showing that the OPA and the Post Office have acted out their responsibilities well in delivering the letter, although the scope of the investigation had been restricted to just this. Note that there is no reference to the addressee of the letter in question in many of OPA's correspondences. This contrasts with Roy's letters, in which he continually refers to the bank as the addressee.

122 LANGUAGE, BUREAUCRACY AND SOCIAL CONTROL

8. In providing 'crucial' information to a 'nagging' client, institutions probably come to recognise the existence of 'professional clients' on the one hand, and the direct consequences for the institution's survival if they deny the client's right to certain bits of information, on the other. It is worth speculating here whether the OPA would have responded differently if the outcome of their enquiry had shown that they or the Post Office were at fault.

9. Whether or not the Post Office would have replied to the OPA if it had not been able to establish receipt of the missing letter by a bank official is another interesting question.

6 The bureaucrat's perspective: citizens as clients

Introduction

In Chapter 5 we looked at how clients can see through the ropes and try getting the best deal out of institutions. In this chapter we will primarily be looking at some of the ways in which institutions construct clients. This will link up with our discussion in Chapter 2 about the introduction of new modes of discourse associated with bureaucracy.

The bureaucratic process can be looked at as a process in which 'all' citizens can potentially become clients – a taxpayer, a registered patient, a licensed driver, an unemployed citizen. Within each category one can find clients with various kinds of experience and various kinds of literacy. What is more, someone who is a 'professional' client in one area may be quite 'naive' when it comes to another client category. In dealing with the public, bureaucracies conduct their routine work with certain client types in mind, which may vary according to the nature of the contact situation. For instance, there is the erring client who is a potential threat to the institutional norms, the foreign client who comes within the remit of the institution, the prospective applicant addressed in a leaflet. In this chapter we shall look at how these client types are constructed in 'bureaucratic' situations. We will focus on a disciplinary situation, a situation where a client applies for an entitlement and a situation where the institution volunteers information to make clients institutionally literate.

Alarming the client

In Chapter 5 we looked at what happened when things go wrong

124 LANGUAGE, BUREAUCRACY AND SOCIAL CONTROL

with the institution and how clients perceive institutional practices in such situations. What sort of perceptions do institutional representatives bring to a situation where the client appears to be 'in the wrong'?

The case we are discussing happened in a university library. ND, a visiting scholar, walks past the alarm point and the alarm goes. Knowing what the alarm means, ND returns to the counter and, unasked, she opens her bag to check its contents. She knew she had no borrowing rights, but only a card entitling her to use the on-site library facilities. An attendant arrives. By that time ND has already found out that she had a book in the bag which she should have left in the library. She says: 'oh I'm so sorry it's just like the size of my diary sorry extremely sorry'. Another library employee arrives and asks: 'How is this book with you?', a question which ND interprets as 'How did this come about?' She replies: 'along with these diaries this small book by mistake I have put it sorry for this'.

The second library employee asks for ND's library card, takes it and goes away to consult with a senior colleague. Meanwhile, ND asks the attendant: 'Shall I go and put the book on the shelf?' She shows the photocopies she has made of the book, which the attendant inspects.

The second employee comes back with the 'offender's form' and asks ND to fill it in. She says: 'generally we call the police in such cases you better fill it in'. ND is worried and says 'you see I'm a government servant in [country] I teach there it's not expected of me it's just a mistake will there be any problem in my service then'. ND was a visitor to the university but as she is employed by the government of her country she cannot afford to have a record. The offender's form was more alarming than the library alarm itself.

ND dutifully fills in the form (part 1). A third (senior) employee arrives and asks: 'Have you got any other identification where is your passport?' ND replies, 'I haven't got the passport here I've given it to the immigration for extending my visa and I'm supposed to get it back tomorrow but my brother is working in the university'. 'What is his name?' 'DR.' The senior employee picks up the phone to contact DR but he was out. The second employee then turns to ND and asks: 'what you have explained to me now how this book came with you you just write here' (part 2 on the back of the form).

THE BUREAUCRAT'S PERSPECTIVE: CITIZENS AS CLIENTS   125

By then, the senior employee comes back and says: 'I've left a message [for your brother] he's not there generally we call police in such matters but we will keep this pass and you may not use the library further.'

The next morning, DR, having received the message from his answerphone, calls the senior employee to clarify the situation. The message on the answerphone included that 'she was trying to remove a book without issuing it'. DR stresses that it was a mistake and asks whether ND could retrieve her library card as she wanted to continue using the library resources during her stay. The card was returned to her the same day.

The sequence of events was clearly determined by asymmetrical perceptions of the situation. ND is perhaps a 'naive' client. She tries very hard to cooperate and admits her mistake. The book indeed resembled the diary and she had taken photocopies of relevant sections. Her passport was indeed at the embassy. However, the fact that she was ready to expand and explain was treated with suspicion. Moreover, her offer of remedial action was interpreted as coming from someone who had been caught and was trying to buy her way out.

The following warning about ticketless travelling on the London Underground further illustrates how client's explanations in cases of non-compliance are treated with suspicion:

Example 1

Our inspectors just don't listen to excuses. They simply take notes.

Rather than specifying the penalty as such, clients' *post hoc* explanations have here been incorporated into the warning. The client is cast in dishonest terms, and the situation is construed in such a way that if a passenger is detected without a ticket there is no room for information gathering beyond registering the offence.

Let us analyse the library incident further from the bureaucratic perspective. The basic policy here is that the institutional representative has the benefit of the doubt. All library users are potential booklifters. From the library staff's point of view it is not possible to go on record as stating that ND had made a genuine mistake.

126   *LANGUAGE, BUREAUCRACY AND SOCIAL CONTROL*

It is important to bear in mind that bureaucrats, in their day-to-day activities, can be held accountable by the institution which they are serving and where absolute power lies. Going through the procedure is their safety net. So the card was immediately withdrawn to see whether the client's statements were correct but also to allow the library staff to back up their actions. It is just possible that the staff actually believed the user from the start.

Likewise, the use of the 'offender's form' reveals the institution's premium on the meaning of actions (rather than a concern with the client's intentions). In the section marked 'for official use', the library staff is required to tick one of the two following boxes:

Example 2a

ii. Item(s) was/were:
[   ] intentionally removed [   ] unintentionally removed.

What matters is the library staff's assessment of the client's intentions. Even if the staff intended to return the card as soon as the user's explanation was confirmed, the offender's form had to be filled in, in order to be filed. This is also evident from the specification of the offence as communicated over the telephone: 'she was trying to remove a book without issuing it'. Let us look more closely at the part of the form under the heading of 'Details of offence':

Example 2b

Details of offence

Date of incident _____ Time of incident _____

Details of item(s) removed from the library without authorisation.

Book(s)   call no. _____   call no. _____
         barcode _____   barcode _____
         author _____   author _____
         title _____   title _____

THE BUREAUCRAT'S PERSPECTIVE: CITIZENS AS CLIENTS 127

Other item(s) _____

Offender's statement: _____

I acknowledge receipt of this record and letter of warning.

Signature of offender: _____

Thus, filling in a form means that the client goes on record about an offence, an application, and so on. In the form above, ND becomes an offender by signature, irrespective of whether library staff later tick the box 'unintentionally removed'. As soon as a form enters a situation, the client is labelled (even before evidential information is processed). Forms are a major anchorage point for institutional classifications. Whether it is in the context of eligibility, or the context of disciplining, it is through forms that citizens are turned into 'clients' and their stories into 'cases'.

Maintaining bureaucracy through official documents: forms and leaflets

The information-seeking role of institutions through application forms and their information-providing role (through leaflets) is multi-functionally targeted at certain client types (e.g. to make sure that the 'old age pensioner' knows what the benefit is about, to make sure that the more streetwise client does reveal the information requested in box 4a). Both these dimensions can be analysed in terms of client needs and bureaucratic perceptions of these needs – it is the latter which informs institutional provisions.

Application forms and leaflets are both text types which emanate from the institution but which have clients as principal addressees. In Chapter 5 we have looked at circulars which indiscriminately address a group of citizens, and how clients may read these as personally addressed. Similarly, one can examine what type of client is implied in leaflets, application forms, and so on. How does this relate to forms of social control? The fact that client needs differ from institutional provisions produces an asymmetry which makes the use of application forms inherently problematic. Thus, leaflets can be seen as moving ambivalently between, on the one hand, intended attempts at reducing this

128   *LANGUAGE, BUREAUCRACY AND SOCIAL CONTROL*

asymmetry and, on the other hand, having the effect of normalising bureaucratic notions of clienthood. A further question arises about how one explains the substantial changes which both these text types have undergone in recent years.

Answering these questions will allow us to develop further the issue of the role relationships bureaucrats enter into: relationships within the institution, relationships with other institutions and relationships with clients. Our thematic focus in this chapter will be on the construction of the 'client' as the 'other' in each of these relationships.

Executing bureaucracy: application forms

In Chapter 3 we claimed that bureaucracy is all about processing people. Most of this processing takes place by examining information collected from clients through application forms, and turning this information into files on the basis of pre-existing categories which follow set institutional criteria. These categories inform institutional decisions.[1]

Let us first discuss a few general properties of application forms.

(1) Forms typically have names which reflect the subroutines, the labour division and the departmentalisation in an organisation in a way which is not transparent to clients (form names are there for the sake of bureaucrats).

(2) The layout of forms heavily constrains the client's activity in that it does not allow clients to tell a whole story. Boxes, dotted lines, multiple choice questions, pre-formulated answers, limited space (e.g. six letter spaces to fill in date of birth) all contribute to the packaging of the client's case. From a bureaucrat's point of view, this is tied up with the efficiency of processing information. There is, however, a recent trend to provide a space where the client can state things not accommodated by the form. This may appear as a move to minimise clients' constraints, but it is a double-edged sword, because it increases the possibilities that clients may give away information which could jeopardise their case.

(3) Forms have also temporal dimensions (deadlines and eligibility periods), which equally constrain the client's

THE BUREAUCRAT'S PERSPECTIVE: CITIZENS AS CLIENTS 129

activities. Clients may be required to declare something ahead of a situation, whether or not it reflects the client's actual needs at that point in time.

(4) Forms are also used to provide information to clients; they have a 'leaflet function' through the occurrence of explicit information about the procedure, entitlements, and so forth, and there is also the implicit 'leaking' of information when clients work out aspects of the procedure and the decision making from the nature of the form.

(5) Forms also have sections for 'office use only' – boxes and diagrams which run parallel to the spaces used for clients' responses. This is where the decision making will leave its traces on the form and the categorisation of an applicant as 'a particular case' will become definite. This is usually done in a non-transparent way (with abundant use of abbreviations and non-transparent codes). This may explain why forms, once filled in and processed, remain the property of the institution and are seldom returned to clients.

The processing of information provided by clients by bureaucratic channels can be captured through the concept of '(re)formulation' (cf. Fairclough 1992a). To (re)formulate a state of affairs is an act of classification but it also amounts to the imposition of a particular interpretation which informs subsequent action. (Re)formulation thus links up with situational power. It also successfully captures the asymmetry and the 'translation' element involved. Bureaucrats' (re)formulations take priority over clients' characterisations. Although forms reduce clients to category-types, this also entails a form of protection in the sense that a legitimate claim does not require more than what the form caters for.

Forms have an information-seeking function. They are often after the same information (e.g. personal particulars, education) but they vary when it comes to the amount of detail needed. For instance, one embassy may require certain personal details not required by another embassy, or embassies may require certain details not required by banks. The wide difference in what information is sought suggests that different institutions regard different types of information as essential and thus assign values to their 'preferred' types of information. Clients are very familiar

130 LANGUAGE, BUREAUCRACY AND SOCIAL CONTROL

with such differential treatment, but they rarely make this an issue and deny information that they deem 'irrelevant' on the basis of their prior experience with similar institutional processing. In fact, this reconciliation points to the fact that clients occupy a compliant/ cooperative role and turn their lives in to 'open books' for bureaucratic 'gaze'.

From the bureaucrat's perspective, it is easy to rationalise why certain bits of information are asked for. This may depend on the following factors:

- immediate processing: 'more information is always better', so that the bureaucrat can act on it without having to send reminders or having to seek further information from other sources. A form may also have a number of sections to be filled in by other institutions before it can be submitted. This reveals the hierarchies between and within institutions;
- traditions in record keeping, background statistical research;
- forms of legitimation (e.g. a client may be entitled to something following a verbal promise, but a form needs to be filled in for the record);
- records of information exchange with an implicit claim of 'objective' treatment (it carries the assumption that clients will be treated in the same way);
- devices to apply for and/or deny entitlement;
- face-redressive functions: apparent distancing from the institution when bureaucrats claim they do what forms require.

One of the questions arising here is whether forms can be offensive in the way they probe and in the way they address a particular type of client. Or do they require of a client some understanding about their immediate functioning? The latter would mean clients must learn to 'distance' themselves from the information asked/provided in the form and not consider the forms as a 'moral grid'! But this also highlights the one-sidedness of information exchange and leaves clients with little power to 'challenge' bureaucratic practices. Forms can be described as a defence which bureaucrats use to protect themselves from accusations of partiality, bias and so on. An unsuccessful outcome is often blamed on the client, because the bureaucratic decision is taken in accordance with the information provided in the form.

THE BUREAUCRAT'S PERSPECTIVE: CITIZENS AS CLIENTS 131

The implied client in application forms

Institutions operate with certain assumptions about the clients they address and process. Institutional assumptions about client categories have implications for the kinds of application forms which are used and for the questions which are put to applicants in a particular form. Let us take the situation of claiming 'incapacity benefit' in Britain. An 'incapacity for work questionnaire' has to be filled in in order to claim this benefit. This questionnaire has various categories related to muscular activity, but there may not be room for people suffering from, say, a skin condition to be able to declare their situation. While client constructs have been built into application forms, the real clients may remain absent from the form.

The questionnaire elicits detailed information about everyday activities, such as 'getting up from a chair', 'walking', 'lifting and carrying' etc. Under 'walking' for instance, the form asks:

Example 3a

You cannot walk, without having to stop or feeling severe discomfort, for more than

* Just a few steps
* 50 metres, this is about 55 yards
* 200 metres, this is about 220 yards
* 400 metres, this is about 440 yards
* 800 metres, this is about half a mile

Questions such as the above objectify (in)abilities and require clients to measure and express abilities in numerical terms. Additionally, there is a tension between 'an activity one ideally should avoid doing because of medical conditions' and 'what one manages to do, even against the medical odds, simply because daily living becomes impossible without it'. The applicant here has to grasp that the objectified measurement is the bit which is going to count – rather than a statement of the difficulties one experiences in coping with these things in daily life. As the manager (Ma) and the deputy manager (DM) of a local Citizen Advice Bureau (CAB) explained to us (See Chapter 7 for details about the role of mediating institutions like the CAB):

132 LANGUAGE, BUREAUCRACY AND SOCIAL CONTROL

Ma: we have difficulty with it [. . .] how far fifty yards is because if you ask me if I can walk fifty yards I have no idea – so this is a problem and the other thing is people tick that and if they tick it in ignorance if they cannot walk fifty yards then everybody is assessed – they have an assessment – they go to the assessment and first thing the doctor says is you ticked fifty yards and you have just walked all the way – and I think that puts them in a position they are thinking they are worse than they are.

DM: I think there are words that are very difficult like walk – what does it mean when you say walk – does it mean can you walk fifty metres and that's not understood by the client from the stuff that explains it – does this mean could I actually get there given all that I get there comfortably – can I do that and I repeat that people don't understand what is meant by that expression – ok there is a box to expand the point if you don't understand what they are after anyway it doesn't occur to you to qualify the tick

Clearly, self-assessment constitutes an important dimension of the filling in of application forms and clients may not only be inclined to under-estimate their needs, they will also be held responsible for the subsequent outcome of the decision-making.

Self-assessment also bears directly on the ways in which certain clients are excluded. Although the incapacity questionnaire addresses a wide range of audiences, certain kinds of clients are excluded if one goes by the range of questions asked in the form, as can be seen from the following comment made by the CAB deputy manager:

DM: [. . .] the questions they are asked on incapacity they are descriptors – the difficulty is that for many people none of these actually fit their conditions – for example this week we had someone with psoriasis – a skin condition – none of the questions got skin conditions none of them are about [. . .] conditions and the only way you can fit people in with that severe condition of that type into those descriptors are – if for example their pain keeps them awake at night or if their skin condition is such that they have lost grip of their hands and their joints cause them problems – but the condition itself does not trigger anything.

THE BUREAUCRAT'S PERSPECTIVE: CITIZENS AS CLIENTS   133

Let us now look closely at a more widely used form (application for income supplement) to illustrate further how clients can be confused and are actually affected by the categories in the application form. One difficulty which clients commonly experience with application form lies in the declaration of their marital identity in institutional terms, This is particularly the case for clients from ethnic minorities who may not quite understand what each category entails. For instance, cases have been noted where 'sharing a flat' was interpreted as 'living together' and communicated accordingly in the application form, without the client realising the consequences of such an interpretation. However, interpretative discrepancies of this kind are not restricted to groups who may or may not share the dominant cultural or linguistic conventions. To quote the CAB manager again:

> DM: [. . .] there are some forms that ask questions about for example the relationship with people who live in the house where they don't perceive that one of the answers is correct because neither of them seem to fit and therefore they usually feel constrained to tick one of the boxes and they are then judged according to this

Let us concentrate on one particular case which involves a woman in her mid-fifties, who applies for income support. She is divorced after a violent marriage and takes in a man in his seventies as a lodger. Early on in the application form the applicant (in this case the woman) is asked about her marital status. She is required to 'tick the boxes that apply to you and your partner' (see appendix 5a for the original, filled-in form (Part I of Form A2)). We reproduce the relevant section here for our analysis:

Example 3b

You				
Married	[ ]	Separated	[ ]	
Living together	[ ]	Divorced	[ ]	
Single	[ ]	Widowed	[ ]	

The applicant first ticks 'living together' and then strikes it out

134   *LANGUAGE, BUREAUCRACY AND SOCIAL CONTROL*

and ticks 'divorced'. The deputy director of the CAB recounts this instance as follows:

> DM: [. . .] it's the lady who herself was divorced but had a lodger living there – she should have ticked that she was divorced and has nothing to do with partner because she doesn't have one – but also she was thoroughly confused as to which bits she was ticking – because it wasn't clear to her where the boxes matched up [refers to form] I mean if you work from this side it's clear that box matches that but if you come over here that box goes with those questions – she ticked this box thinking she was ticking divorced but in fact of course she was ticking living together – you see what I mean [. . .] the boxes are nearer to the next question than to the question they have replied – she meant to tick divorced – but what she did was ticked living together because that box is answering living together not answering divorced – although it looks the other way round [. . .] she ticked it and then she crossed it out when she realised that that box was divorced – in fact the department read it wrong and they actually read it as she ticked living together – so it's their own fault that they've been misled – because the form is so badly designed they actually couldn't work out where the answer was anyway – it meant for these people that this woman had her benefits stopped because she had him there living which resulted in the man saying I can't give you this trouble I will move out – so we ended up with a seventy one year old man living in one unheated bed-sit while we sorted all this out – and this woman who had loads of mental health problems over the years was back on valium for the first time in ten years [. . .] we had to go to the tribunal which took several months to sort this out – he had to go and live in a bed-sit to leave her alone so that she could get her benefit back while we sorted it out – all because the form elicited the wrong information or wrongly interpreted

What we see here is two levels of confusion: the first is at the level of the layout and design of the form. The applicant and the institution associate the boxes and the categories differently. The second level of confusion pertains to the interpretation of the categories. Because 'living together' is a potential label to characterise this client (a divorcee, who shares her house with a

THE BUREAUCRAT'S PERSPECTIVE: CITIZENS AS CLIENTS   135

lodger), the institution in fact applies the 'living together' category to the client without hesitation (see Appendix 5b, in particular point 4, for further details of how the institution processed the information provided by the client). In the appeal procedure which followed, the investigation department adopted the direct surveillance method to verify the applicant's movements, before the misreading could be rectified.[2]

Several general points can be made here on the basis of how actual clients have perceived their information-giving role when filling in application forms:

* Clients may feel that not ticking a box is a risky strategy which could lead to an unfavourable categorisation and outcome. Even when they are confronted with several sections which do not apply to them, having answered the first question (and going by the instructions), they feel that they are expected to answer each of these questions.
* Application forms presuppose a client who is literate to understand the instructions contained in the form, who is prepared to provide the information required and who is in a position to judge whether or not s/he falls within a category. However, the institution denies clients' lived experiences and its associated interpretations, when, informed by notions of uniform and rational treatment, it upgrades certain 'factual' pieces of information (with fixed interpretations) to the central plane of decision-making. This, in its turn, makes it easier for the institution to deny/withdraw an entitlement to a benefit or an allowance.
* Some clients assume that the department already knows from previous correspondence about their condition and that the crucial bits of information are already owned by the institution.

Questions in application forms not only presuppose that clients have a fair idea about organisation procedures, the applicants are also put in a difficult situation – deciding exactly what information to provide, but also worrying about how that information will be processed. There is bound to be mismatches between the institutional construction of client situations and the actual client conditions. As the deputy manager of the CAB notes:

> DM: [. . .] I take a cavalier attitude to forms – and I think that
> the purpose of the form is to actually collect information
> but if you can't put it down the information in the box
> provided just scribble it anyway [...] even our workers have

136   LANGUAGE, BUREAUCRACY AND SOCIAL CONTROL

> to have us to tell them to take that attitude – they feel so
> constrained by the form – they are attempting to answer
> something that doesn't really fit in the box – so I say well
> you know just write across the box what you want to tell
> them even it it's not answering the question because that
> way you can't be accused of not having supplied the
> information [...] that the purpose of the form is to collect
> information not to make it difficult to present it

The construction of clients is not an atypical process. At the heart of application forms then is a presupposition of institutional literacy (cf. the ways in which clients are assumed to know which form number to turn to, know how other institutions play a role in their case, etc.).

Official forms reveal to a certain extent some information about bureaucratic procedure that the client will go through, and about how the work is organised within a bureaucratic organisation (e.g., expert opinions sought from relevant profess-ionals). When the initiating moves have been completed, the information provided by clients about their situation travels in 'files' from one desk to another within the institution. Looking at the type of information which forms seek of clients, one could argue that each form has an 'implicit client' built into it. Thus, forms construct clients in terms of a potential set of common denominators.

Advertising bureaucracy: leaflets

The application forms we have analysed are also interesting in another light. Usually, one column in the form provides information about how to fill in the form and, in that respect, the form functions like a leaflet (cf. the registration form in appendix 2b). Note that in certain cases one application form refers applicants to another leaflet for more information. The leaflet function of the application form is 'limited', for instance, because it does not address the issue of whether the user needs to make the application and how the decision making will take place.

Generally speaking, leaflets exist outside application forms. Private enterprises like banks and insurance companies use leaflets as a way of advertising their services, targeted at potential clients. What kinds of clients are implied in, say, credit card

THE BUREAUCRAT'S PERSPECTIVE: CITIZENS AS CLIENTS   137

leaflets and in welfare leaflets? Do leaflets in the public sector have a similar function, targeted at a particular client type? Are there mismatches between the mode of advertising which is characteristic of leaflets and the intended addressees of these leaflets? In order to answer these questions we shall first examine what kind of client is implied in leaflets and what macro-social forces are responsible for such client- constructs.

The implied client in welfare leaflets

The proliferation of leaflets in the public domain is the result of the realisation that there are gaps in client–institution communication. It forms part of a reaction against frequent accusations that institutions are inaccessible and uninformative. Through leaflets there is also redress of the institution's face, as leaflets imply a hope for a better informed clientele and a more open flow of information. If anything, one would expect leaflets to be more explicit about how the institution functions – for example, making the rules and criteria more transparent. Have institutions really become more accessible with the recent proliferation of leaflets? In order to answer this question, what constitutes a leaflet and what client types are addressed through them has to be analysed in detail.

Let us consider in detail a leaflet from the Department of Social Security about 'family credit'. On the cover it reads:

Example 4a

THIS IS YOUR CLAIM PACK

It contains
* a sheet to help you work out if you could get Family Credit
* a Family Credit claim form

SEE IF YOU MIGHT QUALIFY

The 'claim pack' is designed as a wallet, containing several documents, an information sheet, a claim form and a form which is partly to be filled in by the employer (see Appendix 6). Rather than directing the client to different forms and leaflets, the 'pack' suggests an 'attractive' completeness comparable to the information given about consumer products. In addition, various

138 *LANGUAGE, BUREAUCRACY AND SOCIAL CONTROL*

bits of information are repeated at various points and the jacket of the pack contains a number of summary statements which are expanded upon in the leaflet itself. This is a very common advertising technique. Bold statements are given first to attract the reader who is then expected to find his/her way through various separate sheets with further information (cf. mail order catalogues, for example).

This kind of presentation constructs the citizen in a customer mode, and the sentence ('See if you might qualify') suggests indeed that a client can 'benefit' from 'shopping around'. What contributes to the construction of the client as a consumer is that the text promotes choice wherever it can (although this could be at a fairly trivial level). For instance, on the inner jacket, we read:

Example 4b

you can choose how the money is paid
– into your bank or building society account.
– with a book that you cash at the post office.

In addition, there are various lexical choices which signal a client as consumer: 'family credit' (despite the confusion that may arise from the use of this term), 'payments' (instead of 'benefits'). These lexical choices underpin a shift from 'rightful entitlement' to 'availing oneself of opportunities'. This point comes out very strongly in the reference to 'a worthwhile sum' (inner jacket) and the advice, 'Do not wait or you could lose money' (on the information sheet). Now that we have examined how the leaflet is 'selling', we will next turn to its 'telling' potential.

The leaflet addresses a client as someone who will be able to judge for him/herself the eligibility condition on the basis of the information provided. However, there is a mismatch between the way in which the client is at first addressed ('See if you might qualify') and the condescending explicitness (on the inside of the jacket; see also the definition of 'partner' below):

Example 4c

It's not a loan – you don't have to pay it back.

The idea that the reader can work it out for him/herself disappears as one continues to read the leaflet. It now emerges that the criteria are quite complex. An application involves a detailed enquiry into one's earnings and the employer is responsible for conducting part of the application. Clearly, a 'yes' to the three questions at the beginning of the leaflet functions to 'sharpen the appetite':

Example 4d

Find out if you might qualify

Answer these 3 questions about you, and about your partner if you have one.

We use *partner* to mean a person you are married to or a person you live with as if you are married to them.

1. Are you, or your partner, working for at least 16 hours a week?

2. Do you, or your partner, support at least one child who normally lives with you?

3. Do you, and your partner, have £8,000 or less in savings between you?

If you have ticked YES to these 3 questions you may be able to get Family Credit ⟶

The original promise of a straightforward answer about entitlement has now been toned down to 'you *may* be able to get Family Credit'.

It is clear that accessibility here means sorting out any ambiguities at the client's end when it comes to the information needed for an application – rather than making transparent how the decision will be made. From the bureaucrat's point of view, the accessibility problem can be seen as adequately dealt with by making transparent what is meant by 'partner', 'credit' – and doing this in a 'non-offensive' way. Although trying hard to avoid being offensive, it may in fact be insulting since it presupposes a client who does not know what 'credit' means, what 'partner' means, and so on. It is clear now that, although a leaflet such as FC1-Wallet may carry the assumption of greater institutional accessibility, it is nevertheless tied up in complex processes of information control.

140   *LANGUAGE, BUREAUCRACY AND SOCIAL CONTROL*

Privatising the citizens of a capitalist welfare state

The FC1-Wallet strongly resembles credit card leaflets in the way it advertises the government services (cf. the executive summary which highlights the selling points of the service; the organisation of text blocks around questions such as 'What is [a service]?' and 'Who is it for?'; the hyperbolic rhetoric of guaranteed problem solving). Looked at from this perspective, it has taken on the advertising mode but, in doing so, it has created a problematic addressee. We see here an addressee who is seen as a literate shopper, being invited to 'invest in' and 'choose between' benefits, and who can work out for him/herself whether she/he is entitled, but at the same time, the text maintains at various points, that eligibility will be decided by an official authority.

Although the FC1-Wallet actually addresses citizens who do not have a choice, it purports to offer choice. The issue of 'choice' is at the heart of leaflet construction. Credit card leaflets also operate with this notion, capitalising on the consumer's power to choose and the straightforwardness of the credit card's use. Applications for a credit card, however, are screening devices to decide on who can become a card holder. The introduction of consumerism in the public domain is thus matched by increased social control in the private sector. In short, whereas the state has turned to advertising and has adopted the terminology of banking in the world of welfare state provisions, banks have started to probe into private details to determine entitlements for credit cards, endowment policies, and so on. But, although the two may seem to be moving towards one another, an altogether different financial situation is presupposed as far the client is concerned. The bank's client is the one whose income is big enough to qualify for the use of a credit card, whereas in state institutions it is usually the other way round (citizens qualify for tax reductions, income supplement, local tax exemption) because their income is low enough. What separates the two addressee types is that those who need 'family credit' cannot take the leaflet and throw it away in the same way they could when reading a credit card leaflet.

The use and design of leaflets is caught up in complex socio-economic and political developments, and in recent years they have undergone dramatic transformations. It is not just the accessibility of institutions which is at stake here, but the fact that leaflets have become a major element in attempts at a fundamental redefinition of the social welfare space as based on a free market economy model – an advancement of the private economy model in various domains of social life. Fairclough (1992a) interprets this tendency in terms of a commodification of discourse practices and discusses some of the ambivalences inherent in it. For us, one key notion here is that of the textual construction of a welfare citizen who 'shops around' to find out how he/she 'wants to' become a client of a particular institution.

It is, of course, true that banks and insurance companies (encouraged by governments) have also made a bid for the social welfare space (e.g. sickness insurance, top-up schemes in case of prolonged illness, study loan schemes, pension schemes). This development is intimately connected with a perception of a failure of the state and New Right politics – and, in reality, it entails a re-definition of existing facilities (e.g. personal loans have always been there, but now they are used on a much greater scale). The use of leaflets by government institutions to advertise social services tactically misses the point that similar services offered by the bank are only available for those who can afford it. When it comes to citizens who cannot afford privatised social services, their 'needs' must be addressed at a different level.

Charters: from accessibility to accountability

Leaflets from government institutions do not always adopt an advertising mode, trying to sell the services while telling more about them. For instance, the UK Inland Revenue leaflet has quite consistently restricted itself to 'telling', that is how and what to declare about one's financial situation and revenue. In 1984, the Inland Revenue leaflet stated:

Example 5a

How to fill in your tax return

These notes will tell you what I need to know about your income and capital gains for the tax year ended 5 April 1984 and the allowances you may claim for the tax year ending 5 April 1985.

142 *LANGUAGE, BUREAUCRACY AND SOCIAL CONTROL*

Remember

- It is a serious offence to conceal any part of your income or chargeable gains.
- Keep any vouchers, papers, etc. that you use to fill in your tax return, in case I need to see them later.
- If you made a loss in lettings, in a business, or in any other source of income, you may be able to claim relief. I can give further information on request.

Since 1992, the Inland Revenue has carried a 'Tax Payer's Charter' on its front page. For instance, the front page of the 1993 leaflet reads:

Example 5b

REVENUE

FILLING IN YOUR TAX RETURN

Income, deductions and capital gains for the year ended 5 April 1993 and tax allowances for the year ending 5 April 1994

The Taxpayer's Charter

You are entitled to expect the Inland Revenue

To be fair
- by settling your tax affairs impartially
- by expecting you to pay only what is due under the law
- by treating everyone with equal fairness

To help you
- to get your tax affairs right
- to understand your rights and obligations
- by providing clear leaflets and forms
- by giving you information and assistance at enquiry offices
- by being courteous at all times

To provide an efficient service
- by settling your tax affairs promptly and accurately
- by keeping your private affairs strictly confidential
- by using the information you give us only as allowed by the law
- by keeping to a minimum your costs of complying with the law
- by keeping our costs down

THE BUREAUCRAT'S PERSPECTIVE: CITIZENS AS CLIENTS   143

To be accountable for what to do
- by setting standards for ourselves and publishing how well we live up to them

---

If you are not satisfied
- we will tell you exactly how to complain
- you can ask for your tax affairs to be looked at again
- you can appeal to an independent tribunal
- your MP can refer your complaint to the Ombudsman

In return, we need you
- to be honest
- to give us accurate information
- to pay your tax on time

Comparing the two front pages, several differences can be noted which are the result of socio-political developments. A new dimension has entered leaflets, namely, government institutions now go on record about the quality of their practices, and their accountability, and they offer a new definition of clients' rights and obligations. In short, the irresponsible client presupposed in the 1984 leaflet has made way for a responsible government institution which invites the citizen to enter into a contract with reciprocal guarantees of cooperation. The client is constructed linguistically as being under no legal obligation and, whereas in the past, only clients had to go on record about the completeness and correctness of the information they provided, now the institution makes similar promises.

Have institutions become more accessible and transparent through this? Does this really imply a reduction of the asymmetries in information exchange practices? It is clear from the charter that, proportionally, the institution provides more guarantees and, in return, seems to expect little of the client. The institutions have clearly invested energy into constructing a self-image of accountability towards the public. This image is potentially misleading in a number of ways (cf. the mismatches between the advertising mode and the eligibility conditions in the FC1-leaflet):

1. Although the institution appears to offer help with complaints, in reality this may mean that complaints

144 *LANGUAGE, BUREAUCRACY AND SOCIAL CONTROL*

procedures are brought more tightly within the scope of institutional control. In short, the charter does not reveal that it discourages clients from challenging the social principles on which the institution operates. The encouragement to complain through the Inland Revenue itself shows how institutions attempt to promote a route which can be kept within their control.

2. Although the client is 'invited' throughout to cooperate and references to disciplining have disappeared from the pages, the reality of strictures is still there.

3. What counts as 'accountable' is left for the institution to define and for the institution to make public.

Social control manifests itself in two ways. First, leaflets are principally targeted at naive clients (for instance, by addressing issues of what a particular benefit is, and how to apply), but fail to make institutional decision making more transparent. Secondly, leaflets have become a key element in attempts at redefining the client–institution relationships, that is they have become active instruments in attempts at securing the client's cooperation through apparently non-coercive means and in building up the institution's image of a trustworthy, accountable and equal (?) 'partner'. What is at stake is an ideology of cooperation in a situation where it is far from obvious that institutions have indeed become more accessible.

Conclusion

In this chapter, we have pointed to the relevance of two wider social developments which have had an impact on certain discourse practices. First, disciplining situations often take on counselling dimensions, as shown for example in the bank notice which DG received to inform him about the overdraft (Chapter 5). But 'counselling' also appears now in the Inland Revenue guide to the annual tax declaration. A second macro development has been the colonising of discourse domains by advertising, thus producing such mixtures as the combination of 'selling' and 'telling' in leaflets about social security benefits. Both macro developments are reflected in discourse situations where

THE BUREAUCRAT'S PERSPECTIVE: CITIZENS AS CLIENTS   145

institutions address citizens indiscriminately (e.g. leaflets, application forms, standard format letters).

From our analyses, it emerges that the indiscriminate addressing of individual citizens and the use of standard format correspondence are areas where the institution's perceptions are not informed by clients' actual reading behaviour. Clients may read indiscriminate addresses in a very personal way (and, hence they often find them face threatening), but this escapes the institution's attention. The institution's priority, of course, is 'helping citizens to cooperate in becoming clients'.

In this chapter, we have looked at various situations where citizens are turned into clients. For instance, the Tax Payer's charter (one of the 'Citizens' Charters') in Britain is one such attempt at constructing citizens' clienthood within an institution. What is implicit here is the safeguarding of the institution but it is accomplished in a way which tries to implicate apparent concessions to the clients within institutional control. One aspect of this is the channelling of mediation between clients and institutions and of complaints directed at the institution. Since bureaucracies have taken on this counselling dimension, it is useful to study situated instances of mediation to see what they entail in terms of information exchange, client empowerment and social control. This is the main focus of the next chapter.

Notes

1. We are familiar with the fact that bureaucrats organise their work essentially in terms of a number of files they have to process in a given work shift. The file/case is essentially their 'unit' of work.

2. If the institutional representative who processed the form had taken note of the fact that the section under "your partner" was not filled in at all, s/he could have inferred that the client must have meant "divorced". Careful inspection of the form also reveals that the "tick" next to "living together" is crossed out, whereas the "divorced" box is just "ticked". Probably, rash processing or a priori suspicions about any client's sincerity meant that the officer concerned went for the less favourable (but institutionally safe) reading, which results in a denial of entitlement.

7 The discourse of mediation: bureaucrats' dilemma and clients' wisdom

Introduction

In the preceding chapters, we saw how information exchange between institutions and clients is constrained by various social factors and how it runs essentially asymmetrically despite recent developments in 'user-friendly' leaflets and application forms. There is a communication divide which is difficult to bridge if clients remain 'clients' and bureaucrats continue to control the handling and distribution of state provisions. In this chapter, we will focus on institutionalised attempts at bringing bureaucrat and client back together.

What seems to be at stake is some kind of 'institutional literacy', so that clients can get to know what the options are, and how to go about putting forward their case. As discussed in Chapter 6, this situation has also led to a proliferation of leaflets and the use of advisory booklets across and within institutions; it may be doubted, however, whether real institutional literacy has resulted from this. In this chapter we focus on the various forms of social remedial action which exist in the social space, by looking at the practices of intermediary bodies which, in recent years and in various settings, have emerged as resources for clients to turn to when dealing with government departments.

We will discuss three institutionalised types of 'go-between', their discourse practices and the scope of their intervention. The types are:

(1) Intermediary professions, like social work, which are fully funded by government and local authority resources, but are

THE DISCOURSE OF MEDIATION: BUREAUCRATS' DILEMMA AND CLIENTS' WISDOM   147

thought to be more humane and less bureaucratic in the ways they go about their daily work.

(2) Intermediary bodies like the Citizens Advice Bureau and the Advisory Centre for Education, which may be partly funded with government money but are perceived as essentially outside the formal state or local bureaucracy.

(3) Private courier companies like WorldWide who offer services on the fringe of bureaucratic institutions and, in return for payment, expedite matters which would otherwise go through a painfully slow bureaucratic process. Although they are closely associated with bureaucratic institutions (with standard agreements about the scope and routines of their practices), these bodies do not receive any form of public funding.

The practices of such advisory agents, as we will show, provide a useful site for researching dilemmas in the bureaucratic world. In each of these cases, we will look at how applications and appeals are interactively constructed, with professionals responding to drafts and discussing strategies with clients, a practice which is increasingly seen as a fulfilment of client rights. It is clear that in these developments, institutional literacy cannot be seen as a goal in its own right, having as its sole purpose the empowering of clients. At the same time, bureaucrats are saved from being directly questioned about practices. Expressed in relation to the examples in Chapter 6, when the application is mediated, housing officers no longer have 'to throw out their mothers' and clients can face bureaucrats 'armed with housing points' entitling them to a place to live.

So, while examining the discourse practices of these intermediary institutions, in particular information exchange around troubles talk, we shall bear in mind the following questions: Whose side do these institutions take and whose interests do they serve? What type of client are they likely to attract and what kind of client is likely to benefit from their advisory practices? How are such bodies perceived by clients, bureaucracies and by the government? Are their practices non-bureaucratic and what are the effects of having to operate in the space between client and bureaucrat?[1]

148 *LANGUAGE, BUREAUCRACY AND SOCIAL CONTROL*

Social workers attempting to redress the imbalance

As citizens have found it increasingly difficult to deal with institutions, social workers have been allocated to the institutions to act as intermediaries when clients feel their case has become 'stranded' somewhere in the bureaucratic network, or, conversely, welfare workers may be assigned to clients when their situation seems to be calling for guidance over a longer period of time. In Chapter 5 we also looked at two instances (examples 1 and 2), where the government representative, a housing officer, 'side-stepped' and made an apparent gesture of assisting a 'helpless' client by taking on a 'consulting' role.

Let us examine two excerpts from a situation where a social worker (SW) is in the role of a mediator.[2] Together with the client (CL), he is filling in an application form and from the dialogue it is clear why the client sought professional help: the client's child is guaranteed a place in the nursery school if she can receive welfare assistance.

Example 1a:

SW: Nothing under any of these sections.
CL: No we don't get any of these no.
SW: Yes.
CL: Not at the moment see I'd be going out to work. I'm hoping that if he gets into the nursery should be able to go to work to earn some money. See I mean we've got some rent arrears which we've got to clear up [otherwise] the council will get very tacky about that situation so we've got to clear that up and I thought well if I go out to work. I can help you know to get over these mm things
SW: What kind of work would you do
CL: Office work
SW: Office work yeh you've done that before

[they discuss the kind of work CL would like to do]

SW: this depends on A getting into the Royal
CL: Exactly.
SW: Do you call him A or T?
CL: A A A
SW: A?
CL: A for the children that's what they called him you know

THE DISCOURSE OF MEDIATION: BUREAUCRATS' DILEMMA AND CLIENTS' WISDOM   149

SW: And how old is he?
CL: He's three and three quarters he'll be four in April. You're
nearly four love (to child) Alright shush.
SW: Have you got a nursery place for him?
CL: Well I went over to CH over here and they said ehm I said
to ehm have they got any places and they said well we have
got a few. So she said you do realise it's £-a week now and I
said oh I'm hoping the welfare might be able to help me a
bit you know so she said oh well in that case if the welfare's
going to help you you've definitely got a place.
SW: Yeh.
CL: You know so I mean she said I'll put his name down could
start today I said well I haven't (laughs) seen the welfare
worker yet.
SW: Yes uhm.
CL: You know but ehm if they could help me I mean I know it's
I haven't put down the rent that's £20. Give me that (to the
child).

In the second excerpt, the talk hovers between 'troubles talk'
and the activity of filling in the form.

Example 1b:

CL: I wanted to convert this one back to the ordinary and pay it
off weekly with them it would work out cheaper that way
because it's something like that (. . .) our bill now where as
with the slot my friends got exactly the same as me and
SW: mm
CL: she pay forty her last bill was £56
SW: she pays she pay herself on a meter or by credit
CL: on a quarterly
SW: quarterly credit yes
CL: you see
SW: credit is probably a bit cheaper the only problem is with it is
you know if you're short of money when the bill come to you
CL: exactly that is the problem
SW: it builds up and up and up
CL: well that we had that problem once before
SW: mm
CL: (admonishes child) mm don't get any of this [referring to
form] erm oh we have we have got the £30 we have to pay
£6 a week back to my mother-in-law cause we had to

150 *LANGUAGE, BUREAUCRACY AND SOCIAL CONTROL*

> borrow some money to pay an outstanding debt with the
> court you know and oh
> SW: what kind of debt were you paying off to (. . .) that your
> mother-in-law paid you the money for?
> CL: well they were gonna make us bankrupt see cause it was
> about a washing machine that kept going wrong it's all very
> complicated we were accused of (. . .) and they wouldn't
> come and repair it (child interruptions) so we had to borrow
> money off off B's mum for it well she offered to lend it to us
> so we could – so we weren't made bankrupt so
> SW: I think you should put it down and if you don't mind
> explaining to them about finances they would realise it was
> an important debt
> CL: hm
> SW: that'd have to be paid but
> CL: thirty
> SW: put the amount here
> CL: and how shall I sort of phrase it?
> SW: repayment of debt to mother-in-law do you want to explain
> what the debt was for or would you rather leave it out?
> CL: mm well I don't mind explaining eh but it's putting it in the
> most simplest terms isn't it?
> SW: put in brackets to prevent ban bankruptcy lovely great
> CL: hm
> SW: now do you think that's all that would come under your
> necessary expenditure that's leaving aside food and
> everything else
> CL: yes that's everything there so that's er (counting up debts
> and drawing up balance sheet)
> SW: how much do you think you'll be able to offer towards the
> CL: well I could man I could manage half of it I think
> SW: well put that down then it's always a good idea to suggest
> that you can something because they (writing)
> CL: just sign it
> SW: just sign it and

Although this situation is essentially very similar to one where an
applicant fills in a form at a desk with the bureaucrat present, the
social worker's discursive behaviour is different from that of a
bureaucrat – even when the latter is a sidestepping bureaucrat.
Let us list a number of differences.

THE DISCOURSE OF MEDIATION: BUREAUCRATS' DILEMMA AND CLIENTS' WISDOM   151

(1) The social worker responds to and participates in troubles talk. In an explicitly bureaucratic context (cf. Chapter 3), the client may also talk about her friends' and relatives' experiences and talk about what experiences of financial hardship are like, but this stance is unlikely to be reciprocated by the bureaucrat. In the cases of side-stepping we looked at in Chapter 5, the bureaucrat only sympathises implicitly (by offering 'a way out' for the client). Here the social worker is actually co-narrating a life-world story and there are even indications of role reversal (cf. the social worker's turn 'the only problem is with it is you know if you're short of money when the bill come to you' is followed by the client (!) formulating the situation 'exactly that is the problem').

(2) There are also other signs, which indicate that the social worker, discursively, at least, appears to be siding with the client (e.g. in the second excerpt, example 1b, the decision makers are referred to as 'them' and 'they'). Clearly, social workers see themselves outside 'traditional' bureaucracies. They visit clients at their homes and only certain client types fall within their domain of service (as opposed to the indiscriminate address of citizens by bureaucratic institutions).

(3) Next, there are rather overt indications in the excerpt that the construction of a professional client is an interactional goal. In a more traditional bureaucratic set-up one would expect neither the client nor a side-stepping bureaucrat to be open about this. We can refer to three points in the interaction where this is the case.
  - The social worker anticipates how the information provided in the application will be interpreted by the person who will be processing it (cf. 'if you don't mind explaining to them about finances they would realise it was an important debt').
  - The social worker and the mother also share between them a sense that there are various ways in which one can fill in a form and that this is often a matter of tactical formulations (e.g. in example 1b the social worker's turn, 'do you want to explain what the debt was for or would you rather leave it out?' is responded to by the client with 'well I don't mind explaining but it's putting it in the most

152   *LANGUAGE, BUREAUCRACY AND SOCIAL CONTROL*

> simplest terms isn't it?'; see also e.g. where the client asks 'how shall I sort of phrase it?').
>
> - The social worker advises the client on what can count as an acceptable and effective answer in the space provided for 'necessary expenditure' (cf. 'put in brackets "to prevent ban bankruptcy" ').

(4) Finally, the social worker is much less directive in asking for information and offers the client a choice whether or not to supply certain bits of information (cf. 'do you want to explain what the debt was for'). In a comparable situation, a bureaucrat would also ask the client for the information (e.g. 'what was the debt for?') but he/she could not leave the client with the choice of refusing it. Likewise, the social worker asks the client whether she feels the stated information is complete (cf. 'now do you think that's all that would come under your necessary expenditure'). For a bureaucrat, on the other hand, 'completeness' is entirely the client's responsibility. A bureaucrat should not ask for this, but a side-stepping bureaucrat may hint at its necessity. And, if clients forget to declare something that would speak in their favour, this is of no concern to a bureaucrat. To the contrary, suggesting that more information would increase the client's chances is ruled out. Sidestepping in such circumstances would probably take the form of a request for further information in a fashion which suggests that the information forms an essential part of the procedure.

Although intermediaries, like the social worker in this case, may empower clients in part and relieve bureaucrats from having to take clients through the procedure, their actions are only remedial and do not have the effect of fundamentally challenging the communicative divide. In this case the social worker's primary purpose is to complete the application form and enhance the client's chances of success. For instance, towards the end he explains, 'it's always a good idea to suggest that you can offer something because they'. He does not complete this utterance. At this point, finishing the explanation is less important than getting the form signed. Of course, the client learns here about 'valid answers' and 'efficient ways to declare' a particular situation before the decision is made (cf. clients who, only after an unsuccessful

THE DISCOURSE OF MEDIATION: BUREAUCRATS' DILEMMA AND CLIENTS' WISDOM   153

outcome, learn that, had they declared their situation differently, their application would have stood a better chance of being successful). However, it is not the worker's aim to inform the client maximally about the rules and criteria of decision making.

Counselling institutions

Before clients fill in an application form or lodge an appeal, they may try to gather as much information as possible about, for example, their entitlements and the bureaucratic decision-making procedure. Institutions like the Citizens' Advice Bureau cater for this kind of client need.[3] Nowadays, institutions like the Department of Social Security advise clients to contact mediating bodies for assistance. For instance, the FC1-Wallet we looked at in Chapter 6 reads on the inside of the cover:

Example 2

HELP AND ADVICE. For more information about Family Credit ring Freeline Social Security 0800 666 555. The phone call will be free or get in touch with your Social Security Office. The phone number and address are in the phone book under SOCIAL SECURITY or BENEFITS AGENCY or get in touch with an advice centre like the Citizens Advice Bureau.

To understand the role of these mediating institutions one has to look at their everyday practices. In the earlier example we looked at how the application for welfare assistance formed part of an application for a child's place in a nursery. We paid particular attention to the social worker's coaching activities in submitting an application with good chances of a successful outcome. What happens when this sort of help is not forthcoming? Or, when clients, who did not seek the help of a mediating agency, are faced with an unsuccessful outcome and decide to appeal?

From 'making an application', we now move to the stage of 'lodging an appeal'. We stay within the field of education and concentrate on a case where parents in a London borough enter the stage of a second appeal with the local education authority (LEA) after a place in a primary school was denied to their child and a first appeal proved unsuccessful. At this point they turned

154   *LANGUAGE, BUREAUCRACY AND SOCIAL CONTROL*

to the Advisory Centre for Education. We will discuss the advisory organisation's written response to the appeal draft (see Appendix 7). Interactive construction is in this case presupposed, but is to be inferred from the data.

Local education authority versus Martins: episode 1

Let us first turn to the beginning of the case in September 1990. Jimmy, when four, goes on to Little Oak First School (a state primary school) where he has been offered a place. This is in accordance with the 'rule' that children are first given a place in the school whose catchment area includes their home. As the child is not doing very well, the parents request a transfer to North Oak Combined. The parents' stated reasons, as re-formulated by Oak borough education authorities, are three-fold:

Example 3a

1. Jimmy's development at school has been poor. He is losing confidence and finds school boring.

2. Music and drama is limited at Little Oak First – areas of curriculum which are important to the parents. There is also no reading scheme.

3. Parents feel that there is a breakdown of communication with the school over Jimmy's education.

After attending an interview with the Principal and the Director of Education, the parents learn of the decision not to allocate Jimmy to the preferred school. In the advice to the education committee, the Director of Education adduces the following responses to the parents' stated reasons:

Example 3b

1. As Little Oak First School caters for children of First School age, the curriculum provided will be suited to children of that age range, with emphasis given to the development of educational, social and practical skills. The acquisition of those skills is essential and all schools would be expected to provide these opportunities for young children.

THE DISCOURSE OF MEDIATION: BUREAUCRATS' DILEMMA AND CLIENTS' WISDOM

2. Whilst the reasons for making this request are understood, it is not possible to give priority on this basis to a school which is oversubscribed and where other applicants with higher priority have been refused.
3. Priority cannot be given on the grounds of parental preference for the ethos, organisation or curriculum when high priority applications have been refused.

In addition, the Director states:

Example 3c

. . . Having taken account of the circumstances of this case and those of other applicants, the appeal committee is advised that the reasons given for requesting the school do not outweigh the prejudicial effect of making further admissions to North Oak School.

The Director's advice is accepted by the education committee and the reasons for refusal communicated to the parents:

Example 3d

. . . the Committee have decided to refuse your appeal on the grounds (1) that to comply with the parental preference would prejudice the provision of efficient education or the efficient use of resources at North Oak CFM School and (2) that this prejudicial effect is not outweighed by your preference or any of the other circumstances stated.

What we see here is a mismatch between the basis on which the parents lodge the appeal and the reasons given by the LEA to ignore the parents' story. From the Director of Education's response to the parents' stated reasons it emerges that their first and third argument – Jimmy's poor development and the communication breakdown with the school – are not being responded to. On the other hand, the second argument is countered by the first of the director's reasons for refusal: Little Oak is a school suitable for children like Jimmy. The reply again refers to the criteria on the basis of which a decision can be reached – the number of places available and Jimmy's ranking on a waiting list.

Bureaucracies like the LEA will act upon the assumption that

156 *LANGUAGE, BUREAUCRACY AND SOCIAL CONTROL*

complaints have to be warded off as much as possible: if a client complains about school *x*, she/he can also be expected to complain about school *y*. Although for the parents the child's well-being and the relationship with the school are more important, the education authority's priority is the provision of education (seen in terms of quantity, e.g. pupil–staff ratio, having an effect on quality). The quality of educational provision – i.e. the quality of interaction and the curricular content – stands beyond doubt.[4]

It is clear from the LEA's viewpoint that parents should follow the leaflet instructions about what can constitute a valid basis for appeal.[5] When parents deviate from this 'path' and try to tell their story, institutions ignore 'parental preference'. The reasons adduced by the LEA against the transfer bypass the implicit accusations: North Oak Combined is full and to comply with parental prejudice would endanger the school's provision of education.

The phrase 'would prejudice the provision of efficient education' is used by the LEA here in a legal sense. Thus, the stated reason is that further admissions to North Oak would endanger the quality of provisions there. The parents may very well have seen this as an easy – quantifiable and irreversible – way out for the education authority.

Let us now turn to what may have prompted the parents to invoke certain reasons, rather than others, in the appeal procedure. If from the appeal leaflet they could have worked out that the decision would be made in terms of educational provisions in the preferred school, why did they go ahead and base their appeal on an assessment of the quality of education in Little Oak First School? And why did their appeal fail to say anything about North Oak Combined? In short, despite the knowledge that a decision would be made on the basis of whether or not Jimmy's transfer would prejudice the provisions in North Oak Combined, they persisted in criticising Little Oak and reporting Jimmy's disappointing development.

It is also worth noting that the parents are commenting on Jimmy's development at school in a situation where only trained school personnel are expected to assess pupils. Obviously, the parents had very strong feelings about the situation, drawing mainly on perceptions from their lifeworld. This situation not only

THE DISCOURSE OF MEDIATION: BUREAUCRATS' DILEMMA AND CLIENTS' WISDOM 157

shows their lack of institutional 'literacy', but also that the leaflet with the notes on how to appeal failed to direct their efforts.

The outcome of this appeal is that Jimmy is put on a waiting list and, in a further letter from the local Education Service, the parents are invited to consider an alternative school. In their response addressed to the Director of Education (dated 6 February 1991), the parents outline the circumstances at Little Oak with reference to the position of Jimmy, whom they now wish to place in Elm First School. Let us now look at how their perceptions develop after this failed appeal and as they turn to the Advisory Centre for Education (ACE) to improve their chances of a successful outcome.

Local education authority versus Martins plus ACE: episode 2

Let us first say a few words about the ACE. The Advisory Centre for Education was founded in 1960. It describes itself (in a leaflet, p. 1) as acting

> as a consumer organisation covering the statutory school years of the maintained education service. The Centre provides free advice through its telephone service, and publishes handbooks and information sheets written for parents and governors about the education system.

Parallel with advice work, the ACE runs projects which look in depth at specific aspects of edcuational provision in order to develop models of good practice.

As explained in the ACE's introductory leaflet (p.1),

> Most of our calls come from parents who are involved in formal procedures concerning their children's education.

> We can advise parents on where they stand legally, explaining the respective roles and powers of the headteacher, the school governors, the Local Education Authority and the Government; and on effective ways of making their own views known.

The Martins call upon the ACE on two occasions: a first time, over the telephone before drawing up the appeal and a second time, when they send the appeal draft to the organisation for feedback. We shall analyse both the encounters. In our analysis

158   *LANGUAGE, BUREAUCRACY AND SOCIAL CONTROL*

below we will concentrate on the 'turns' in the 'conversation' between ACE and the parents and focus on the discursive processes in the drafting of the appeal – which will be presented in person.[6] In other words, our aim is to examine what 'restating' and 'channelling' of complaints precisely entail (e.g. which arguments can enter the appeal, which cannot enter the appeal, and for those that can enter, how they are best put).

ACE's advice before the draft: try not to put any backs up

Let us now look at with preliminary advice which the parents noted down when talking to the ACE over the telephone. We have numbered the points.[7]

Example 3e

Jimmy's School
Advies van de Advisory Centre for Education
18 Victoria Park Square
London E2 9PB
tel 081-980 4596

(1) Don't be nasty about the old school, find all the points why your child should be in the new school.

(2) Be very positive about the new school, and list why he should do better (more formal, old school too free for him.

more art and music used to concentrate very well, can't now anymore)

(3) New school in line with your thoughts on education.

(4) Just say there is a breakdown in communication with the headteacher (don't be nasty about her) and there is a basic difference in philosophie about his education.

(5) That you can't see yourself for the next four years going up and down to the school all time time, because the difference stays.

(6) Say their approach is fine for others but doesn't work for your child (we know because have been helping in class).

(7) Don't say things you can't back up, like saying your child can't cope.

(8) Be as honest as you can

THE DISCOURSE OF MEDIATION: BUREAUCRATS' DILEMMA AND CLIENTS' WISDOM 159

(9) You believe that in the next school there will be a true partnership between you and the school (Artscouncil).

(10) Try not to put any backs up.

From this text, the role of the ACE becomes clear: either classify a point as not worth making or argue that it needs modification. The basic strategy is that of phrasing one's case by appealing to established and acceptable propositions and categories, but to do so in a way which makes one's case salient and genuine. Thus, parents are advised to stress the benefits of the new school, especially what the child would gain from it (points (2), (3) and (9)). They are also advised to transform their criticism of the old school into a statement that, while being generally fine, the school is not well-suited to Jimmy (points (4), (5) and (6)). The underlying assumption is that the school's reputation as an adequate provider of education is kept intact. But, of course, some statement of negative experience is needed, otherwise there could be no reason to move the child. On the other hand point (7) shows that the thing which really matters to parents, namely how Jimmy is doing in the old school, cannot enter the appeal.

Finally, note that point (8) reflects that parents stand a better chance if they come across as sincere (whereas the LEA does not have to make any pretence at all about it not being sincerely concerned with the quality of educational provision).

ACE's comments on the appeal draft

After having spoken to the ACE, the parents prepare the appeal draft. The parents pass on the draft to the ACE and it is returned, accompanied with detailed comments. Being the result of 'brain storming', this appeal draft is probably trying to include everything they can think of, but the parents must have realised they may eventually have to be selective in their presentation.[8]

In our analysis we will refer to excerpts from the appeal. The complete text of the draft can be found in Appendix 7. We will focus on the parts of the parents' text which receive feedback from the ACE. In the background there is also the question about the nature of the relationship between the ACE, the LEA and the government.

160   *LANGUAGE, BUREAUCRACY AND SOCIAL CONTROL*

Knocking Little Oak down
Despite the original advice not to be too negative about the old
school, the parents commence with one page of criticism.

Example 3f

[. . .] extremely poor concentration in the class.
[. . .] no reading scheme.
[. . .] little or no control on learning to write properly.
[. . .] no attempt to give guidance on spelling.
[. . .] The class teacher seldom hears Jimmy read.
[. . .] this is an exceptional case of a probationary teacher not
coping particularly well.
[. . .] the school's resources appear to be diminishing rapidly.
[. . .] There is now neither a music nor a drama specialist in
the school

ACE comments:

Example 3g

1. An appeal is to balance 'parental considerations' against
'prejudice to efficient education'.
2. You may knock Little Oak School, but it could have the effect
of putting the Appeal Committee against you. It is better to just
state the particular aspects of Elm that suit you.
2a. Appeal Cttee will not consider criticism of one school as valid
reason for move to another school. Reasons for appeal should all
be positive in favour of new school.

[. . .]

I'm sorry but your arguments about poor teaching at Little Oak
are not for Appeal Committees, they should be the subject of (a)
complaint to Head, (b) complaint to governors, (c) formal
complaint to Director of Education.

In their comments, the ACE points to restrictions on the
procedural agenda and advises the parents to observe these
restrictions of what will count as 'relevant information'. It
reiterates earlier advice – parents stand to gain more from
praising the preferred school than from criticising the old school
and the quantity of educational provisions in the new school is
what will matter. At the same time, the ACE also channels the

THE DISCOURSE OF MEDIATION: BUREAUCRATS' DILEMMA AND CLIENTS' WISDOM   161

parents' complaints when stating that arguments about the quality of teaching in a school cannot enter an appeal for transfer, but should be voiced through other channels. The ACE is trying to draw a line between what is and what is not – in principle – an appeal (point (1)).

In doing so, the ACE also contributes to the construction of two distinct types of clients by suggesting a particular parent identity for parents who are involved in making an appeal against an educational decision. The underlying assumption is that it is all right for someone to criticise the educational policies in the political sphere through certain channels, but parents like the Martins (although journalists) should behave like troubled parents for whom it is better that they go along with the decision-making procedure rather than adopt a 'political' voice.

Note how the ACE's role has changed. Whereas during the initial telephone contact, the organisation offered general guidelines and warnings which would apply for all clients, its response to the parents' draft is geared at a successful outcome for a particular appeal case. Therefore when it comes to a written draft, the ACE processes the appeal from the LEA's perspective.

Politically significant facts about 'real books'

In a more specific complaint, the parents show their institutional literacy and there is a clear signal that they are aware of the political situation in the background.

Example 3h

There is no reading scheme. There is a total reliance on 'real books', a method that, when used exclusively, has been widely disproved. Earlier this month the Education Secretary Kenneth Clarke described the 'real books' method as cranky and other new schemes as eccentric. 'All reports show that where phonics is used teachers have an overwhelming record of success,' he said. They are not used in Jimmy's class.

ACE comments:

Example 3i

Your point about real books is incorrect. The National Curriculum contains much reference to real books and in fact the

162   *LANGUAGE, BUREAUCRACY AND SOCIAL CONTROL*

> recommended reading at Key Stage 1 lists 51 of them. In addition, most schools use a mixture of methods & in 80% of schools they are teaching reading successfully.
>
> Unless you can get a written statement from Little Oak that they only use 'real books' & a different statement from Elm, this very delicate point is not likely to stand.

The parents' criticism is met with the advice that it is better not to dig their own grave by producing facts which will not be acknowledged as true. At this point, the ACE discourages parents from entering into a discussion over the spread and quality of certain educational practices and methods, a role reserved for social scientists and educational specialists. Is the point about 'reading schemes' probably also 'delicate' because a politician's voice is introduced to lend support to it? Educational specialists and practitioners are likely to see politicians as having no authority in matters such as the effectiveness of educational methods. At a lower level, claims also need to be backed by 'written evidence' ahead of opinions/observations. Parents are certainly entitled to their opinions, and there are occasions for voicing these, but they should not enter an appeal procedure about the placement of a child in a particular school.

Voting with your feet

In the appeal draft, the parents use whatever resources they have available. From their point of view, it is important to come on strongly, signalling they cannot easily be pushed aside. Here the father – who is a journalist – draws on the professional discourse format of a newspaper column article as a resource for making a political point.

> **Example 3j**
> I know that some parents in this class are concerned about the standards, but their reaction has been, like ours, to provide a strong presence in the class. (. . .) Other parents have simply moved out of the borough, which accounts for the falling numbers. (. . .) This seems to be an early example of what the Councillor calls 'voting with your feet'. As he says, 'Under LMS the money follows the pupil and if the parents don't like what is being done by the school then the school will have to change.'

THE DISCOURSE OF MEDIATION: BUREAUCRATS' DILEMMA AND CLIENTS' WISDOM 163

ACE comments:

Example 3k

'Voting with your feet' is an erroneous suggestion.

Even if 85% (April 1993) of the school funding depends on pupil
numbers there will be insufficient money to build an extra
classroom. Popular schools will always be full.

In its response, the ACE also acknowledges that it is dealing with
a parent who is well-informed about political decision making in
the area of education. But it advises against making these points,
probably because of their politically sensitive content.[9] One can
also expect the future of educational institutions to be an area of
struggle between LEAs, the council and the government. It may
rebound unfavourably on parents if they evoke this struggle when
arguing about the day-to-day management of the LEA. Implicitly,
the advice also reads that one cannot invoke the authority of a
'political voice' from the borough council when dealing with one
of its subsidiaries.

Language is our livelihood
The parents' own educational background and institutional
literacy comes up again in the following argument, now used as a
demand that their son receive an equivalent educational standard.

Example 3l

. . . high academic standards are important to us. Language –
speaking, reading and writing – is our livelihood. I work in higher
education – teach and direct plays at GMSD. I work as a theatre
critic for *The Guardian* and feature writer for *The Times*. I write
books.

Wife – foreign correspondent for Dutch press, radio and TV.

Language is important to us and we try to convey those values to
our son. That is why we expect him to have a first class academic
education.

ACE comments:

164 *LANGUAGE, BUREAUCRACY AND SOCIAL CONTROL*

Example 3m

Everyone wants a first class academic education. This is not an argument for an appeal committee.

Here the clients are advised not to state what appears to be an obvious demand for all parents. Their professional situation and life style do not warrant special treatment, a point we shall return to further on. At the same time, this is a reiteration that statements about the quality of education cannot enter the appeal – partly because representatives of the education system cannot afford to be seen admitting that it is not always offering the standards required by law.

Overcrowding problems, desks and coat pegs
At this point in the 'conversation', the ACE changes its stance. While earlier points were more about 'what not to say', the ACE now turns to 'what to say'. Parents are advised to turn to those details that bear on the criterion 'prejudice the provision of education'.

Example 3n

Overcrowding problems

The Education Authority has stated that Elm is full. Classes in Jimmy's year are at capacity. And people are, like Jimmy, on a waiting list hoping to get in.

ACE comments:

Example 3o

Elm at Appeal must prove that it is full.

1) How many desks has it?

2) Does it have enough space for another desk?

3) Are there enough coat pegs for an extra child, etc.

Although the arguments here may seem trivial from the parents' point of view, they are not from the ACE's or the LEA's point of view. This shows another dimension of the role relationship

THE DISCOURSE OF MEDIATION: BUREAUCRATS' DILEMMA AND CLIENTS' WISDOM   165

between government bodies and the ACE. The ACE adopts here the role of a bureaucratic spokesperson who endorses institutional practices, rather than challenging them. Of course, at one level, the comments also make rules more transparent.

The decision of the appeal committee is not just based on parents' motivations, but on considerations about the facilities in the preferred school (e.g. enough room for one more child, extra cost, practical arrangements). The target school is also an area to which the committee will turn for reasons to deny the child a place. So, strategically, parents are advised to preempt this aspect of the procedure and to incorporate information about the preferred school in their appeal. In fact, already from the LEA's response to the first appeal, the parents could have inferred that (i) criticism of the school and its curriculum will not bring about a favourable outcome, as the education provisions count as 'adequate' and (ii) that the decision (not) to allocate will be based on 'numbers & places' in the preferred school. But the parents persisted. As is clear from the first sections of the appeal draft, they were very reluctant to change their strategy. Obviously, they must have felt that they had been brushed aside by the LEA and that their reasons were very well founded, and the next stage of the case, for them, is part of a 'warrior' fight over principles of decision making.

At this point in the ACE's response, the logic of a smooth, minimally problematic procedure comes clearly into the foreground, especially one that will not be face-threatening to any of the decision makers. If the topics of decision making can appear to be of a practical, measurable nature, it is easier to win over the committee members. But from the appeal draft it is clear that the parents saw things differently: they assumed that institutions will want to deal with things in terms which matter to them!

The following excerpt and the ACE's response to it further illustrate this trivialisation of criteria. Physical nearness of the school is picked up as the 'best argument so far'.

Example 3p

Third: As for closeness to the school, we can also reach the school quickly – less than 5 minutes drive.

166 *LANGUAGE, BUREAUCRACY AND SOCIAL CONTROL*

ACE comments:

Example 3q

Third: this is your best argument so far.

What you or your child bring to the school does not matter
The trivialisation of arguments also extends to the contributions
which parents can make to the working of the school.

Example 3r

First, Elm is known to have a mobile population. [. . .]

Second. Jimmy is known to be a very bright, well-balanced child
[. . .] and will be a credit to the school.

Third. His command of English is above average for his age. And
because of his bi-lingual background (he is fluent in Dutch) and
his very international upbringing, he is used to racial and cultural
differences [. . .] In classes like those at Elm he can be a
valuable bridge between foreign children and those from a more
conventional English background.

Fourth: [. . .] My point is that there is a very good context of
music and drama at Elm. I am prepared to bring my own
expertise to help enrich the drama work.

ACE comments:

Example 3s

First: a good point.

Third: if you can show that there are more foreign children at
Elm and this would benefit Jimmy this is a good point.

Fourth re: earlier I said that Jimmy must benefit from drama.
What you bring to the school doesn't matter.

That the parent could assist in drama activities at school is a
point better not made, because in the event of a favourable
outcome, the case may become open to allegation of preferential
treatment, which can invite an angry reaction from other parents.
Rather than the parents, the well-being of the child as a recipient

THE DISCOURSE OF MEDIATION: BUREAUCRATS' DILEMMA AND CLIENTS' WISDOM 167

of educational practice should be the focus of attention. The parents' point that Jimmy's foreign origin is a strength is reversed. They are advised to draw the multicultural card only when Jimmy can be the beneficiary, not the benefactor.

Here one can see one of the fundamental assumptions behind the provision of education. The child can only enter an action scenario in which he/she is seen at the receiving end of educational provision, benefiting from the new school (rather than bringing something to the new school by his/her presence).

This is the state of affairs

In a final response, the ACE finally acknowledges the legitimacy of the parents' outrage and expresses their solidarity with them.

Example 3t

Does this mean we have no way of upholding the right to choose the best education for our child – in line with the philosophy of the Government. We're happy to appeal to your discretion. It would be a sad state of affairs if there is basically no freedom of education and children are denied a good, or even competent education; if you can't get the best education without paying for it.

ACE comments:

Example 3u

THIS IS THE STATE OF AFFAIRS for some children. At the moment Jimmy is one of them.

From its response, it is clear that the ACE may be relatively powerless in the context of the day-to-day decision-making within the LEA. But, at the same time, it is also clear that the ACE functions to ward off certain arguments from entering the procedure – partly because appeal procedures generate some kind of self-censorship. To lodge an appeal is a twofold activity of expressing complaint and dissatisfaction with a procedural outcome, while, on the other hand, acting strategically to secure a favourable outcome. In the process of lodging an appeal, clients can be expected to develop from a stage of outrage at an institutional decision (that which prompts the appeal) to a stage

168   *LANGUAGE, BUREAUCRACY AND SOCIAL CONTROL*

where a favourable decision becomes the top priority. In this process, clients gradually adopt the institutional categorisations of, and restrictions on, what can enter the appeal. This is a reflection of the actual powers of the institutions which clients have to deal with (e.g. an appeal can be thrown out because it violates the institutional restrictions on the appeal agenda). As bodies like ACE see their function as assisting clients in the appeal activity, they accelerate the process in which clients adopt the institutional frames of reference. This may have the effect of saving clients from having to appeal twice or from being at a loss how to go about it. But another side-effect is undoubtedly that institutional control over what can enter the appeal procedure is even better secured. Nor is it unthinkable that mediating bodies may strive to monopolise a social space for themselves.

How the parents' account is being turned into a case

One basic message which runs through the ACE's responses is that clients are discouraged from telling their own story, but are instead advised to attend to those details which the Appeal Committee can act upon and find easy to rationalise decisions about. Parents are advised to omit information which will not be taken into consideration or which may be politically sensitive or face-threatening to committee members. The procedures thus transform the case into a situation where the criteria can easily be made salient without the risk of face loss for any of the institutions involved. Thus, parents are advised to refrain from commenting on any matter related to educational policy and from expressing personal views about the quality of educational provision, be it in a particular school or in general. Bodies like the ACE therefore can be ascribed a 'ventilation' function. Clients are given a forum to voice their frustrations but the ACE channels these in such a way that parents, out of pragmatic necessity, develop from being 'angry warrior' clients into 'professional' clients who, at the end of the day, are content to reduce their initial demands for far-reaching political and social change to the hope of a successful outcome for their particular application or appeal.

Through its mediation efforts, ACE helps maintain existing practices, together with all the possible 'ways out' for the local education authority or the schools involved. A general observation can be made here: once political decisions have resulted in bureaucratic procedures, there is a strong pressure to treat them as 'objective', self-sufficient entities. This, in turn, affects institutions' orientations towards the procedures, as decision making on overtly political grounds is ruled out, or – when it does occur – it must assume the disguise of measurable and acceptable, non-political criteria.

However, we should not underestimate the contradictory aspects inherent in the ACE's role. Through the discourse of advising, the ACE tries to adopt an insiders' perspective into the bureaucratic appeal procedure. This way it acts out the go-between role it is invested with. A clear illustration of this is the selection of arguments for the appeal draft, with advice on how they should be worded (cf. recasting the multicultural argument). At the same time, the ACE's comments also reveal their sympathy towards the parents' point of view, based on a shared middle-class worldview. On the one hand, the ACE helps the parents to prepare a 'suitable' appeal which must facilitate preferential treatment of the appeal case, but, on the other hand, this also means transforming the parents' 'sharp middle-class elbows' (as Frank Field, the Labour MP would put it). Consider again the advice: 'Everybody wants a first class academic education. This is not an argument for an appeal committee.' Here members of the ACE react both as professional advisers and as members of the middle class with conflicting ideologies. Arguably, the comment above (together with other comments) hints that the ACE feels that parents should refrain from using their social status to try to persuade the LEA to accept their case for a different school. A conflicting (more radical) middle-class discourse which wants good education for all children may view appeals like this as special pleading by an already advantaged group.

Institutional monopolies over mediation

So far we have looked at (semi)-bureaucratic professions and institutions acting bureaucratically and thus contributing to the asymmetricality between client needs and institutional provisions.

170 LANGUAGE, BUREAUCRACY AND SOCIAL CONTROL

In this final section of the chapter, we shall show how the bureaucratisation process also affects private bodies when they take on an intermediary role in the bureaucratic domain. This becomes particularly visible when we examine their discourse practices and their relationships with the traditional bureaucracies which they purport to represent.

Let us consider the following case where an international courier agency, WorldWide, steps in – unasked – to deal with a set of books which a British publisher sends to a Belgian university for exhibition purposes during a conference which will be attended by its representative. At the airport, WorldWide had handled the 'import' and paid the duties which the customs felt were due.[10] Neither the publisher nor the conference organisers knew about this. During the conference the books were displayed. At the end of the conference, the publishers' representative exported the books via the local railway station, as she was taking a ferry back to England.

The assigned client is asked to pay up

About two weeks after the conference, the organisers received an invoice from WorldWide for some BF 3,000 in customs duty. Stated reason: VAT on imported books, which WorldWide had paid on behalf of the conference and which it was now reclaiming. The invoice was accompanied by the following letter (we provide here a translated version of the first paragraphs, see Appendix 8a for the original).

Example 4a

Dear client,

Goods, imported from abroad, have to be declared at the customs and cleared by WorldWide.

To speed up this customs routine, WorldWide pays the VAT and/or excise duty as soon as the goods arrive in Belgium. This is subsequently invoiced to the client.

Therefore, we ask you to pay this amount within 7 days. If you have questions about the exactness of the clearance, please contact us before the invoice expires.

THE DISCOURSE OF MEDIATION: BUREAUCRATS' DILEMMA AND CLIENTS' WISDOM   171

The main purpose of this letter is to explain WorldWide's mediating role between the Belgian customs and importers/exporters. In it, WorldWide claims to be a legitimate part of the customs procedure (see, for instance, the opening sentence which uses a modal of external obligation ('have to') and also the technical term 'cleared'). There is an implicit agreement with the customs 'to speed up the customs routine'.

WorldWide also casts itself in a 'customer-assisting role', which includes the handling of goods for importers from whom they have no mandate. This explains why WorldWide stepped in and paid import duties on behalf of the conference (the addressee, and hence also the alleged importer of the goods). In doing so, they acted on their own initiative: they pay VAT where due and reclaim the money afterwards from the addressee. Note that, unlike the ACE, WorldWide is a client-assisting body which has secured for itself not only a monopoly over the expertise but also over participation in the procedure![11] Therefore, it is clear that WorldWide only sides with the client, in so far as she/he is paying for this, and it is even in a position to assign clienthood to someone, without the person's or organisation's prior consent! Unlike the ACE, the role of such agencies is exclusively oriented towards the demands of a particular case as there is no attempt to take on a role of representation with a government department to influence legislation and practice.

On receiving the invoice, one of the conference organisers rang up WorldWide to find out exactly where things had 'gone wrong'. It emerged that, because the box had failed to state the import was temporary, the customs officers had assumed it concerned books the addressees were 'buying' from the British publisher and therefore they had charged VAT before they could 'clear' the box. Had the travel documents on the cardboard box stated that the books were to be used for an exhibition, no VAT would have been due.[12]

From the conference organisers' viewpoint, WorldWide's unsolicited involvement in 'clearing' the books has resulted in an unwarranted assignment of clienthood. Had WorldWide not stepped in, the customs officers would have had to contact the university about the box which needed to be cleared. This would have made it possible for the organisers to explain the situation and the misunderstanding would have been sorted out before any

172 *LANGUAGE, BUREAUCRACY AND SOCIAL CONTROL*

damage had been done. In short, WorldWide and the customs had followed routine practice, and therefore they had acted rashly.

The assigned client is advised to mediate

But WorldWide saw things differently. As far as they were concerned, they had done the organisers a service at their own expense (because this kind of service brings along administrative costs which they could well do without and there was no surcharge for WorldWide's intervention). They also saw it as a contribution to the smooth flow of transactions at the customs in the airport. From WorldWide's viewpoint, since the VAT has already been paid, the next step is to find out how the money could be reclaimed from the customs, because, after all, the books had been imported temporarily and, normally speaking, no duties should have been paid.

WorldWide obviously knows how to play the game. They have a vested interest here, and it is also clear that, under 'normal circumstances', WorldWide keep their expertise to themselves – this way guaranteeing a monopoly on their mediating role in international transactions! At the same time, WorldWide are unwilling to go back to the customs to rectify the situation. They want the addressee to declare (and prove with evidence) that the books have left the country again. If WorldWide were to do this, their standing with the customs could be affected: first, they would have to alter the 'default truth' (that the conference organisers must have bought these books) and secondly, they would have to provide evidence, which might involve correspondence with the publishers.[13]

Consequently, WorldWide forces a scenario in which whoever is responsible has to refund the conference. They advised the organisers to pay the invoice and to reclaim the money from the publishers (as the publishers were responsible for the misunderstanding at the airport). WorldWide's logic here is probably: if the organisers can reclaim the money from the publishers, they will not mind honouring the invoice.[14]

But the conference organisers thought differently. As far as they were concerned, they were not involved in this transaction. They got involved because of the customs' and WorldWide's

THE DISCOURSE OF MEDIATION: BUREAUCRATS' DILEMMA AND CLIENTS' WISDOM   173

interpretation of the transaction. Discussing the matter at length, they decided to 'freeze' the affair and take no action whatsoever (unless pressurised by WorldWide – in which case they would pass the matter on to the publishers). Legally speaking, there was no way that WorldWide could reclaim the money from the conference. Nor was there a need to worry about what the customs at the airport would do. WorldWide had paid the VAT. For Customs and Excise, this would also be the end of the story.[15]

One could say the conference organisers take on a 'warrior'-role here, as they reject the practices of WorldWide in principle and refuse to pay for a service done on their behalf but unasked for. However, this rejection is self-protectingly limited by the boundaries of the organisation's own interests.

Client as reluctant mediator

Although it is now established that the conference organisers were not importing the books, WorldWide continues to use them to recover the VAT expenses. Following normal customs practice, it is the addressee who is liable to account for what is 'imported' into the country. The basis for this is the 'suspicion' that the client may be playing up. So, they have to provide either evidence of 'innocence' or settle the invoice first and then recover the money from the sender, in this case the British publisher. What WorldWide has been trying to do is to cast the conference organisers in exactly the same role as its own is with Customs and Excise. From WorldWide's viewpoint, therefore, the client can easily take on the role of mediator between the British publisher and WorldWide.

To the organisers' surprise, one month later, WorldWide sends the following reminder (translated from Dutch, see Appendix 8b for the original):

Example 4b

Dear Madam/Sir,

Please find enclosed the statement of the account as sent monthly to all our debtors. As you can read from this statement the deadline for payment, set at 30 days after the date of invoice, has already passed.

174   *LANGUAGE, BUREAUCRACY AND SOCIAL CONTROL*

> Whatever may have been the cause for this, we would prefer not to include you among those customers who need to be reminded every month. A permanent control of debtors consumes time and energy, which could be much better spent on improving our customer services.
>
> Therefore, may we kindly ask you to rectify this omission and settle the payment of all your invoices which are older than 30 days this very week.
>
> We thank you for your confidence in our firm and hope for a further smooth cooperation in the future.
>
> [name]
> Credit Control
> [telephone number]
>
> If you have already paid, please ignore this letter.

Note that this is a standard letter which makes no reference to the discussion between the conference organisers and one of World- Wide's representatives. This situation is similar to one where bureaucrats ignore the initiatives which clients have taken, thus preferring to follow the pre-established agenda of institutional routines. On the one hand, like bureaucratic reminders, the letter aims at sustaining the assigned clienthood by continuing to address the addressee as a client of a particular type (here, as a late payer). On the other hand, however, the text of this letter is very unbureaucratic. For instance, the claim that chasing late payers consumes time and energy, which could be better spent on improving their services, reflects private economy logic. A bureaucratic institution would not say anything of the kind, but probably threaten with a fine, or impose one immediately.

Additionally, we see WorldWide's text to be full of customer rhetoric. It borders on the moral level when it attempts to draw a line between those who need a reminder every month and those who settle their invoices without such reminders. It sounds patronising: 'whatever may have been the cause for non-payment'.[16] Nevertheless, WorldWide emphasises its commitment to the consumer's cause in global terms, not individually as institutions from the service industry such as banks and insurance companies tend to do. This is the basis for

THE DISCOURSE OF MEDIATION: BUREAUCRATS' DILEMMA AND CLIENTS' WISDOM 175

the ensuing warning. Note that a typical government reminder will not go on record about a waste of time and energy.[17]

As agreed earlier, the organisers at this point write a letter to the British publisher's commercial department and pass on the original of the invoice together with the accompanying documents. It is also worth noting that although WorldWide made no reference to the telephone conversation in their reminder, the conference organisers choose to base their next action not on the 'text' of the reminder, but on what had transpired by telephone.

How do we account for this? The organisers interpret the reminder in the light of their own action-logic, and not on the text. They take on the role of mediator rather than that of customer (which is what the reminder addresses itself to). This shows that WorldWide is not really interested in whether the conference organisers actually take up the matter with the publisher. Their major interest is in the honouring of the invoice: the route by which this happens does not matter to them.

In their letter, the conference organisers advise the British publisher to ignore WorldWide's claim:

Example 4c

[name]
Senior Promotions Executive
[address]
England

6 November 1992

Dear Ms [name],

[name] INTERNATIONAL CONFERENCE 1992

May I take this opportunity to thank you for the financial help which you gave us with the conference in September. It was, I believe, a great success and I understand that [the representative] found the occasion very satisfactory from a professional point of view. I hope so.

Unfortunately, I am now writing to you about something which may possibly cause a further drain on the coffers of [British publisher] with regard to our conference. When the consignment of books for display at the conference arrived at Brussels airport,

176 LANGUAGE, BUREAUCRACY AND SOCIAL CONTROL

the labelling of the box did not specify that this was a temporary import only. As a result the couriers WorldWide paid the VAT due on the contents.

When the time came to send the books back to England, they were sent via [name] railway station. Because of this, the import and export of the books were not connected so it was not possible for WorldWide to reclaim the VAT.

Accordingly, they have sent us an invoice which, together with relevant documentation, you find enclosed here.

I am sorry to be the bearer of ill tidings. I hope you can sort this out as I don't see why you should have to pay for something that you didn't actually do (i.e. import the books into Belgium).

Best wishes,

Yours sincerely,

[organiser]

As the first paragraph reveals, the letter has a double focus: (i) to congratulate and thank the publisher for its involvement in the conference, and (ii) to raise the WorldWide-matter. This face-redressive strategy contributes to playing down the importance of the affair. The letter also recounts the various stages with factual details, rather than leaving it to the publishers to find out on their own. In this respect, the organisers do take on the mediator role. The letter tries to coordinate three voices: WorldWide's, that of the conference organisers and that of the British publisher. The organisers are also taking the publisher's side by being generous with information (something which is also obvious from the suggestion – 'I don't see why you should have to pay . . . '.

In the meantime, WorldWide issues yet another reminder in the form of an updated invoice (despite its earlier warning about this being time and energy wasting). Once again, it ignores any previous correspondence in the matter. Their advice to hold the British publisher responsible is seen as a one-off generous information-providing gesture. As is clear from the letter (example 4c), WorldWide has succeeded in turning its client (the conference organisers) into a mediator who deals with another institution on WorldWide's behalf. However, there are limits on

THE DISCOURSE OF MEDIATION: BUREAUCRATS' DILEMMA AND CLIENTS' WISDOM   177

what the organisers are willing to do in this role, as is clear from their faxed response to WorldWide's reminder (in translation, see Appendix 8c for original):

Example 4d

WorldWide
[address]

Dear Sir/Madam,

In reply to the reminder which you sent us on December 7 (SETB250), I would like to inform you that a month or so ago we passed on the invoice to [British publisher], because the (temporary) import/export of the books mentioned on the invoice is really to be charged to their account.

I presume that they will contact you.

Yours faithfully,

[name organiser]

The fax to WorldWide reiterates the point that the matter should be settled between WorldWide and the British publisher and that the conference organisers wish neither to remain a client of World-Wide nor to act further on WorldWide's behalf in the matter.

About a month later, the organisers received a letter from the bank, telling them the bank had received BF 2,914 from the British publisher destined for WorldWide Express. The fact that the publisher paid without any resistance shows perhaps that they thought it was their fault, contrary to the conference organisers' reading of the events.[18]

Conclusion: socio-economic struggles over multi-tier bureaucracy

From each of the cases we looked at in this chapter, it is clear that bureaucratic procedures have expanded in such a way and to such an extent that clienthood is no longer a self-evident matter – if it ever was. In short, although leaflets and institutions with 'leaflet' functions may, at one level, appear to turn 'naive' clients into 'literate' users, new mechanisms for social control have been brought into existence as well, while leaving the older forms largely

178 *LANGUAGE, BUREAUCRACY AND SOCIAL CONTROL*

untouched. This way institutions are becoming even less account-able to the public, as 'backchannels' have become institutionalised and, their use, in some cases, has become subject to payment.

Historically, the institutions may have come some way from 'withholding information'. Undoubtedly this constitutes some form of increased cooperation on the information exchange side of procedures. However, institutions are still unwilling to make explicit the bases of their decisions. In fact, one could argue that institutions – as a result of the transfer of communication problems to 'new' institutions – have distanced themselves even further from their information-providing function.

Far from mitigating the asymmetries, the discourse practices of intermediary institutions help sustain the communicative divide between clients and institutions. However, one can only account for this unstable status quo by paying attention to the forms of social struggle in which these institutions are caught up. The rise of mediating institutions is clearly implicated in contradictory movements. Armed with the knowledge that clients may stand a better chance if they can 'tune into' the institutional way of doing things, their practices serve to empower clients by improving their chances of eligibility. But, at the same time, they also make citizens increasingly dependent on a flow of information which is controlled by institutional networks. Clienthood and appeal are channelled through institutions like the ACE or WorldWide, whose existence is located on the fringe of bureaucracies. This leads to multi-tier bureaucracy, with mediating institutions being financially dependent upon client illiteracy.

Notes

1. Although there is no dearth of literature on the subject of mediation in legal settings (e.g. Dingwall and Eekelaar (1988) on divorce), there have been fewer attempts to study mediation practices from a linguistic perspective (see, for instance, Candlin and Maley (forthcoming) on mediation and conflict resolution in court cases). This picture contrasts with the work done on the discourse of 'counselling', say, in the field of education (Erickson 1976 and Erickson and Shultz 1982) or in the field of health care and family planning (Tannen and Wallat 1982). See also Abbott and Wallace (1990) on social work and the nursing professions.
2. The data excerpt is taken from Stenson (1989).

THE DISCOURSE OF MEDIATION: BUREAUCRATS' DILEMMA AND CLIENTS' WISDOM   179

3. Citizens' Advice Bureaux are a national network of information offices, set up in 1939 to inform the public about emergency wartime regulations. They have remained in operation since the end of the war to provide free and confidential information, particularly concerning the social services, housing, legal aid, consumer services, and family matters. There are about 900 offices, staffed by trained counsellors, mostly volunteers. Each office is funded by the local authority and by the Department of Trade and Industry.
4. The reason why an LEA cannot allow issues like curriculum to be brought into the appeal procedure may be linked to legislative restrictions, which are to limit the movement of children between various schools.
5. Note that the reason for the refusal (and its wording) is already there in the notes of the leaflet, 'Notes of Guidance on how to appeal against a school place which has been allocated':

   > The Appeal Committee has to decide whether to comply with the parental preference would prejudice the provision of efficient education or the efficient use of resources at the school concerned and whether this prejudicial effect is outweighed by the parental preference or any other circumstances stated by the parents.

6. At the appeal hearing there will be a representative of the LEA, the school, its board of governors, and the town council. The third school is not represented on the committee, but, of course, its story will be heard too.
7. This is the parents' reflection of what the ACE people have said, and hence a mixture of what the ACE said and what parents already had in mind for an appeal text. We have retained oversights and lapses.
8. The data is in a hybrid form: it is not a finalised text, it is like a speech which is being prepared for delivery; it bears traces of the dialogic processes of oral text which is under construction, anticipating the issues which may arise before the appeal committee.
9. The LMS scheme, which was then being tried out, went into full operation in 1993. It involves a delegation of budgetary and staffing decisions from the town hall to the school head and its board of governors.
10. WorldWide's unsolicited involvement is very similar to the situation in some countries, where mediating institutions have adopted the structure of actual agencies, such as the export agencies at Belgian frontier posts where in return for payment customs documents are filled in, with the result that customs officers simply direct arriving importers and exporters to the agent across the road rather than talk to them about anything that may have to be imported as, say, a car.

180 *LANGUAGE, BUREAUCRACY AND SOCIAL CONTROL*

11. Although the ACE addresses all citizens as potential clients via leaflets and literature, it is less likely to assign clienthood. Nor is it likely to be involved in the actual procedure of appeal.
12. At this point the question arises as to why the publisher did not specify on the box that the books were for exhibition purposes. There are a number of possible explanations: (a) their commercial department did not know about the exact destination of the books, (b) or, knowing that their representative often sells some books at conferences, it was risky to go on record adopting an 'exhibition' script, or (c) the publishers were simply not familiar with the way agencies step into the customs context and assumed that the protocol of entry would be sorted out between the Belgian customs and the conference organisers.
13. But in this case, identity of goods would be hard to prove. The British publisher's representative had exported the books via the railway station, carrying with her all the documents that had accompanied the box. Moreover, proof of 'identity of goods' was only possible if established by the railway staff during the export procedure. The chances that this would have happened were incredibly small.
14. Also in this respect, WorldWide is different from the ACE in that its representation of the client with the government institution does not extend beyond its standing, routine role.
15. As reported to us by the organisers, the logic behind this was two-fold: in all likelihood the British publishers, when asked, would refuse to pay. The chances that WorldWide would chase them for BF 3,000 were even smaller. The conference organisers' backs, would be covered as well, because it was WorldWide's view that the publisher was ultimately responsible for leading customs officers to believe that the organisers were 'buying' the books.
16. This situation is comparable with the way the bank dealt with Roy's overdraft (Chapter 5), the difference being that the bank offered a counselling option by constructing the client in pathological terms. As opposed to this, WorldWide clearly considers such an option as 'time and energy consuming'.
17. In Chapter 6, we have drawn attention to the citizen's charter, which also adopts a moral stance when it comes to 'favoured' forms of client behaviour. As a matter of speculation, one may therefore wonder how long it will take before reminders from government institutions begin to take on this 'moral' tone as well.
18. The author of the letter is making a factual error ('it was not possible for WorldWide to reclaim . . .' should really have been 'it was not possible for us to reclaim'). Maybe this affected the British publisher's response.

8 *Instead of a conclusion*

We call this chapter 'Instead of a conclusion', because our approach has not been solution-orientated and in that sense it defies a closure of the problematic issues we have been dealing with. We will attempt two things. First of all, we tie together the key issues which arise from the various analyses, highlighting in particular the complex interplay of notions like 'accountability', 'choice' and 'accessibility' associated with the more recent forms of bureaucracy. It is the social construction of client identity which provides an anchor point for examining these connections further, especially the ways in which this is constituted in the discourse practices of institutions and their members (clients and personnel). Secondly, we contextualise our findings within contemporary social-theoretical debate about the conditions of late capitalist society.

Information exchange has emerged as the unifying theme of this book and it is through our analysis of information exchange in contemporary bureaucratic processes that we have been able to set our work aside from previous research in this area. In theoretical terms, we have attempted to integrate two frameworks – the pragmatics of information exchange, and the social-theoretical debate about client construction *vis-à-vis* transformations of the public domain. This integrated approach has been central to our selection and interpretation of data from hitherto unbureaucratic domains in the private sector – such as banks, educational institutions and even courier services – rather than concentrating on traditional bureaucracies and tracing their socio-historical origin or detailing the linguistic features of their text output. Our interest has been process-orientated so as to account for some of the subtle changes which occur in the contemporary scene. The rich and varied data source has enabled us to extend our analysis

182 *LANGUAGE, BUREAUCRACY AND SOCIAL CONTROL*

to the interactional level of client–institution encounters and to the level of contact situations between institutions. The mainstay of our argument has been that the asymmetrical divide between clients and institutions is constituted in the ways in which information is (not) exchanged or can(not) be exchanged, or, in the ways in which information is transformed in the processes that make up institutional contacts. We have also raised the issue of how clients, when faced with unfavourable outcomes, challenge some of the asymmetries and may, at times, come to be perceived as having an edge over the institutional procedures. This viewpoint contrasts sharply with earlier studies of institutional discourse which conceptualise the asymmetry in terms of a clash of frames resulting from the institutional representatives' attempt at fitting the client into the organisational ways of thinking. Inherent in the latter characterisation is an *a priori* asymmetry as a definitive feature of all bureaucrat–client encounters. For us, it is not simply a matter of clash of frames. What is going on here can be captured under the notion of bureaupretation (Chapter 3). This implies that preferred readings of client situations are mediated through the superimposition of the socio-economic climate (e.g. slumping resources) in which the institutions are embedded.[1] Obviously, this affects the ways in which client situations are processed and outcomes are decided upon. Some institutions have recently been addressing clients as partners, customers, and so on while portraying the institution's role primarily in advisory terms, helping clients towards achieving their (clients') goals. This has often meant that all clients are assumed to need basic help with, say, their claims to benefits. The tendency thus is towards an increasing toning down of asymmetricality, certainly as far as the threshold of information supply is concerned.

In a general sense, in constructing their clients in a particular way, institutions tend to underestimate the actual range of client behaviour we come across. Agar (1985: 164) talks about the existence of different types of clients:

> Clients come with varying degrees of sophistication in the institutional frameworks, with widely different client frameworks, with different abilities to psych out an institution, and with different personal styles and manipulative abilities.

INSTEAD OF A CONCLUSION 183

But this observation does not address the following questions: How can we explain the occurrence of a 'naive client'? Is he/she the one who has been brought up to trust institutions? By a similar token, how can we explain the existence of 'professional clients'? Is he/she the one who deploys the rationality condition of the institution? Or, is he/she the one who persistently and unnecessarily complains? This is also a question of *habitus* and *cultural capital* (Bourdieu 1991) which is unequally divided over social groups: the occurrence of kinds of discursive behaviour is a result of the actual distribution of symbolic resources over groups of the population. In short, the question is whether there is a particular type of client who is 'favoured' in the current socio-economic climate? With privatisation and the advance of consumerism in public institutions and the launch of 'citizen charters' (as is the case in Britain), what are the effects in the social welfare 'market'? While creating the impression that institutions are increasingly becoming more accessible through the provision of leaflets and user-friendlier application forms, in reality, the chances of entitlement may have remained the same (if they have not already become smaller).[2] Does this sort of development encourage one to act professionally (making the most of available expertise) and discourage one from becoming a rebellious warrior (fighting the institution on moral and political principles)? Additionally, is this development a matter of client professionalism being transformed, as institutions are increasingly becoming more demanding in the ways in which eligibility claims have to be backed by adequate evidence? Or, should we conclude that, despite fundamental changes at the bureaucratic end, clients have essentially continued to behave according to old recipes? For instance, have clients actually started shopping around, as expected, for social benefits and do they familiarise themselves with the rationality criteria of a particular institution before they decide to start a procedure?

As Giddens (1991) points out, late capitalist society is characterised by the salience and systematic use of expert systems, systems constituted by doctors, therapists, lawyers, scientists and technicians with highly specialised technical knowledge. This also includes the expert systems of government, administration and, indeed, as has become clear in the course of this book, corresponding expert systems of clienthood and

184 LANGUAGE, BUREAUCRACY AND SOCIAL CONTROL

negotiation. Discursive practices themselves are one domain of reflexivity and expertise and even self-identity has become a reflexive project.[3]

Giddens' analysis is highly relevant to the increased role of mediators and mediation in institutional domains, as it helps throw light on how clients arm themselves with all sorts of knowledge when they have to deal with institutions. But, if the self has become an emancipatory project, one cannot deny the extent to which clients' identities are being transformed in the process of dealing with institutions. Let us return for a moment to the parents' education appeal (see Chapter 7 and Appendix 7), where they – rather cynically – go on record:

Example 1

Before our last appeal several people advised us what to do in order to succeed. Some were teachers. They told us that it might be effective if we could show a report from a child psychologist proving that Jimmy was disturbed. Or that we ourselves were on valium because of the whole saga. Or even that a note from our GP about Jimmy might be useful. But we brushed this advice aside and prepared a rational argument based on facts. We lost.

It is interesting to note that clients like the Martins highlight the 'rational' basis of their appeal. They 'brush aside' the counselling of friends and teachers who suggest devious practices, thus stressing their sincerity and, at the same time, setting themselves aside from others who would take advantage of the institution. What we see here is a moral dilemma in which clients are caught up. The above extract suggests that the Martins are aware of the backdoor method of manipulating institutional rules for their own private benefit and the possibility of adducing medical or psychological 'evidence' to that purpose. Yet, they state their preference to fight the case on moral and rational grounds.

Let us look at another self-reflexive account, which interestingly combines issues of rationality and morality with truth conditions. In the following extract where Roy is responding to our analysis of the case 'lost post' in Chapter 5, he writes (the full text of Roy's reaction is in Appendix 9b):

INSTEAD OF A CONCLUSION 185

Example 2:

You explain my letter to the GPO in terms of an awareness of institutional mismatches. Perhaps, but I was also trying, more crudely, just to speed up the process of tracing the letter and assigning blame, especially in the light of the OPA's warning that the trace might take a month or so.

At a later point in the story, when I am about to ask the OPA for concrete proof of the letter's delivery, you refer to this as the only way for me to restore my face with the bank. Of course, face was important to me at this stage, but I was certain that the bank would only accept a GPO (i.e. British) document as evidence that the letter had been delivered and that without this I would not be able to claim reimbursement for my expenses. As you point out later, my face is more threatened by the bank's failure to respond to earlier correspondence and their implication that I was lying.

Roy's *post hoc* explanation reflects the ways in which he has been able to anticipate institutional procedures, partly enabling him to deal with the problem situation. Additionally, his aim was to counter the implicit accusation of having been lying. This raises an important question. Clients appear to be motivated to act in ways which correspond to what institutions expect from them: speed, efficiency, rationality and sincerity. The pillars of bureaucracy have clearly not crumbled and continue to dominate client perceptions.

This point also ties up with the notion of accountability which we have discussed as a factor of contemporary bureaucracy. Cast in moral and rational terms, Roy's and the Martins' actions conform to the accountability criteria traditionally propagated by institutions. When we look at accountability at the institutional end, shifts can be noted in recent years. Earlier on there was a stress on citizens' rights of entitlement to the provisions of the welfare state (including the right to good education) and the institutional fairness in treating every citizen in the same way. Nowadays, the stress is on accountability in terms of how slumping resources are spent by institutions, the insistence on the sincerity of clients, and so on. On the one hand, accountability has brought to the forefront assumptions about, for instance, equal rights and opportunities, fairness, honesty. On the other hand, institutions have come into the open in proclaiming their

186 *LANGUAGE, BUREAUCRACY AND SOCIAL CONTROL*

values and codes of practice, yet, in return, demanding a corresponding effort from clients (see our analysis of the tax payer's charter in Chapter 6).

One aspect of accountability is making institutions accessible, often via linguistic means such as 'Plain English', but there is also the promotion of choice wherever available. Accessibility, choice and diversity are increasingly becoming cornerstones of the bureaucratic set-up. A moral basis for action is called for, while choice is being promoted. But it is worth considering what these choices actually mean to clients. In the appeal draft, the Martins deny the desirability of available choices when it comes to their son's education:

Example 3:

We feel strongly that we want to keep him [Jimmy] in the state system. It is important for him to grow up with children of all backgrounds, but in an academically stimulating environment. We feel it is unacceptable if the school system should force us to send him to a single-sex, private school. That is something which we emphatically do not want. We want to make one move, that will be the right move and will last. We therefore appeal most urgently to your discretion.

From the parents' point of view the provision of private education is not a desirable choice. Their position is that choice within the state education system should align with parental preference and they channel their efforts through the Advisory Centre for Education. In taking this position, the Martins are trying to force the education authority to bend its ways since forcing parents into a position where a single-sex private school is the only option left would undermine the educational ethos of the state-run schools.

This brings us to the status of negotiating bodies and their communicative capacities in late capitalist society, as traditions have to be negotiated against alternative possibilities, yielding an openness with greater possibilities but also greater risks (cf. Fairclough 1993: 140). For instance, the preparatory talk between the Martins and the Advisory Centre for Education is a clear example of this newly created discursive room for negotiation. The question this poses for us is this: Which client

INSTEAD OF A CONCLUSION   187

group is well equipped with the dialogic negotiative skills necessary to influence the institutional outcomes? Looked at in this way, client empowerment can never simply be a matter of assisting clients to participate in an institutional routine. It should always presuppose a critical analysis of the institution's projected realities and categories, and clients' willingness to take risks. This is quite contrary to the ways in which institutions in recent years have adopted promotional discourses to channel choice, thus minimising risk-taking on the clients' part.

Late capitalist society has been characterised in terms of the salience of consumer culture (Featherstone 1991) and promotional culture (Wernick 1991). Consumer culture and promotional culture are intimately interwoven. The increasing demands on institutions to give clients 'value-for-money' has made institutions turn to promotional discourse forms (e.g. advertising benefits), but also promoting a consumer-friendly image (e.g. the publication of research into quality of service has become part of the information exchange). Here we can refer back to the research findings presented in the Post Office Code of Practice brochure in Chapter 1. Similar publications of quality audit can now be found in student brochures. Increasingly, traditional institutions have to justify their existence against possible alternatives and promote new forms of role relationships and client identities. As Fairclough (1993: 141) points out, one of the net results of this tendency is a widespread instrumentalisation of discursive practices, in which meaning becomes subordinated to instrumental effect.

In our view, the importance of the promotional condition is not just applicable to institutions addressing clients manipulatively but also to clients addressing institutions. With slumping resources and tightened scrutiny of applications, clients have come to see the profit that comes from presenting their cases in a self-promotional mode. What is more, within some institutions (e.g. higher education) self-promotion is made a condition for socio-economic survival. Our analysis of the teaching profile in Chapter 2 bears witness to this. In Fairclough's (1993: 142) terms,

> it is increasingly difficult not to be involved oneself in promoting, because many people have to as part and parcel of their jobs, but

188 *LANGUAGE, BUREAUCRACY AND SOCIAL CONTROL*

also because self-promotion is becoming part and parcel of self-identity in contemporary societies.

The promotional dimension of discourse can also be seen in the education appeal draft, where the Martins refer to Jimmy's bilingual background, and the parents' capacity to contribute to drama in the school, as a kind of uncalled-for selling point.

Especially in Chapter 7, we have elaborated the point that for clients, the political promise of a consumer culture has entailed the hope that institutions will become more sensitive to the specific properties of an individual case, hence the use of case-promoting strategies has become an important – but ethically problematic – aspect of client applications and appeals. It is possible to argue (with Wernick 1991) that with more and more self-promotional discourse comes the risk of direct and traceable face loss.[4] This is parallelled by increased control of the private life-sphere and institutional probing which is inherent in contemporary societies characterised by the state surveillance of health, schooling, and so on.

This trend does not exclude the so-called private economy institutions like banks which are also increasingly invading people's private life by asking for the sort of information which used to be the forte of bureaucratic institutions. Following Beck (1992), this situation can be interpreted as resulting from the contradictory pressures of a society which increasingly wants to insure itself against future risks, thus necessitating an increase in the probing of members' lives. Although such institutional probing itself is often resented by clients, it is possible to argue that in individual cases compliance with more and more institutional scrutiny is seen as potentially rewarding. On the other hand, it is also true that promotional practices present themselves as a possible device for disguising the probing face of institutions.[5]

All these contradictory tendencies point to an overflow of information exchange. The restructuring of relational identities between institutions and clients, and within institutions, has, of course, meant that more information is being processed on both sides. The challenge which this proliferation of discourse throws down for linguistic research is unavoidable. As far as our analysis goes, we have been constantly shifting between different frameworks, but the socio-pragmatic approach has proved to be

INSTEAD OF A CONCLUSION   189

particularly fruitful. Of course we have focused on individual cases in bureaucratic settings, but far from being rare instances, these cases have thrown light on patterns of client-institution interaction. If we want to mould information exchange into strictly formal principles with an arithmetical calculus, as is the case in many linguistic-pragmatic analyses, we run the risk of precisely missing out what is most essential to information exchange, namely that it bears on social identity, that it is a relational entity and that its specific forms stand in a particular relationship with socio-cultural values. Hence, it is important to achieve an analytic balance between looking at the behaviour of an individual client in a specific situation, and doing this from within a macro-societal perspective.

As a concluding caveat, if one of the key techniques of modern power resides in the institutional 'gaze' of various types of administration and institutions of public service, then a book about bureaucracy is not meant to be a critique of bad institutional practice, but instead its theme goes to the very heart of the exercise of power in modern society: wide-scale community-funded practices of record-keeping and procedurally monitored surveillance of all aspects of social life.

Notes

1. This is not to suggest that institutions always readily endorse and act out the current political ideologies. One needs to keep political manifestoes separate from bureaucratic procedures, although in many cases political agendas are translated into bureaucratic rules.

2. Consider, for instance, the recently introduced guidance relating to who can claim family credit in Britain. The new rule specifies that this is now available only to full-time workers, that is to say, those employed for 16 hours a week or more over a calendar year. Among those affected are many part-timers in the education sector. Consider the following testimony from Ms Walker, a single mother and a nursery school teacher:

    My real gripe is they gave me no warning this was going to happen. I would have understood it better if they had said I could have family credit for another six months only, giving me a chance to get myself sorted out (*The Guardian*, 29 October 1994, p. 11).

    The above quote challenges the governmental self-image of better

190   *LANGUAGE, BUREAUCRACY AND SOCIAL CONTROL*

information supply and exposes how leaflets do not warn you that the criteria for entitlement may be likely to change in the future.

3. Reflexivity, for Giddens, is a condition of late capitalist society as well as a solution to some of its problems. By one reading, Giddens's answer to some of the negative effects of (high) modernity is to have more modernity. This can be compared with Habermas's (1981) analysis, which, as Thompson (1984: 294) notes, lends support to the 'thesis that the major problems facing advanced industrial societies today have to do with the self-destructive consequences of system growth – a growth which threatens to silence the potential for reflection which, with the rationalisation of the life-world, has become accessible to us'.

4. Wernick (1991) in his concluding chapter on the promotional condition of contemporary society suggests a direct link between the condition of self-promotion and individual face concerns in Goffman's sense.

5. In Habermas's (1981) terms, one can talk of a two-way process of colonisation at the level of the systems (the invasion of state administration by private economy logic, and, conversely, the increasing bureaucratisation of private economy institutions). Both are perhaps trends which Habermas's model does not foresee at first sight, as more is at stake than the pathological effects resulting from an inner colonisation of the life-worlds by the systems.

Bibliography

Abbott P and Wallace C (eds) 1990 *The Sociology of the Caring Professions.* London: The Falmer Press.

Agar M 1985 Institutional discourse, *Text* 5, 3, 147– 68.

Alatis J and G Tucker (eds) *Language in Public life.* Georgetown University Press.

Austin J L 1962 *How to do Things with Words.* Oxford: Clarendon Press.

Beck U 1992 *Risk Society.* London: Sage.

Berger P L and Luckmann T 1972 *The Social Construction of Reality: a Treaty in the Sociology of Knowledge.* Harmondsworth: Penguin.

Bourdieu P 1991 *Language and Symbolic Power.* Edited and introduced by John B Thompson, translated by Gino Raymond and Matthew Adamson. Cambridge, Mass.: Polity Press.

Brown P and Levinson S 1978 Universals in language use: politeness phenomena. In Goody E (ed) *Questions and Politeness: Strategies in Social Interaction.* Cambridge: Cambridge University Press, pp. 56–310.

Brown P and Levinson S 1987 *Politeness. Some Universals in Language Use.* Cambridge: Cambridge University Press.

Candlin C and Maley Y forthcoming Intertextuality and interdiscursivity in the discourse of alternative dispute resolution. In Gunnarsson B, Linell P and Nordberg B (eds) *The Construction of Professional Discourse.* London: Longman.

Charrow V R 1982 Language in the bureaucracy. In di Pietro R J (ed) *Linguistics and the Professions.* Norwood, NJ: Ablex Publishing Corporation.

Collins J 1987 Conversation and knowledge in bureaucratic settings. *Discourse Processes*, 10, 303–19.

Dews P 1987 *Logics of Disintegration. Post-Structuralist Thought and the Claims of Critical Theory.* London: Verso.

Dickens C 1966 *Little Dorrit.* Oxford: Oxford University Press.

Dingwall R and Eekelaar J 1988 *Divorce Mediation and the Legal Process.* Oxford: Clarendon Press.

192 LANGUAGE, BUREAUCRACY AND SOCIAL CONTROL

Dunleavy P 1991 *Democracy, Bureaucracy and Public Choice.* New York: Harvester.

Erickson F 1976 Gatekeeping encounters: a social selection process. In Sandy P (ed) *Anthropology and Public Interest.* New York: Academic Press, pp. 111–45.

Erickson F and Shultz J 1982 *The Counsellor as Gatekeeper: Social Interaction in Interviews.* New York: Academic Press.

Fairclough N 1985 Critical and descriptive goals in discourse analysis. *Journal of Pragmatics,* 9, 739–63.

Fairclough N 1989 *Language and Power.* London: Longman.

Fairclough N 1992a *Discourse and Social Change.* Cambridge: Polity Press.

Fairclough N 1992b Discourse and text: linguistic and intertextual analysis within discourse analysis. *Discourse and Society,* 3, 2, 193–217.

Fairclough N 1993 Critical discourse analysis and the marketisation of public discourse. *Discourse and Society,* 4, 2, 133–68.

Featherstone M 1991 *Consumer Culture and Postmodernism.* London: Sage.

Foucault M 1971 *L'ordre du discours.* Paris: Gallimard.

Foucault M 1972 *The Archaeology of Knowledge.* Translated by A Sheridan-Smith. London: Tavistock.

Foucault M 1973 *The Birth of the Clinic: An Archaeology of Medical Perception.* Translated by A Sheridan-Smith. New York: Vintage.

Foucault M 1977 *Discipline and Punish: the Birth of the Prison.* Translated by A Sheridan-Smith. New York: Vintage.

Fowler R, Hodge B, Kress G and Trew T 1979 *Language and Control.* London: Routledge.

Fraser N 1989 *Unruly Practices: Power, Discourse and Gender in Contemporary Social Theory.* Cambridge: Polity Press.

Giddens A 1991 *Modernity and Self-Identity: Self and Society in the Late Modern Age.* Cambridge: Polity Press.

Goffman E 1955 On face work: an analysis of ritual elements in social interaction. *Psychiatry,* 18, 213–31.

Goffman E 1959 *The Presentation of Self in Everyday Life.* Harmondsworth: Penguin.

Goffman E 1981 *Forms of Talk.* Oxford: Blackwell.

Gramsci, A 1971 *Selections from the Prison Notebooks.* Edited and translated by Q Hoare and G N Smith. New York: Lawrence and Wishart.

Grice H P 1975 Logic and conversation. In Cole P (ed) *Syntax and Semantics, Vol 3: Speech Acts.* New York: Academic Press.

Gumperz J 1982 *Discourse Strategies.* Cambridge: Cambridge University Press.

BIBLIOGRAPHY 193

Gyford J 1991 *Citizens, Consumers and Councils: Local Government and the Public*. London: Macmillan.

Habermas J 1968 Thesen zur Theorie der Sozialisation. In Jurgen Habermas ed *Arbeiterkenntnis, Sozialisation*. Amsterdam: De Munter.

Habermas J 1970 Vorbereitende Bemerkungen zu einer Theorie der kommunikativen Kompetenz. In Habermas J and Luhmann N (eds) *Theorie der Gesellschaft oder Sozialtechnologie?* Frankfurt: Suhrkamp.

Habermas Jurgen 1974. Zur Entwicklung der Interactionskompetenz. Unpublished manuscript.

Habermas Jurgen 1981. *Theorie des kommunikativen Handelns, Vol I and II*. Frankfurt: Suhrkamp.

Hall C, Sarangi S and Slembrouck S forthcoming Moral construction in social work discourse. In Gunnarsson B, Linell P and Nordberg B (eds) *The Construction of Professional Discourse*. London: Longman.

Halliday M A K 1978 *Language as Social Semiotic*. London: Longman.

Heath S B 1979 The context of professional languages: an historical overview. In Alatis J and Tucker G (eds) *Language in Public Life*. Washington, DC: Georgetown University Press, pp.102–18.

Hymes D 1977 *Foundations in Sociolinguistics: an Ethnographic Approach*. London: Tavistock.

Iedema R 1994 *The Language of Administration*. WIR Industry Monograph Series, Vol. iii. DSP, Met East. Sydney: Disadvantaged Schools Program.

Kress G 1989 *Linguistic Processes in Sociocultural Practice*. Oxford: Oxford University Press.

Kress G and Hodge B 1979 *Language as Ideology*. London: Routledge.

Leech G 1983 *The Principles of Pragmatics*. London: Longman.

Levinson S 1979 Activity types and language. *Linguistics* 17, 365–399.

Levinson S 1981 Explicating concept of participant-role. Paper read at workshop of British Sociological Society, Plymouth 1981.

McCarthy T 1984 *The Critical Theory of Jurgen Habermas*. Cambridge: Polity Press.

Mey J 1987 Poet and peasant: a pragmatic comedy in five acts, *Journal of Pragmatics*, 11, 281–297.

Philips S U 1987 The social organisation of knowledge and its consequences for discourse in bureaucratic settings, *Discourse Processes* 10, 429–33.

Pratt M L 1981 The ideology of speech act theory, *Centrum* (New series), 1, 5–18.

Redish J C 1983 The language of bureaucracy. In Bailey R E and Fosheim R M (eds) *Literacy for Life: the Demand for Reading and Writing*. New York: The Modern Language Association of America, pp. 154–74.

Sarangi S and Slembrouck S 1992 Non-cooperation in communication: a reassessment of Gricean pragmatics, *Journal of Pragmatics*, 17, 117–54.

Stenson K 1989 Social Work Discourse and the Social Work Interview. Unpublished PhD thesis. Brunel University.

Tannen D and Wallat C 1982 Interactive frames and knowledge structure schemas in interaction: examples from a pediatric examination. Paper presented at US-France joint seminar on Natural Language Comprehension. Saint Paul les Durances, France.

Thomas J 1985 The language of power: towards a dynamic pragmatics, *Journal of Pragmatics*, 9, 6, 765–83.

Thomas J 1986 The Dynamics of Discourse: a Pragmatic Analysis of Confrontational Interaction. Unpublished doctoral dissertation. University of Lancaster.

Thompson J B 1984 *Studies in the Theory of Ideology*. Cambridge: Polity Press.

Tolson A 1991 Televised chat and synthetic personality. In P Scannell (ed) *Broadcast Talk*. London: Sage, pp. 178–200.

Weber M 1930 *The Protestant Ethic and the Spirit of Capitalism*. Translated by Parsons T, with a foreword by Tawney R H. London: George Allen and Unwin.

Weber M 1922 *Economy and Society: an Outline of Interpretive Sociology*. New York: Bedminster Press (1968).

Weber M 1947 *The Theory of Social and Economic Organisation*. Translated by Henderson A M and Parsons T, with an introduction by Parsons T. Glencoe, Ill.: The Free Press.

Wernick A 1991 *Promotional Culture*. London: Sage.

Williams R 1976 *Keywords: A Vocabulary of Culture and Society*. London: Fontana Press.

Wittgenstein L 1958 *Philosophical Investigations*. Oxford: Basil Blackwell.

Appendices

APPENDICES 197

Appendix 1: Teaching profile

LANCASTER UNIVERSITY
Staff Development

Creating a Teaching Profile

Guidance Notes for Staff with Teaching Responsibilities August, 1994

Creating a Teaching Profile – Guidelines

The Teaching Profile is now a compulsory part of any case being submitted for approval of probation, transfer from Lecturer A to Lecturer B and promotion from Lecturer to Senior Lecturer, following the decision of Senate at its meetings on 1 June, 1994.

The notes which follow are intended to assist in the development of a full and comprehensive profile which will not only give the Promotions Committee as complete as possible a picture of an individual's teaching work but will also allow for reflection upon and development of a person's teaching.

Creating a Teaching Profile

The Purposes of the Profile
The Teaching Profile has two principal purposes. Firstly it is a method by which a lecturer may reflect upon their professional practice and evaluate their development through the collection and analysis of a range of information about their teaching.

Secondly, the completed Teaching Profile document can provide evidence to the Promotions Committee on the range and quality of teaching undertaken by a candidate for promotion.

Collection of Material
The various headings under which material may be presented will be given later in these guidelines. It helps to collect material as teaching proceeds. Examination papers, results, handouts, student evaluations, teaching materials, and so on, should be filed as they are produced. As experience grows the process will become refined. Each individual can decide whether or not to include evidence under any heading. Moreover, candidates for promotion can add information on any other aspect of their teaching at the end of their profile. Where ever possible statements made should be substantiated by evidence of colleagues, students, or persons from outside the University (e.g. external examiners or colleagues from other relevant institutions).

198   *LANGUAGE, BUREAUCRACY AND SOCIAL CONTROL*

It is recognised that profiles are going to vary, for example from one discipline to another and between undergraduate and postgraduate teaching. Evidence of research and administrative activities will be submitted as they are at present, separately from the teaching profile. The profiles of candidates would be considered first at Departmental level and then by the Area Committee, to ensure that they are seen by those with experience of the teaching contexts described. In effect, these two stages of consideration will validate the profiles. The Promotions Committee will then receive the profiles of those candidates who are short-listed.

To illustrate the idea of profiles these guidelines include two real, but anonymous profiles. One or two sides of A4 paper will be sufficient to provide a summary of the much larger amount of material that a lecturer has on file. Lecturers may also find that the information collected for their profiles could be useful in the self-appraisal aspect of the University's appraisal system.

A one-off 'snapshot' of teaching cannot offer the range of evidence desirable for the preparation of a full profile. Where practicable, evidence on particular aspects of teaching would be gathered from different sources to avoid possible bias or distortion. Those preparing or interpreting profiles should appreciate that evidence from sources external to the candidate will have a stronger influence than that from self-appraisal. For example, evidence on course presentation might include information from current and/or previous students; on course content from colleagues or possibly a course committee drawn from a wider constituency; on course management from students and from colleagues; and on development work from the Head of Department and from self-appraisal. The Staff Development Officer can give advice about the design of questionnaires to obtain feedback from students.

Elements of the Profile

Examples of the kinds of entries which might be made under the various headings are given in the appendix.

Teaching Responsibilities
A statement of the courses taught and the associated teaching loads. Service as a Course Director, Senior Tutor, membership of a Course Committee, or similar post concerned with teaching, should also be mentioned.

Educational Aims and Objectives
A statement or statements showing what you are trying to achieve in different areas of your teaching. This will provide a context for the

APPENDICES 199

interpretation of statements about the methods of teaching and assessment, outcomes of student learning, and so on, which will be presented later in the profile.

Teaching Methods
Statements of the way in which you go about your teaching and whether any special methods or materials have been introduced. It is recognised that 'special' is a relative term and what is established practice in one discipline may be highly innovative in another.

Assessment and Evidence of the Outcomes of Teaching
A description of the way in which students are assessed, and how they are given feedback about their work. Information should be given about what students seem to have achieved and what they have subsequently done. The effectiveness of the assessment methods might be commented upon, in relation to the relevant aims and objectives.

Course Evaluation
Description of course evaluation processes and outcomes, the evidence so obtained, and the light it throws on the teaching which has taken place. Normally teachers should be devising systematic and objective methods of obtaining feedback on courses, at least from students. Such activities should be continuously maintained.

Evidence of the Continued Study of Teaching and Learning
Measures taken to improve your own teaching and that of your discipline and institution. Courses and workshops which have been attended, or offered for the benefit of others, and materials which have been published about teaching and learning.

Teaching References
A statement should be submitted from an appropriate internal or external referee. The statement should include any other appropriate features of your teaching. This teaching reference is in addition to the references for research. There must also be written assessment from your head of department or experienced colleague of teaching sessions observed.

Appendix 2: Community charge

Appendix 2a: About the canvass (leaflet)

Lancaster City Council

THE COMMUNITY CHARGE

"ABOUT THE CANVASS"

THIS LEAFLET IS

DESIGNED TO ASSIST IN THE

COMPLETION OF THE

ENCLOSED CANVASS FORM.

PLEASE READ IT CAREFULLY.

FURTHER ASSISTANCE IS

AVAILABLE BY TELEPHONING

382288.

PART 5 Only complete this section if the property is not used as someone's sole or main residence; for example a property which is empty or used for commercial purposes, or as a second or holiday home.
Please state the name and address of the person currently in possession or dealing with the affairs concerning the property and tick the appropriate box on the right.
In the box below please indicate the reason the property is unoccupied.

PART 6 The declaration should be signed by a responsible adult living in the property or a legal representative.

BEING RESPONSIBLE FOR COMPLETING THIS FORM * DOES NOT MEAN YOU WILL HAVE TO PAY A COMMUNITY CHARGE FOR OTHER PERSONS SHOWN IN PART 2.

WARNING!
TO GIVE FALSE INFORMATION COULD LEAD TO CIVIL PENALTIES BEING IMPOSED AND TO PROSECUTION.

Please return the form in the prepaid envelope as quickly as possible or at latest by the due date shown on the front of the form.
If you cannot return the form by the due date please ring the *HELPLINE 382288*, so that the Registration Officer can be made aware of your circumstances. Civil Penalties will only be imposed where there is an outright refusal to provide information.

THANK YOU FOR YOUR CO-OPERATION

* HUSBANDS/WIVES AND COUPLES LIVING TOGETHER AS MAN & WIFE MAY BE RESPONSIBLE FOR THEIR PARTNERS COMMUNITY CHARGE.

EXEMPTIONS *(continued)*

BOX 5 Adults resident in a property for the better performance of their duties as a Care Worker.

BOX 6 Persons detained in legal custody.

BOX 7 Foreign Diplomats, Members of visiting forces and International Headquarters staff and their dependants.

STUDENTS

If someone at the address is a student undertaking a full time course of education he/she will only be liable to pay 20% of the Personal Community Charge. See **PART 4** below for details.
Further proof of student status will be requested later.

PART 3 If anyone else lives in the property and is not listed in Part 2 then tick YES ☑ and give details. If no one else lives in the property tick NO ☑ and go on to Part 4.

PART 4 Please complete this section if anyone in your household is over 18, but is still in full time education and this is their **TERM TIME ADDRESS**.

Please ensure that you have also entered a tick in the column marked **S** in **Part 2**.

"ABOUT THE CANVASS"

The **Community Charge** is an amount which most people over 18 will have to pay towards the cost of local services such as Education, Refuse Collection, Libraries etc., and will replace domestic rates (or any contribution towards rates paid with your rent), from 1st April, 1990.

The Community Charge Registration Officer for Lancaster City Council is required by law to compile a register of every adult in the District. He will set up a register of everyone who has to pay, using the information given on the enclosed form.
It will be an Offence to give false information

The Canvassers - Your Security

In most cases it is hoped that there will be no need for a canvasser to make personal contact with the person required to complete the form **which should be filled in and returned by post** in the envelope provided.

All canvassers have been issued with an identification card and have been instructed to conduct a doorstep interview only. If, for any reason a canvasser is required to call to interview a resident, for example, blind persons, the elderly, etc., a request for such a visit should be made in writing or by telephone. A friend, relative or neighbour may help. Contact telephone number is 382288.

DO NOT ALLOW ANYONE INTO YOUR HOME UNLESS THEY PRODUCE PROPER IDENTIFICATION. IF YOU ARE IN ANY DOUBT ASK THEM TO CALL BACK AND RING HELPLINE 382288 OR 63333 (POLICE).

FOLLOW THIS STEP BY STEP GUIDE TO ASSIST YOU TO COMPLETE THE FORM

The form has been addressed to the person who, according to the Council's current records, is the ratepayer/tenant. If this information is incorrect you should still complete the form as the occupier. Any adult who lives at the address shown on the form can fill it in. Failure to do so will lead to the Registration Officer making someone responsible for completing the form and issuing penalties for further non-completion.

If no one is solely or mainly resident at the address on the form and you are the owner, tenant, sub-tenant or a legal representative - Go to Part 5 on the back of the form.

PART 1

Make sure that the full and correct address for this property is entered. Also please indicate the type of property, i.e. bedsit, house, flat (please state flat number or floor level as appropriate) etc.

PART 2

This part is very important. Please list everyone who is * solely or mainly resident at the address who is aged 16 years or over. The date of birth of persons aged between 16 and 18 is also requested.

* A person's sole or main residence is the address they consider to be their permanent home. However, a student's sole or main residence is deemed to be the place where they are living for the purpose of undertaking their course.

EXEMPTIONS FROM PERSONAL COMMUNITY CHARGE

The small boxes on the right hand side of Part 2 are to enable you to tick ✓ where a claim for an exemption is to be made. Read the list below which describes the various groups of people who may be exempt and tick ✓ the box which applies. *(For example if the person on the list of residents is still eligible for child benefit tick ✓ box 1 alongside their name).*

The list of exemptions given below does not set out all the requirements to claim an exemption; for further details telephone HELPLINE 382288. The Registration Officer will send a further form requesting all the information necessary to grant the exemption.

WHO WILL BE EXEMPT?

NB. Reference to 'Adults' means anyone over 18.

BOX 1 People who are over 18 for whom Child Benefit is still payable.

BOX 2 Adults whose sole or main residence is a NHS Hospital. This will include those people who have given up their homes to live in hospital. Also those adults whose sole or main residence is a nursing home, residential care home or hostel providing a substantial level of care, and who are receiving care or treatment there.

BOX 3 Adults who are severely mentally impaired.

BOX 4 Adults who are members of religious communities devoted to prayer, contemplation, education or the relief of suffering and who have no income or capital of their own.

SEE OTHER SIDE

202 LANGUAGE, BUREAUCRACY AND SOCIAL CONTROL

Appendix 2b: Community charge registration (form)

PLEASE REFER TO THE ENCLOSED LEAFLET "ABOUT THE CANVASS"

Lancaster City Council

COMMUNITY CHARGE REGISTRATION OFFICER
TOWN HALL
LANCASTER
LA1 1PJ
HELPLINE TELEPHONE (0524) 65272

OFFICE HOURS
9.00am-5.00pm Mon-Fri

THE OWNER OR OCCUPIER	PROPERTY REFERENCE NUMBER
THE OCCUPIER FLAT 7 BOWLAND COLLEGE UNIVERSITY OF LANCASTER BAILRIGG LANCASTER LA1 4YT	1001005173370
	DATE FORM ISSUED 20/11/89
	THIS FORM MUST BE RETURNED BY: 11/12/89

COMMUNITY CHARGE REGISTRATION

The enclosed note "ABOUT THE CANVASS" explains why this form has been issued to you, together with an easy-to-follow guide on how to complete your registration form. IT IS IMPORTANT THAT YOU READ THESE NOTES AS YOU COMPLETE THE FORM. For further information, help or advice, please ring the HELPLINE number above.

The PENALTY for failure to supply this information is £50 for the FIRST OFFENCE and £200 for the SECOND AND SUBSEQUENT OFFENCES.
Please use CAPITAL LETTERS.

1 The FULL POSTAL ADDRESS(or location) of the property is....   The address of my previous property was . . .

Postcode   Postcode

2 The following PEOPLE AGED 16 OR OVER live at the above address, and it is their SOLE OR MAIN RESIDENCE....

TITLE Mr/Mrs Miss etc	SURNAME	FORENAMES (in full)	If over 18	Otherwise please state Date of Birth Day : Month : Year	EXEMPTIONS OR REDUCTIONS If you think anyone is entitled to an exemption or a reduction mentioned in the leaflet, please ✓ below							
					1	2	3	4	5	6	7	8*

* In order to claim a reduction in respect of a STUDENT please enter FULL DETAILS in SECTION 4 overleaf.

POSSIBLE EXEMPTIONS:

If you claim one of the above exemptions, the Community Charge Registration Officer will send you a claim form for completion. You may also be required to prove your claim with supporting documents (on request only).

1. Persons aged 18 years old who are still at school and where child benefit is still payable.
2. Persons whose sole or main residence is in a hospital, nursing home or residential home.
3. Persons who are severely mentally impaired.
4. Members of religious communities with no income or capital of their own.
5. Persons resident in a property due to their employment as a care worker, by a charity or similar institution.
6. Persons serving prison sentences or held on remand.
7. Diplomats and members of Visiting Forces International Headquarters.

(P.T.O.)

APPENDICES 203

Appendix 3: TV licence

Appendix 3a

[Naam]
[Adres]

UW BRIEF VAN   UW KENMERK   ONS KENMERK (1) BIJLAGE(N)
[reference]
Aanhalen a.u.b.

Betreft: Identificatie van uw inschrijving voor autoradio- en/of
televisietoestel.
Uw inschrijvingsnummer: -----

~~Mevrouw~~, Mijnheer,

Er wordt vastgesteld dat uw voornaam ontbreekt in uw inschrijving
bij mijn dienst.

Om alle verwarring te vermijden die hierdoor zou kunnen ontstaan,
verzoek ik u binnen 10 dagen deze brief gefrankeerd terug te sturen, na
uw voornaam en geboortedatum in onderstaand vak te hebben ingevuld.

Hoogachtend,

VR. DE DIRECTEUR-GENERAAL
DE ADMINISTRATIEF AFDELINGSCHEF,
[naam]

Voornaam van de houder:

Geboortedatum van de houder:

---

(1) Gelieve ons kenmerk evenals uw inschrijvingsnummer(s) van 8 cijfers
(zie deel B van uw betaalbiljet) te vermelden bij elke betaling of
briefwisseling met de Dienst Kijk- en Luistergeld.

204 *LANGUAGE, BUREAUCRACY AND SOCIAL CONTROL*

Appendix 3b

Aan [naam]
Administratieve Afdelingschef
Dienst Kijk- en Luistergeld
[adres]

Geachte Heer/Mevrouw,

Hierbij bezorg ik u het overschrijvingsformulier terug dat u ons enkele dagen geleden hebt toegestuurd. Ik kan er geen gebruik van maken want we bezitten geen kleurentelevisie en nergens op dit formulier wordt vermeld hoeveel kijk- en luistergeld we zouden moeten betalen voor het draagbare zwart/wit-toestel dat wij in bruikleen hebben.

Ik stel me trouwens een aantal vragen bij de werking van uw dienst. Even kort de gebeurtenissen op een rijtje zetten. Begin maart schrijft mijn vrouw een brief naar uw dienst om informatie te vragen over de reglementen van het kijk- en luistergeld. Deze informatie hebben we tot nu toe nog altijd niet ontvangen. In de plaats daarvan heb ik een brief gekregen waarin u me vraagt naar mijn voornaam en geboortedatum (RT 1307 NL). Ik heb u die informatie bezorgd en nu stuurt u mij een betalingsformulier waarin staat dat we kijk- en luistergeld verschuldigd zijn voor een kleurentelevisie (die we niet hebben) en dat wij dit toestel als gebruiken sinds 7 maart jl. (wat jullie niet eens zeker kunnen weten). Dat het formulier onbruikbaar is verwondert mij niet, gezien niemand op uw dienst zich ook maar de moeite getroost heeft om ons te vragen welk toestel we hebben en sinds wanneer. Als iemand om meer informatie over het betalen van kijk- en luistergeld vraagt dan betekent dat niet automatisch dat hij of zij daadwerkelijk een toestel bezit. Ik vraag me trouwens af waar de dienst kijk- en luistergeld het recht vandaan haalt om op eigen houtje te beslissen over wat mensen al dan niet bezitten en hoelang ze al iets bezitten. En, wat nog het meeste van al stoort is dat in antwoord op een brief geschreven door mijn echtgenote beslist wordt mij in te schrijven bij uw dienst. Als dit geen diskriminatie van de vrouw is!

Hoogachtend,

[naam]
[adres]

APPENDICES 205

Appendix 3c

[Naam]
[Adres]

UW BRIEF VAN   UW KENMERK   ONS KENMERK (1) BIJLAGE(N)
                              [reference]
                              Aanhalen a.u.b.
Betreft: Wettelijke en reglementaire voorschriften inzake kijk -en luistergeld.
           Uw inschrijvingsnummer: *[nummer]*

Mijnheer,
~~Mevrouw~~,

Ik zou u dank weten kennis te nemen van de inlichtingen in de
hiernastaande rubriek(en) nummer(s): 7 *en* 12 *(zie keerzijde)*

1. Het kijk- en luistergeld is verschuldigd voor periodes van twaalf
   achtereenvolgende maanden. De datum waarop de periodes
   aanvangen wordt bepaald door de eerste letter van de naam of de
   benaming van de houder.
   Uw periode van 12 maand begint ieder jaar vanaf _____ daar uw
   vergunning op naam staat van _____
   onder het nummber _____.
   Ik vestig er uw aandacht op dat het kijk- en luistergeld moet worden
   betaald met de door de Dienst Kijk- en Luistergeld toegestuurde
   betalingsformulieren.
   Zou u uitzonderling geen betalingsuitnodiging ontvangen hebben
   binnen de eerste maand van uw periode dan moet u bij de Dienst
   Kijk- en Luistergeld onmiddellijk een betalingsformulier aanvragen.

   Indien u vaststelt dat de gegevens op uw voorbedrukte
   betalingsuitnodiging niet juist zijn, gelieve dan in een afzonderlijke
   brief mijn dienst in te lichten.
2. Daar de bestendige opdracht (domiciliëring) bij een financiële
   instelling niet wordt aanvaard voor het kwijten van het kijk- en
   luistergeld wordt u verzocht het verschuldigde bedrag uitsluitend
   met de u door de Dienst en Kijk- en Luistergeld toegestuurde
   betalingsformulieren te betalen.
3. De inschrijving onder nummer _____ voor _____ wordt
   geschrapt. De vergunning voor _____ is voortaan ingeschreven
   onder het nummer _____ op naam van _____.
4. De inschrijving onder het nummer _____ op naam van
   _____ zal voortaan ingeschreven zijn onder het nummer
   _____ en derhalve vervallen op _____.

206 LANGUAGE, BUREAUCRACY AND SOCIAL CONTROL

Deze wijziging heeft tot gevolg dat nog moet worden bijbetaald voor de periode van _____ tot _____, dit is _____ maand. Er zal u eerlang een betalingsuitnodiging worden toegestuurd van _____ frank.

5. Er wordt nota genomen dat u geen enkel _____ (vast of draagbaar) meer hebt.
   Derhalve wordt uw inschrijving geschrapt voor het volgende vervalstel (dit is vanaf _____). De taks blijft evenwel verschuldigd/verworven voor de lopende periode, dit is van _____ tot _____.

6. Daar de betalingsuitnodigingen reeds verzonden zijn, wordt u verzocht het kijkgeld voor uw kleurentelevisie te betalen met de u reeds toegestuurde betalingsuitnodiging voor uw zwart-wit-televisie. Zo spoedig mogelijk zal u een voorbedrukte betalingsuitnodiging voor het kleursupplement worden toegestuurd.
   Betaal in geen geval met een ander formulier.

7. De betalingsuitnodiging(en) in uw bezit (nr. *[nummer]* voor *kleurentelevisie*) mag (~~mogen~~) worden vernietigd.

8. Gelieve uitsluitend te betalen met de toegestuurde uitnodigingen, of degene die u zullen worden toegestuurd.

9. De nodige schikkingen worden getroffen om u het teveel betaalde bedrag van _____ fr. terug te betalen (verminderd met de portkosten als de terugbetaling per postassignatie gebeurt).
   Reden van deze terugbetaling:

10. Kabeltelevisie.
    Daar het kijkgeld niet begrepen is in het abonnement en de aansluitingskosten op het teledistributienet, moeten de abonnees hun wettelijke verplichtingen nakomen inzake het kwijten van het verschuldigde kijkgeld bij de Dienst Kijk- en Luistergeld voor het houden van hun televisietoestellen.

11. Uit het onderzoek blijkt dat u op _____ wel degelijk de taks hebt betaald voor _____ voor de periode van _____ tot _____ en ingeschreven onder nummer _____.
    De betalingsuitnodiging voor _____ mag worden vernietigd.

12. *In de loop van juli e.k. zal U een betaaluitnodiging worden toegezonden voor de vereffening van het kijkgeld voor het houden van een zwart/wit-televisie.*

Hoogachtend,

VR. DE DIRECTEUR-GENERAAL
DE ADMINISTRATIEF AFDELINGSCHEF,

[naam]

APPENDICES 207

Appendix 4: Interrogation

Mr.D: Waarvoor is 't?
Agent: 'k Weet het niet. Men heeft me niks gezegd.
Mr.D: Ik vind het nogal onbeleefd om ons te doen komen voor een ondervraging als we niet mogen weten waarover 't gaat.
Agent: Beschuldigt u mij ervan onbeleefd te zijn?
Mr.D: Nee. Ik beschuldig de persoon die dit geschreven heeft.
Agent: 't Gaat over uw huis.

LANGUAGE, BUREAUCRACY AND SOCIAL CONTROL

Appendix 5a: Part 1 of Form A2 of income support form

About you and your partner – continued

page 2

Marital status
Tick the boxes that apply to you and your partner.

You	Your partner
☐ Married	☐ Married ☐ Separated
☐ Separated	☐ Living together ☑
☑ Divorced	☐ Divorced
☐ Living together	☐ Single
☐ Widowed	☐ Widowed
☐ Single	

Please tell us the name and address of the post office where you want to get your money.
Tell us about your post office even if your Income Support is paid directly into a bank or building society account.
If you are not sure of the address, you can ask the post office to stamp the form here.

Postcode

APPENDICES 209

Appendix 5b

(Extracts from the appeal documents)

Summary of facts

(1) Mrs W is a divorced lady aged 56. She has no savings and lives in local authority property. She has been in receipt of Income Support/Supplementary Benefit for many years.

(2) On [date], the local office sent Mrs W a form A2 to obtain up to date details of her circumstances.

(3) The information held in Mrs W's claim at the time form A2 was issued, was that she was a local authority tennant [sic] with a lodger Mr L. Mr L had been accepted as such by the Adjudication Officer.

(4) On [date] Mrs W returned form A2 to the local office and reported that her circumstances had remained unchanged. However, at Part I of form A2 she had ticked that she was "living together" with a partner (see page 2).

(5) Because Mrs W had ticked this "living together" box, the Adjudication Officer arranged for Mrs W to be visited, and details of her living arrangements obtained (see pages 26–35).

(6) On receipt of the information obtained by the Visiting Officer the Adjudication Officer made the decision documented at Part I of this decision.

(7) On receipt of Mrs W's letter of appeal, the Adjudication Officer felt there were no new grounds on which to review and revise her earlier decision.

210 LANGUAGE, BUREAUCRACY AND SOCIAL CONTROL

Appendix 6: FC1-wallet (cover page + first few papes)

The inside of the wallet and two papers are reproduced on the following four pages. This pack is constantly reviewed and improved on, and several major changes have been made since the 1992 print.

Can you get Family Credit?

Family Credit

- Read this leaflet to find out who may be able to get Family Credit

WHAT IS FAMILY CREDIT?

Family Credit is a regular tax-free cash payment for working people with children.

The amount that you can get depends on the number of children you have, how old they are and how much money is coming into your home at the time you claim.

WHO IS IT FOR?

Family Credit is for people who are working for 16 hours or more a week and who have at least one child.

It's for self-employed people as well as people who have an employer.

It's for lone parents as well as couples.

Some more facts about Family Credit

- It's not a loan – you don't have to pay it back.
- It lasts for 26 weeks at a time – so it can add up to a worthwhile sum. And the payments stay the same even if earnings go up during that time.
- You can choose how the money is paid
  - into your bank or building society account
  - with a book that you cash at the post office.

While you get Family Credit you and your family can also get free NHS prescriptions, dental treatment and sight tests, and help with the cost of glasses.

HELP AND ADVICE

For more information about Family Credit

ring Freeline Social Security on 0800 666 555. The phone call will be free

or get in touch with your Social Security office. The phone number and address are in the phone book under SOCIAL SECURITY or BENEFITS AGENCY

or get in touch with an advice centre like the Citizens Advice Bureau.

Can you get Family Credit?

Family Credit

- Read this leaflet to find out who may be able to get Family Credit
- Then fill in the claim form if you think you should be claiming.

Find out if you might qualify.
Answer these 3 questions about you, and about your partner if you have one. We use *partner* to mean a person you are married to or a person you live with as if you are married to them.

1 Are you, or your partner, working for at least 16 hours a week?

☐ No
☐ Yes

2 Do you, or your partner, support at least one child who normally lives with you?

☐ No
☐ Yes

3 Do you, and your partner, have £8,000 or less in savings between you?

☐ No
☐ Yes

If you have ticked YES to these 3 questions you may be able to get Family Credit

▲

How Family Credit is worked out

These notes are to give you an idea of how Family Credit is worked out.

The amounts on this page are the ones that will be used from April 1992.

Remember Family Credit is based on

- how many children you have
- how old they are
- how much money is coming in each week
- how much you have in savings.

The figures on this page assume savings of £3,000 or less. See PART 6 of the claim form for more information about how savings affect Family Credit.

How much you can get

If you have less than £66.60 coming in each week, you can get the full amount of Family Credit for your family.

For example a family with 2 children aged 12 and 14 could get £75.50 a week.

If you have more than £66.60 coming in each week you will get less Family Credit. Very roughly, 70 pence will be taken off the full amount for every pound you have coming in over £66.60.

For example a family with 2 children aged 12 and 14 could have £130 a week coming in and still get over £30 a week in Family Credit.

For example a family with 3 children aged 3, 8 and 11 could have £140 a week coming in and still get over £27 a week in Family Credit.

Family Credit is made up of money for you and money for each child. These amounts are

£41.00 for you
The amount is the same for lone parents and couples.

£10.40 for each child under 11

£17.25 for each child 11 to 15

£21.45 for each child 16 to 17 who is doing a full-time course not above A level standard

£29.90 for each child aged 18 who is doing a full-time course not above A level standard

Printed in the UK for C.B. Derry Ltd, St. Ives PLC/2/92/47924/7123L

FC2 (1992)

See if you might qualify

Please look at the second page of your Child Benefit order book. It will tell you if you may be able to get Family Credit.

or If you are paid your Child Benefit directly into an account, look at the letter we sent you about this. It will tell you if you may be able to get Family Credit.

or Pick out your family in the chart opposite. Claim if the amount of money coming into your home each week is the amount shown or less.

- These amounts apply to both lone parents and couples
- The chart is just a guide – even if your family is not shown here, you could still qualify
- If you're still in doubt, fill in the claim form.

Money coming in includes

- Take-home pay
- Business profits *after allowable expenses*
- Social Security benefits *but not Child Benefit or One Parent Benefit or Attendance Allowance or Disability Living Allowance or Housing Benefit or Community Charge Benefit*
- Other money *for example, maintenance (except the first £15) or money from boarders or sub-tenants*

KEY — Child under 11 years — Child between 11-15 years — Child between 16-17 years at school — Child 18 years at school

KEY	Child under 11 years	Child between 11-15 years	Child between 16-17 years at school
£139 or less	£154 or less	£169 or less	£193 or less
£149 or less	£163 or less	£178 or less	£203 or less
£155 or less	£169 or less	£184 or less	£219 or less
£167 or less	£173 or less	£188 or less	£221 or less
	£179 or less	£194 or less	£237 or less
	£191 or less	£222 or less	
	£197 or less		

214 LANGUAGE, BUREAUCRACY AND SOCIAL CONTROL

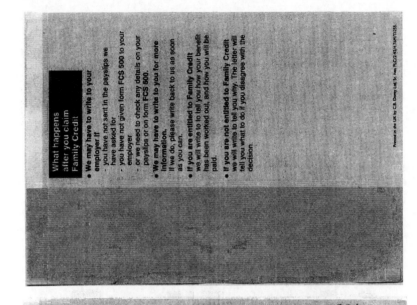

APPENDICES   215

Appendix 7: The Martins' appeal

EDUCATION APPEAL

28 March 1991

[Name]
[Place]

LITTLE OAK SCHOOL

We accept that Little Oak provides a friendly environment and is right for some parents. But it is not right for us. Our concerns are based on the fact that, compared with what other schools in Oak are achieving, Jimmy is reaching very poor levels of attainment. This is even more disturbing because he is regarded by his teacher as one of the most advanced in the class.

I don't want to knock this school unduly. There are some good things happening there. But surely the whole point of this appeal is that I must demonstrate why Jimmy needs to leave Little Oak and why he needs to go to Elm. In describing conditions at Little Oak I will confine myself to known facts. Therefore I must speak frankly.

The following information is based on personal observation.

There is extremely poor concentration in the class. Even with an attendance of as little as 16, pupils will often leave an activity after ten minutes or so then walk around disrupting the others, or play with the Lego.

There is no reading scheme. There is a total reliance on 'real books', a method that, when used exclusively, has been widely disproved.

Earlier this month the education secretary Kenneth Clarke described the 'real books' method as cranky and other new schemes as eccentric. 'All reports show that where phonics is used teachers have an overwhelming record of success,' he said. They are not used in Jimmy's class.

There is little or no control on learning to write properly or form the letters competently. Yet Jimmy's handwriting is regarded by his teacher as very good for his age. He still uses mirror letters and mixes capitals and lower case. Elm is way ahead.

There is no attempt to give guidance on spelling, no corrections, nor do the pupils have a personal dictionary or word book as other schools in Oak have. Jimmy's teacher is hoping to put him on Breakthrough card system next term. But at Elm there are children already using this in the reception class.

216 *LANGUAGE, BUREAUCRACY AND SOCIAL CONTROL*

Understandably, the pupils have very poor attainment levels in their language books: one simple sentence, misspelt, is regarded as a satisfactory morning's work (in the same year at Elm, some pupils have produced three pages).

The pupils have access to a computer to write stories, but this is generally without supervision and there is no check on the spelling of simple words before the work is printed out.

The class teacher seldom hears Jimmy read. To take two recent examples, she did not hear him read between 11th December and 29th January, a period of four school weeks, nor between 11th February and 12th March; a month. Other teachers in Oak hear each child read at least once or twice a week. This cannot be a case of overwork because there are only 18 children on the roll.

To put it bluntly, Jimmy's class at Little Oak is, in many ways, a year behind the equivalent class at Elm.

It could be argued that this is an exceptional example of a probationary teacher not coping particularly well. However the Head Teacher has said she is very pleased with the performance of this teacher and intends to give her a favourable assessment. This means that the class standards, the teaching policies and the attainment levels are implicitly endorsed by the Head Teacher. When my wife challenged her on Jimmy's lack of progress, the Head Teacher's reply was, 'Just by being here he learns.'

Furthermore, the school's resources appear to be diminishing rapidly. There is now neither a music nor a drama specialist in the school, nor any generalist teacher with special teaching skills in these fields, nor even anyone who can play a keyboard instrument. There are moves to see if a parent can be found to play the piano sometimes. Meanwhile an excellent collection of percussion instruments lies in the hall, unused.

In October of last year, class teachers complained of a shortage of paper for pupils to write on and requested parents to help provide paper.

I know that some of the parents in this class are concerned about the standards, but their reaction has been, like ours, to provide a strong presence in the class. Sometimes there will be two parent helpers working with the class teacher: that makes a ratio of about one to six. And still the concentration is poor. Other parents have simply moved out of the borough, which accounts for the falling numbers.

This seems to be an early example of what the Councillor calls 'voting with your feet.'

APPENDICES 217

As he says, 'Under LMS the money follows the pupil and if the parents don't like what is being done by the school then the school will have to change.'

In two years I have seen no evidence of change for the better nor any indication of change in the future. So those of us who are left behind at Little Oak appear to be stuck.

OUR ACTION

We have approached the situation patiently and positively, taking an active part in parent-teacher events and meetings. We have provided regular support in the classroom and on several occasions I have given drama lessons for Jimmy's class.

We have also increased Jimmy's reading and writing practice at home.

But once it became clear that a change of school was necessary, we pursued the matter relentlessly and actively, doing everything we could to speed up the transfer, for we regarded the task as urgent. We appealed for North Oak combined school in January and lost. Immediately afterwards, we set up this appeal.

RESEARCH

We visited the following schools (some of them more than once):

Hawthorn
Beech
Cypress
Elm
North Oak

Birch House
Willow Lodge
Sycamore House.

WHY ELM?

First let me tell you

Why high academic standards are important to us.

Language – speaking, reading and writing – is our livelihood. I work in higher education – teach and direct plays at GSMD. I work as a theatre critic for *The Guardian* and feature writer for *The Times*. I write books.

Wife – foreign correspondent for Dutch press, radio and TV. Language is

218 *LANGUAGE, BUREAUCRACY AND SOCIAL CONTROL*

important to us and we try to convey those values to our son. That is why we expect him to have a first class academic education.

The situation

We have been very patient and supportive, but after nearly two years at Little Oak, hope has run out.

Jimmy's development has fallen back so much that we have urgently to make up for this.

In November, tested at Birch House – a full year behind.

He was the brightest in his class at Oak Montessori – and that is not a cramming school.

A shock to discover that a child can be allowed to fall back so far in so little time.

Most disturbing – he has lost his former joy for learning.

Furthermore, his teacher reports that he has recently become quiet and withdrawn in the classroom.

An intense programme of work at home means that he can now read.
But we want him to learn to write and to begin to learn to spell. From what we've seen and heard, that is standard practice in other schools.

I asked his class teacher recently when the pupils learn to spell. She said, 'I don't know. As far as I can see, we're just supposed to go on doing developmental writing. Even in the Sevens some of them are still writing as they hear.'

We feel that under the circumstances because our child has so much catching up to do, it is our duty as parents to do our utmost to get him into the very best academic school available.

Obviously one can brush aside the state provision and go straight to the independent sector.

Our research covered both. Birch House – place offered, but we declined – commitment to the state sector, and we feel strongly that we want him to have a co-educational upbringing. Having taken many days off work to investigate at first hand the conditions and attainment levels in Oak, we feel sure that Elm is the school best suited to do this.

Qualities of Elm

The Head Teacher has a sound philosophy of education and heads a well-organized team.

APPENDICES 219

From a number of meetings I have had with her, concerning this case and concerning Arts Council business, I can say I have the greatest admiration for her ideas and the manner inwhich she runs the school.

The classes are well-disciplined and well-structured, with excellent concentration.

The attainment standards in reading and writing (for Jimmy's age group) are some of the highest we saw from the state sector and certainly on a par with some of the private schools.

There is a reading scheme as well as a selection of good books. We were impressed by the staff – we found them enthusiastic, confident and committed.

The school has a rich multi-cultural mix which we believe is important for a child growing up in today's Britain. Altogether, we believe in this more formal situation, Jimmy will catch up and achieve his potential.

Drama and Music

We also want a good grounding in music and drama.

From September 1992, increasing attention will be placed on the role drama can play across the curriculum.

The drama and performance work at Elm exceeds what almost all the others are achieving.

Also has a network of contacts to provide a richer input than others are getting. Has had prestigious companies visit the school.

Music lessons are available and children combine with middle school pupils in the school orchestra.

It has a tradition of staging a school production each year.

Overcrowding problems

The Education Authority has stated that Elm is full. Classes at Jimmy's year are at capacity. And people are, like Jimmy, on a waiting list hoping to get in.

So we come to the crux of the argument.

Taking into account Oak's selection criteria:

220 *LANGUAGE, BUREAUCRACY AND SOCIAL CONTROL*

<u>Why should Jimmy take preference over others?</u>

First: The fact facing the local Borough is that all of the best schools have reached or exceeded their standard allocation. However, despite the fact that teachers have to cope with large numbers, Elm has a much higher attainment level with big classes, than Little Oak does with a class of only 18.

Taking the best academic schools in the state sector: Elm, North Oak, Cypress, these other two schools are also full.

North Oak – classes of 32 and 34 with a long waiting list.

Cypress – two classes of 33 with a long waiting list.

So equally little chance of getting him in there.

Second: We have spoken at length with the Head Teacher of Elm about Jimmy. We have shown her examples of his work and explained his situation. She felt confident that she could help him catch up quite quickly. That confidence is vital to us.

Third: As for closeness to the school, we can also reach the school quickly – less than five minutes drive.

Fourth: A few weeks ago I asked the Councillor what advice he would give to parents who wanted to get their child into a better school. 'The trouble is,' he said, 'Around here the only advice you can give is to move.'

We moved two years ago and we like it where we are. Even if we were to find a house in the Elm catchment area of the same value (which is most unlikely) and to succeed in selling our own house, the moving costs would be at least 10,000 pounds. The simple answer to the Councillor, and to you, is that we can't afford to move.

Should our child therefore be denied the best education because he happens to live a few streets too far?

We have shown why our Jimmy needs Elm.

But do the benefits to our child outweigh any detriment to the school as a whole?

I believe they do.

First, Elm is known to have a mobile population. Therefore even if the addition of one more child means that a class will be overcrowded, the effect is likely to be temporary since more places will soon become available.

Second, Jimmy is known to be a very bright, well-balanced child, the kind who is likely to do well academically and artistically and will be a credit to the school.

Third. His command of English is above average for his age. And because of his bi-lingual background (he is fluent in Dutch) and his very international upbringing, he is used to racial and cultural differences to a degree that many children of his age are not. In classes like those at Elm he can be a valuable bridge between foreign children and those from a more conventional English background. In other words he would be very good in the group.

Fourth. When you take on the child, to some extent you also take on the parent. With tight budgets, schools are increasingly looking to make use of the resources parents can provide. Independent schools do this quite blatantly. There's nothing to be ashamed of in that, but it is something to consider.

My point is that there is a very good context of music and drama at Elm. I am prepared to bring my own expertise to help enrich the drama work.

In terms of musical input, I may also be able to help forge links between the school and GSMD. Guildhall, one of the finest music colleges in the world, is at present looking to expand its community work.

CONCLUSION

The chilling reality if we lose yet another appeal, is that, for all our work, for all the nightmare and the worry of this long episode (which began in early October), the door to the best education will be closed on us.

To be honest, our desperation is now at an intense level, and it is becoming increasingly difficult to hide our anxiety from our child. Our confidence in the system of parental choice has been severely crushed through our experiences so far, and we are beginning to feel like the protagonist in a Kafka novel. Are we trapped in a dismal educational situation?

I don't know what we'll do if we lose this appeal.

This is a genuine case for appeal because, for all its good intentions and helpfulness, the Local Education Authority has actually been able to do nothing at all to help us. I believe the officers would like to help us, but they can't.

222 *LANGUAGE, BUREAUCRACY AND SOCIAL CONTROL*

All they can say is that they are officially satisfied with the standard of education at Little Oak, and the other schools we want to get into are full. All we have to go on is, 'Wait a little longer, there is hope of getting your child into Elm.'

For six months we have waited. For six months we have worked relentlessly.

Does this mean that we have no way of upholding the right to choose the best education for our child – in line with the philosophy of the Government.

We are here today to appeal to your discretion.

It would be a sad state of affairs if there is basically no freedom of choice; if some children are denied a good, or even competent education; if you can't get the best education without paying for it.

That isn't the vision of the Government, and I'm sure it's not the vision of the local Borough.

We have not made this request lightly, but have done an enormous amount of research, and have invested a huge amount of our time, to identify the best.

I challenge any other parent to have done the same.

To put it crudely, we feel we've done the work, and we deserve at least some reward for our diligence and integrity.

I emphasise the urgency of the issue. As days go by, Jimmy is slipping back further and further, which means that he has more to catch up on if he is to have a decent chance in later life. That is why he needs Elm. But now. Not in six months time.

We want to make one move, and we want that to be the decisive move – not to tamper with this school and that, disrupting the child's whole social orientation.

As I mentioned before, we also have something to offer the school. Not only will we be supportive parents, willing and able to co-operate with the school's educational work, but I am prepared to bring my own expertise and contacts to help enrich the music and drama work.

For the reasons I have outlined, I hope you will share my view that this is a special case, and we as parents are gravely concerned to improve, urgently, the educational provision for our son.

Before our last appeal several people advised us what to do in order to

APPENDICES   223

succeed. Some were teachers. They told us that it might be effective if we could show a report from a child psychologist proving that Jimmy was disturbed. Or that we ourselves were on valium because of the whole saga. Or even that a note from our GP about Jimmy might be useful. But we brushed this advice aside and prepared a rational argument based on facts. We lost.

Jimmy is not going out of his mind, nor is he physically handicapped. We have an intelligent, well-adjusted child. Ironically that may prove to be the real handicap. Because he is not a 'problem child' in the classroom, he gets little attention and no real encouragement. Consequently, he is not learning.

We have kept our faith with the Oak Education authority, and we believe Elm is a very fine school.

We do not want to have to give up and send Jimmy to a single-sex, private school.

We've done our side of it. Please, use your discretion wisely and help us.

SUMMARY

We accept that Little Oak is right for some people, but it is not right for us.

Despite the official line that all the schools are satisfactory, Jimmy is in an unacceptable situation where he is. We have given you evidence to support this.

Nevertheless, we have been patient and positive, and have given lots of help at home.

Once we knew what had to be done, we didn't leave Jimmy on a waiting list, but pursued the transfer urgently.

Out research has been wide and thorough.

Jimmy has a lot of catching up to do, but the head teacher at Elm feels she can help him, and we have faith in her, in her team and what they have achieved at Elm.

An appeal is necessary because all the best schools have reached or exceeded their standard allocation.

Yet they still do better with 30 or more than Jimmy's present class does with almost half that number.

We can reach Elm easily and quickly.

224 LANGUAGE, BUREAUCRACY AND SOCIAL CONTROL

We can't afford to move into the catchment area.

We have also argued that the benefits to our son outweigh any detriment to the school:

Elm has a mobile population and as places do become available, overcrowding caused by adding Jimmy to the roll could soon be eased.

Jimmy is likely to be, artistically and academically, a credit to the school.

His international background gives him a deeper understanding of racial and cultural differences, which is valuable in a school like Elm.

As parents, we will be supportive and are prepared to offer our own expertise, if needed, to help the school, especially through music and drama.

We have worked hard at this, but we are desperate.

It is beyond the power of the Education Authority to help.

We feel strongly that we want to keep him in the state system. It is important for him to grow up with children of all backgrounds, but in an academically stimulating environment. We feel it is unacceptable if the system should force us to send him to a single-sex, private school. That is something we emphatically do not want.

We want to make one move, that will be the right move and will last.

We therefore appeal most urgently to your discretion.

COMMENTS FROM ACE

1. An appeal is to balance 'parental considerations' against 'prejudice to efficient education'.

2. You may knock Little Oak School, but it could have the effect of putting the Appeal Committee against you. It is better to just state the particular aspects of Elm that suit you.

2b. Appeal Cttee will not consider criticism of one school as valid reason for move to another school. Reasons for appeal should all be positive in favour of new school.

3. Your point about real books is incorrect. The National Curriculum contains much reference to real books and in fact the recommended reading at Key Stage 1 lists 51 of them. In addition, most schools use a mixture of methods & in 80% of schools they are teaching reading successfully.

APPENDICES 225

Unless you can get a written statement from Little Oak that they only use 'real books' & a different statement from Elm, this very delicate point is not likely to stand.

I'm sorry but your arguments about poor teaching at Little Oak are not for Appeal Committees, they should be the subject of (a) complaint to Head, (b) complaint to governors, (c) formal complaint to Director of Education.

You are best to describe your child's aptitude at music & drama & therefore prove a particular need.

'Voting with your feet' is an erroneous suggestion.

Even if 85% (April 1993) of the school depends on pupil numbers there will be insufficient money to build an extra classroom. Popular schools will always be full.

Everyone wants a first class academic education. This is not an argument for an appeal committee.

Elm at Appeal <u>must</u> prove that it is full.

1) How many desks has it?

2) Does it have space for another desk?

3) Are there enough coat pegs for an extra child, etc.

Third: this is your best argument so far.

First: a good point.

Third: if you can show that there are more foreign children at Elm and this would <u>benefit Jimmy</u> this is a good point.

Fourth re: earlier I said that <u>Jimmy</u> must benefit from drama. What <u>you</u> bring to the school doesn't matter.

THIS <u>IS</u> THE STATE OF AFFAIRS for some children. At the moment Jimmy is one of them.

226 LANGUAGE, BUREAUCRACY AND SOCIAL CONTROL

Appendix 8: WorldWide couriers

Appendix 8a

Geachte klant,

Goederen, geïmporteerd vanuit het buitenland, moeten aangegeven worden bij de douane en door WorldWide worden ingeklaard. Om deze doauneformaliteiten te bespoedigen, betaalt WorldWide de BTW en/of invoerrechten van zodra de goederen in België zijn. Vervolgens worden deze doorgefaktureerd aan de klant.

Daarvoor verzoeken wij U dit bedrag binnen de 7 dagen te vereffenen. Indien U vragen heeft omtrent de juistheid van de inklaring, gelieve ons dan te kontakteren voor de vervaldatum van de faktuur.

Appendix 8b

Geachte Heer/Mevrouw,

Hierbij ingesloten vindt U het rekeninguitreksel zoals wij er maandelijks één naar al onze debiteuren versturen. Daarop kan U met ons vaststellen dat de betalingstermijn, bepaald op 30 dagen na de factuurdatum, reeds is overschreden.

Welke er ook de oorzaak van moge zijn, wij zouden U liefst niet tot die klanten rekenen die elke maand een diepgaande opvolging behoeven. Een permanente kontrole van de debiteuren vergt veel tijd en energie die wij liever zouden willen besteden aan het verbeteren van onze service ten behoeve van de klanten.

Mogen wij U dan ook vriendelijk verzoeken deze vergetelheid ongedaan te maken en nog deze week een betaling te verrichten voor al uw facturen ouder dan 30 dagen.

Wij danken U voor het vertrouwen in onze firma en hopen op een verdere vlotte samenwerking.

[naam]
Credit Control
[telefoonnnummer]

Indien U inmiddels reeds betaald heeft, gelieve deze brief als onbestaande te beschouwen.

APPENDICES 227

Appendix 8c

WorldWide
[address]

Geachte Mevrouw, Meneer,

In antwoord op uw betalingsherinnering van 7 december jl. (SETB250), wou ik u meedelen dat we een goeie maand geleden de faktuur doorogestuurd hebben naar [Britse uitgever] – omdat het (tijdelijk) in/uitvoeren van de boeken waarop de faktuur betrekking heeft eigenlijk voor hun rekening is.

Ik vermoed dat zij met jullie kontakt zullen opnemen.

Hoogachtend,

[naam]

228 LANGUAGE, BUREAUCRACY AND SOCIAL CONTROL

Appendix 9: The Lost Mail Case

Appendix 9a Roy's gloss on events

(References to countries have been changed, but initials of bank personnel have been retained)

Response to bank's standard letter of 5.11.92

It became clear during the telephone conversation with KL that as far as the bank was concerned, it had received nothing from me. (KL checked the book which records registered letters received and found nothing). At that point in time, I tended to think that the letter had been lost through the incompetence of one of the postal administrations, probably the British.

First written communication to the bank

In my fax of 11.11.92, I appealed to the bank, in the person of KL, to make an enquiry at her end to try to establish whether the GPO had received the item from [country of origin], in the same way as I would have asked a friend/relative in similar circumstances. This appeal was necessarily framed tentatively because I realised that the bank would regard such a request as inappropriate to a bank/client relationship, narrowly defined. Had there been a personal relationship with one of the bank officers, I suspect the approach to the GPO might have been made. However, I had established no such relationship since my account had been automatically transferred to that branch, while I remained abroad, on the closure of the branch where my account had previously been located.

Letters to GPO

Similarly, I knew it was unlikely that the GPO would entertain an enquiry about the missing letter from me in [country of origin], since I was not a customer of theirs. Nevertheless, I wrote twice to the GPO in London, hoping that it might sidestep its role and inform me about the whereabouts of the letter in London. (OPA had already claimed over the phone that the letter had been despatched). I might also have been trying to trade on my British citizenship! This action and the appeal to the bank were attempts to speed up the process of tracing the missing item.

OPA

The claim contained in OPA's letter of 24.12.92 that the letter had been

APPENDICES   229

'duly delivered' posed a problem. I suspected that the bank would not accept such an unsubstantiated claim from a foreign postal administration. Fortunately OPA substantiated their claim by providing a copy of the documentary proof that the GPO had sent them.

The bank's belated response and the reimbursement of my expenses

On the same day as I wrote to OPA (6.1.93), I wrote to the bank informing them of OPA's claim and requesting them once more to check their records. On 13.1.93 I wrote again, enclosing a photocopy of the GPO receipt and making it clear that I now considered them to be at fault. As I had suspected, the bank wrote only in response to receiving a copy of the signed receipt. Although IG claimed to be replying to my letter of 6.1.93, he was in fact replying to the letter of 13.1.93, since he referred to the enclosed copy:

'With the benefit of the copy receipt enclosed with your letter . . .'

Although the bank admitted fault in this letter, in my reply of 3.2.93 I listed all the expenses and wrongly attributed bank charges, enclosing as much documentary evidence as possible, because I suspected the bank would attempt to evade reimbursement. I was also trying to behave as much like an accountant/bookkeeper as possible, maybe even trying to outdo the bank in terms of professionalism. I also made a claim for financial compensation for time and energy, using a phrase which was designed to make it clear that I would regard such a payment as exceptional ('an ex-gratia payment'). I did not specify the amount because I had no idea of the possible range of such a payment. I asked for compensation because I was angry at the bank's rudeness in not replying to earlier letters, for genuine reasons of redress, and to see what value they put on the concealment of their incompetence from the public.

Compensation

I was surprised that the bank paid all the itemised amounts in full. I was also surprised that IG even entertained the notion of compensation by offering forty pounds. However, I read the amount offered as an insult and as perversely arbitrary. (No explanation was given of how such an amount had been derived.) In asking for one hundred and five pounds without explanation, I was intending to parody the bank's arbitrariness as well as seek adequate compensation. In a sense, this backfired since IG, in reply (24.3.93) asked for a 'breakdown', either ignoring or failing to read my parody. I had no way of knowing why the bank was willing to offer forty pounds without any account but required a breakdown for

230 *LANGUAGE, BUREAUCRACY AND SOCIAL CONTROL*

my claim of one hundred and five. I thought that one hundred and five pounds might exceed the amount that could be disbursed under a 'petty cash' voucher without going outside the branch to a higher level and revealing the branch's incompetence. However, I thought it was more likely that IG suspected I would be unable to substantiate such an amount and that he would be able to save money. While assuming that IG must be as aware as I was that my time and energy could be costed professionally (cf. damages), I wished to avoid mentioning recourse to a third party, hoping to keep things between the two of us. In response to IG's request for a breakdown, I reiterated the basis of my claim, explicitly referring to a previous letter, to make it clear that I regarded his request as superfluous. I also drew his attention to the exact wording of my original claim for one hundred and five pounds ('a sum in the region of . . .') in order to make it clear that I was willing to negotiate.

Appendix 9b Roy's response to the analysis in chapter 5

In the following I explain my reactions to various details of the narration and analysis of the events in the bank story.

With regard to your comments on the standard letter sent to me by KL, I had no expectation that the bank would notice or mention that the monthly draft from overseas had not been paid in for October. I was therefore not at all surprised at the standard nature of the letter nor was I surprised that I had to take the trouble of phoning to find out the cause of the overdraft. (On a point of fact, the debit which caused the overdraft was a cheque paid to a building society savings account, not the standing order for the mortgage repayments.) During that phone call I arranged for the transfer from my reserve account to minimize the penalty but also to take temporary responsibility, assuming that the bank was not at fault and that the postal authorities, to whom I had delegated the delivery of the draft, were responsible (thus making me indirectly responsible). In retrospect I am surprised that I did not point out to the bank my previous practice of sending a more or less monthly draft by registered post.

In paragraph one of my fax to KL, I was offering the bank the chance to (a) believe my claim that I had sent a draft and (b) show that their inquiry on my behalf to the GPO would be a legitimate extension of customer services (my account had been with the bank for twenty years, although with this particular branch for only six months). It seemed that they took no such step since the bank had not lost anything (indeed they had gained by charging me hefty overdraft fees).

The second transfer of money requested in the second paragraph of the

APPENDICES   231

same fax should not be interpreted as a sign of conscientiousness since it was necessitated by an unrelated event (the failure of one of my tenants to pay his rent on time but I don't want to go on record about having paying tenants!).

You explain my letter to the GPO in terms of an awareness of institutional mismatches. Perhaps, but I was also trying, more crudely, just to speed up the process of tracing the letter and assigning blame, especially in the light of the OPA's warning that the trace might take a month or more.

At a later point in the story, when I am about to ask the OPA for concrete proof of the letter's delivery, you refer to this as the only way for me to restore my face with bank. Of course, face was important to me at this stage, but I was certain that the bank would only accept a GPO (ie British) document as evidence that the letter had been delivered and that without this I would not be able to claim reimbursement for my expenses. As you point out later, my face is more threatened by the bank's failure to reply to earlier correspondence and their implication that I was lying. In fact, the bank has still failed to apologise for this insult. It is interesting that you use the word 'risk' here: 'Roy is prepared to take risks as far as OPA and GPO are concerned, because this will help to restore his face with bank'. I saw the letter to OPA as the only course of action available to me, given the circumstances. Maybe I am interpreting your use of the word 'risk' too narrowly.

Index of authors

Abbott P 178n1
Agar M 16n5, 43, 182
Austin J 45

Beck U 188
Berger P L 15n1, 86n1
Bourdieu P 183
Brown P 88

Candlin C 178n1
Charrow V R 7, 8
Collins J 16n5

Dews P 4, 5, 16n4
Dickens C, *Little Dorrit* 15n3
Dingwall R 178n1
Dunleavy P 20

Eekelaar J 178n1
Erickson F 178n1

Fairclough N 11, 14, 33, 45,
    59n2, 129, 141, 186, 187–8
Featherstone M 187
Field F 169
Foucault M 4–6, 12, 14, 16n9,
    36, 58, 80, 86n5
Fowler R 11
Fraser N 34n1, 120

Giddens A 183–4, 190n3
Goffman E 12, 86n1, 88, 190n4

Gramsci A 20
Grice H P 46, 47, 59n2, 120
Gumperz J 16n5
Gyford J 34n5

Habermas J 15n2, 19, 34n1,
    86n5, 120, 190n3, 190n5
Hall C 86n2
Halliday M 86n3
Heath S B 16n6, 46
Hodge B 11
Hymes D 86n1

Iedema R 7, 16n7

Kress G 11

Leech G 59n3, 88
Levinson S 86n1, 88
Luckmann 15n1, 86n1

Maley Y 178n1
Marx K 16n4
McCarthy T 86n5
Mey J 46

Philips S U 16n5
Pratt M-L 59n2, 66, 80

Redish J C 7, 8

Sarangi S 46, 60n4, 86n2, 120

INDEX OF AUTHORS 233

Shultz J 178n1
Slembrouck S 46, 60n4, 86n2, 120
Stenson K 178n2

Tannen D 178n1
Thomas J 66–7, 68, 71, 86n1
Thompson J B 34n1, 190n3
Tolson A 60n7

Trew T 11

Wallace C 178n1
Wallat C 178n1
Weber M 2, 5–6, 9, 15n2
Wernick A 187–8, 190n4
Williams R 1–2
Wittgenstein L 37

Index of terms

access to information 32, 33,
34n5, 78, 100, 108, 113, 137,
139–40
see also information exchange
accessibility 15, 20, 135,
139–41, 181, 186
see also symmetry
accessibility and accountability
141–4, 186
accessibility and entitlement 183
accessible language use 8–9, 22,
27, 139, 186
see also user-friendly documents
accountability 15, 33, 109, 126,
141–4, 173, 178, 181, 185–6
activity types 37, 6
address 13, 14, 38, 54, 182
conversational address 22,
30–1
denial of unsolicited address
93–4
direct address 22
indiscriminate and individual
address 28, 95, 96, 97, 123,
127, 130, 145, 151
manipulative address 187
(im)personal address 83–4, 95
see also client assignment, client
identity construction
advertising
advertising bureaucratic
warnings 21, 22–3, 26–9

advertising social services
136–41
colonising capacities of 34,
144, 187
analyst, position of 14
asymmetry 13–14, 167, 182
asymmetrical perceptions of
role 82
discoursal asymmetry
asymmetrical assumptions
about information exchange
48–9, 61, 125, 182
asymmetries and information
processing 129
asymmetry and shifts in talk
62
asymmetry in information
exchange 38, 45–6
clients challenging discoursal
asymmetries 90, 150, 182
institutional attempts at
reducing asymmetries 15,
127–8, 141, 146, 152,
178, 182
see also address ((im)personal
address), formulation,
client types, cultural
capital, unequal encounter
authority 13, 36, 67, 90, 96, 97,
162–3

bureau 1

INDEX OF TERMS

bureaucracy
as a (social and discursive) process 3–4, 10, 12, 19, 36–7, 87, 123, 147, 181
see also bureaucratisation, debureaucratisation
definition of 1–4, 9, 17, 189
experience of 3–4, 9, 17–19, 29
multi-tier bureaucracy 177–8
origins of 2, 5, 15n1, 15n3
synonyms of 3
bureaucratic language, previous research into 7–11, 12, 29, 34
bureaucratisation 6, 19–21, 23–6, 33–4, 36, 58, 62, 84–5, 170, 190n5
in the private economy 3, 21, 29, 78, 181, 188, 190n5
see also debureaucratisation
bureaupretation 43–5, 182

capitalism 2, 5, 15n1, 16n4, 19
late capitalism 15, 181, 183, 186, 187, 190n3
see also marketisation of the public sphere, consumer culture, promotional culture, expert systems
chat 45, 60n7, 63, 64
choice 15, 138–9, 140, 152, 181, 186–7
client assignment 55, 93, 170–2, 174
see also implied client
client empowerment 145, 146, 150, 178, 187
client identity construction 10–11, 14, 19, 28, 38, 78, 79–80, 88, 121n1, 128, 131–6, 137, 138, 143, 145, 146, 151, 161, 174, 181–2
see also rights and obligations, labelling/typing of clients, role

client literacy, *see* institutional literacy
client types 87, 95, 117–20, 123, 127, 136–7, 147, 151, 161, 168, 182–3
bureaucratic client 109
hopping client 91
naive client 120, 123, 125, 144, 177, 183
professional client 109, 122n8, 117, 119–20, 123, 151, 183
warrior client 119–20, 165, 168, 173, 183
communication divide, *see* asymmetry
Community Charge, *see* practices in institutional domains (local taxation)
confrontation 13, 84, 87
consumer culture 187, 188
see also discourse type (citizen charter)
consumer logic in the private economy 10–11, 78, 174
consumer movement 8, 157
consumerism and the marketisation of the public sphere 20, 26, 33, 34n3, 34n4, 137–41, 183
conventions of discourse 26, 34, 37, 59, 60n7, 64
visual 27
conversation 16n5, 19, 24
analysis of 12, 46, 59n2
colonising capacities of 34
see also chat, address (conversational address)
conversational practice 39, 43–4, 51–2, 61, 63, 68
conversationalisation 33
cooperation 13, 29, 46–7, 49, 53, 61, 178
as an archetype 59

236 *INDEX OF TERMS*

tactical cooperation 120, 130
 see also client types
  (professional clients)
 reciprocal guarantees of 143–4
 see also ideology (ideology of
  cooperation), client types
  (naive clients)
cooperative principle, *see*
 cooperation
counselling 30, 65, 67–8, 97, 114,
 144–5, 178n1, 180n16, 184
counselling institutions 153–69
 see also practices in
  institutional domains
  (mediators)
critical linguistics 11–13, 14,
 16n9, 45, 46
cross-examination 3, 40, 58
 see also discourse types
  (interrogation)
cultural capital 183, 37
 see also institutional literacy
cultural values
 and information exchange 189
 capitalist 2
 see also rationality, protestant
  ethic, consumer culture,
  promotional culture,
  reflexivity

debureaucratisation 19–21,
 21–3, 31–3, 33–4, 36, 52
 see also bureaucratisation,
  marketisation of the public
  sphere, counselling, consumer
  culture, conversationalisation
demodalisation 8, 16n7
disciplinary measures 70, 83–5,
 113, 123–7, 144
discipline 5, 58–9
discourse
 conflict model of 12, 82, 86n5
 consensus model of 82

critical analysis of 10–12, 16n9
 see also critical linguistics
definitions of 12
discourse and social change 6,
 8–9, 10–11, 13, 14, 15,
 19–21, 21–3, 26, 27, 30,
 33–4, 115, 168, 189n2
 see also
  conversationalisation,
  consumer culture,
  marketisation of the public
  sphere, expert systems,
  promotional culture
discourse practices
 commodification of discourse
  practices 138
 constitutive properties of 12,
  29–30, 36, 80, 181
 see also bureaucracy (as a
  (social and discursive) process)
discourse type 36, 86n4
 see also genre, modes of talk
discourse types
 advice to committee 154–5
 advisory booklet 146
 appeal 14, 15, 18, 145,
  153–69, 179n4, 188
 appeal draft 159–69, 179n7,
  179n8, 184–6, 188, 215–24
 appeal hearing 179n6
 appeal notes 209
 application 14, 17–18, 43,
  139, 147, 153, 188
 application for grant 7, 36
 application for visa 47–8
 birth certificate 7
 circular 93–4, 127
 citizen charter 20, 141–4,
  180n17, 186
 complaint 143–4, 145
 credit agreement 7
 discussing an application form
  148–53

INDEX OF TERMS 237

forms
application form 4, 9, 14,
18, 21, 27, 41, 42,
127–30, 131–6, 137,
145n2, 146, 183, 208
complaint form 36
holiday leave form 42, 59n1
immigration card 52–3
medical form 7
offenders form 124–5, 126–7
registration form 30–1, 33,
202
tax form 7
guidance notes 23–6
hoarding poster 21–3, 26–9,
33, 95
interrogation 39, 42, 43–5,
49–52, 78, 121n2
interview
by decision-makers 154
media interview 81–2
research and internal review
interview 64–6, 67–8,
79–80, 131–6
invitation for interrogation 69,
121n2
leaflet 7, 9–10, 14, 18, 21, 27,
30–4, 95, 121n1, 123, 127,
137–45, 146, 153, 156–7,
177, 179n5, 183, 189n2,
200–1, 210–14
letter
of advice 72, 155
of complaint 71–9, 93–5, 204
of debt 170–1
standard letter 18, 72, 76–8,
95, 97, 121n1, 121n4,
173–5, 176, 205–6
mail order catalogue 138
medical consultation 16n8, 46
memorandum 70–1, 82–5,
86n6
newspaper column 162

notes taken over telephone
157–9
notice of overdraft 95–8
off-the-record revelation 60n10
on-record declaration 4, 48,
172
personnel profile 21, 23–6, 29,
33, 34n3, 187, 197–9
public notices 7, 125
questionnaire 131–2
reports
audit report 10–11, 187
financial report 16n7
medical report 16n8
report of progress 21
reporting missing items 49,
52
rules and regulations 7
service encounters 16n8
small print 8, 22, 27, 30, 31,
43, 58, 98
specification of visa
entitlement 55–6, 61
talk at client's home 68–70,
91–3, 121n2, 121n3, 207
talk at the service desk 18–19,
37, 39–41, 47–8, 49–52,
60n5, 62–4, 67–8, 88–90,
124–5, 148–53
telephone conversation 37, 49,
52, 55–6, 61, 98, 121n6,
161, 171
travel documents 171,
180n12, 180n13
work diary 21
written correspondence 9, 14,
18, 53–5, 57, 60n9, 71–9,
93–5, 95–117, 121n7, 121n8,
121n9, 157, 169–77,
180n18, 203–6, 226–7
written gloss of events by
participant 121n5, 184–5,
189, 227–9

238　*INDEX OF TERMS*

written response to analysis
121n5, 229–30
written response to appeal
draft 159–69, 179n7,
179n8, 224–5

eligibility 3, 6, 58, 61, 88, 89,
114, 127, 128, 131–5, 138,
140–1, 143, 145n2, 178, 183
emancipation of the self 184
see also client empowerment
evidence 6, 23–6, 44–5, 90,
105–10, 111, 114, 119, 127,
135, 162, 172, 173, 183, 184–5
expert systems 183–4

face 14, 46, 87–8, 96–120, 121n1
conflicting face demands 100,
108
face-threatening acts 48, 51,
92–3, 97, 100, 108, 118,
145, 165, 168, 185
face damage/loss 74, 102, 105,
110, 119, 168, 188, 190n4
face redress 57, 113, 116, 118,
130, 176
reciprocating face redress 117
face repair/restoration 51, 74,
98, 99, 100, 105, 108–9, 185
face saving 94, 97, 98, 114
face wants 87–8, 92–3, 97, 98,
110
negative and positive face 88
of third parties 88, 97–8, 101,
108
recognising the face wants of
clients 88, 108, 114
see also address ((im)personal
address,
indiscriminate/individual
address)
safeguarding face 104, 137,
147

fairness/equity 2–3, 4, 42, 57,
120, 140, 185
formulation 49, 84, 85, 88, 128,
129, 150–2, 154
frame of reference
(clients/institutions) 16n5, 38,
43, 87, 90, 117, 168, 182

gatekeeping 37
genre 28, 33–4, 60n7, 86n3
see also modes of talk,
discourse type
genre analysis 12

habitus 183
hegemony 20

ideological investment 12
ideology
and power 12, 46
conflicting middle-class
ideologies 169
naturalisation of 13
of accountability to the
consumer 33
of cooperation 144
political ideology 189n1
illiteracy, *see* institutional literacy
implicature 45, 47
implicit assumptions underlying
information exchange 13, 14,
38, 41, 44, 46–9, 55, 59n3, 78,
87, 93, 100, 113, 130, 139,
155–6, 159, 167, 185
see also information
exchange (principles of),
client identity construction
implied client 131–41
indirectness 46, 63, 117
inference 51, 52, 105, 165
information exchange 9, 13,
17–18, 36–8, 83, 87, 95, 143,
145, 146, 147, 181–2, 189

INDEX OF TERMS   239

as a relational entity 189
client failure/refusal to supply
   31–2
control of 32, 45, 51, 57–9,
   139, 143–4, 145, 168, 178
institution seeking/client
   supplying 30–2, 36–8, 38–45,
   45–53, 57–9, 63–4, 87, 103–4,
   114, 125, 127, 129–30,
   131–6, 139, 152, 165, 188
institution supplying/client
   seeking 21, 30, 34, 34n5,
   36–8, 53–7, 57–9, 60n7,
   60n9, 89–90, 91, 93, 94–5,
   103, 104, 107, 109, 117,
   119, 122n8, 123, 127, 129,
   136–9, 153, 157, 176, 178,
   179n3, 187, 189n2
institutional failure/refusal to
   supply 53–7, 58, 97, 109
open flow of information 137,
   189n2
   see also accessibility
overflow of information 188
principles of (e.g. tactical
   insincerity, being generous
   with information, providing
   relevant information,
   withholding information,
   etc.) 13, 45–53, 59, 60n5,
   88, 143, 145n2, 152, 160,
   168, 176, 178
processing of information 25,
   36, 100, 107, 127, 128, 130,
   134–5, 145n2, 151, 182
threshold of institutional
   information supply 182
institutional decision-making 2,
   3, 4, 6, 9–10, 14, 15n1, 18, 19,
   24, 36, 37–8, 42, 50, 51–2, 57,
   68, 79, 89, 117, 120, 128–9,
   130, 134–5, 136, 139, 140,
   144, 152–3, 154–5, 156, 161,

163, 165, 167–9, 178, 179n5,
   179n9, 182
institutional literacy 9, 123, 133,
   135, 136, 139–40, 146–7,
   156–7, 161, 163, 178
interpretation of discourse
   practices 12, 14, 82

jargon 7, 8, 12

keywords of culture 2–3

labelling/typing of clients 3–4, 6,
   9, 10, 41, 42–3, 65–6, 79–80,
   123, 125, 127, 129, 130, 174
   see also client identity
      construction, client types,
      role, implied client
language games 37
lifeworld voices 59, 89–90,
   134–5, 156–7
   see also conversation, chat,
      asymmetry

marketisation of the public sphere
   33, 34n3, 141, 183, 190n5
   see also consumer culture
mediation 15, 81, 145, 146–80,
   184
   see also practices in institutional
      domains (mediators)
modernity, see capitalism, late
   capitalism
modes of talk 10, 19, 30, 33,
   61, 62–6, 71, 79, 80, 86n3,
   86n4

New Right 20–1, 141
non-cooperation 60n10, 79–80,
   116–17

objectivity 2, 3, 15n1, 17, 24,
   130, 131, 169

240 INDEX OF TERMS

officialese 8
orders of discourse 12, 33, 36–7

plain language campaign, *see*
  accessible language use,
  user-friendly documents
politeness 46
  accusation of impoliteness 92–3
  politeness strategies 31, 88, 90
  see also face (face redress)
Poll Tax, *see* practices in
  institutional domains (taxation,
  local tax)
postmodernity, *see* late capitalism
power
  absolute power 126
  consumer power 138
  distribution of 12, 20, 33, 61,
    65, 68, 80, 109, 130, 167–8
    see also asymmetry
  in the modern state 3, 4–6, 58,
    188–9
  political power 20–1
  productive power 4–5
  situtational power 96, 114, 129
  struggle for 82
  techniques of modern power 58
  see also ideology (and power)
practices in institutional domains
  banking 1, 3, 6, 10, 62–4,
    67–8, 71–4 78–9, 95–117,
    136, 140–1, 180n16, 184–5,
    188, 227–30
  child nurseries 148–53
  contexts of immigration 21,
    29, 56–7
  customs and immigration
    points 49–53, 60n5,
    169–77, 179n10, 180n11
  education 1, 3
  educational inspection 81–2
  embassies 37, 43, 47–8, 55–7,
    60n10, 61

employment in higher
  education 21, 23–6, 29, 33,
    34n2, 34n3, 42, 57, 59n1,
    70–1, 82–5, 86n6, 187, 197–9
higher education 34n3, 36
insurance 134, 138–9
legal settings 178n1, 179n3
libraries 124–7
local education 119, 153–69,
  179nn4–9, 184–6, 188,
  215–25
media 20, 21, 81–2
mediators
  Advisory Centre for
    Education 15, 131–6, 147,
    153–70, 172, 178, 180n11,
    180n14, 186, 224–5
  Citizens Advice Bureau 147,
    153, 179n3
  export agencies 179n10
  private courier agencies 147,
    170–8, 180n14, 180n15,
    180n16, 226–7
  social work 15, 62, 64–6,
    67–8, 79–80, 146–7,
    148–53, 178n1
medical institutions 3, 16n8,
  46, 178n1
public housing 88–90, 93–5,
  121n4, 148, 179n3
public transport 125
post 10–11, 95–117, 121n6,
  121n7, 122n8, 122n9,
  184–5, 187, 227–30
police 39, 42, 43–5, 49,
  68–70, 78, 91–3, 121n2,
  121n3, 207
private companies 2–3, 6
social security
  (un)employment 3–4, 6, 21,
    37
  family income supplement
    39–41, 133–5, 136–41,

INDEX OF TERMS 241

145n2, 153, 189n2, 208–9, 210–14
incapacity benefit 131–2
private social security schemes 140–1
social welfare 1, 10, 21, 29, 137, 179n3, 183
state institutions 2–3
supermarkets 11
taxation 1, 6, 9, 19, 29
  income tax 64, 140, 141–4, 186
  local tax 30–4, 34–5n6, 58, 140, 200–2
  television licensing 53–5, 60n8, 60n9, 71, 74–9, 93–5, 203–6
  vehicle licensing 4, 21–3, 26–9, 33–4, 37, 95
pragmatics 12, 13–14, 45–6, 59, 59n3, 62, 66, 86n1, 181, 189
pre-formulation, *see* formulation
private and public lifeworlds and systems 19–20, 136–41, 188, 190n5
privatisation 21, 141, 183
promotional culture 187–8
promotional practices 10–11, 33, 35n8, 187–9
  promoting choice 138, 186, 187
  promoting accessibility 33
  self-promotion 29, 187–8
  self-promotion and face wants 188, 190n4
  see also advertising
protestant ethic 2
public watchdog 94

rationality 2–3, 9, 19, 42, 84, 183
  and counselling 184
  and information exchange 36, 130, 135, 168

and moral values 184–5
and reflexivity 190n3
parody of 15n3
strategic and communicative rationality 15n2
reflexivity 184
  see also rationality and reflexivity
reformulation, *see* formulation
register 16n6, 86n3
rights and obligations 4, 21, 33, 34n5, 94, 124, 143, 147, 185
  discoursal rights and obligations 37, 51, 58, 59n3, 61, 78, 84, 94
role 14, 62, 86n1
  commitment to role, *see* role interpretation and perception
  conventional role theory 86n5
  discourse role 14, 62, 66–71, 86n1
    in relation to social role 67
    categories (author, overhearer, bystander, mouthpiece and spokesperson) 60, 68–71, 84, 91, 97, 165
  role assignment 71, 79, 93, 148, 170, 171–2, 174, 180n11
  role barriers 10
  role configurations and modes of talk 10, 30, 61–6, 95, 97, 148
    see also social subject (dispersed social subject)
  role distancing, *see* role interpretation and perception
  role interpretation and perception 64–6, 80–2, 83–5, 86n5, 87, 120, 135
  role-less self, *see* social subject (essentialist social subject)

242 *INDEX OF TERMS*

role mandate 68, 70, 162, 171
role relationships 24, 61, 87,
95, 110, 123, 164, 187
role reversal 38, 53, 151
role slippage 80
social roles in discourse 86n3
and the construction of social
identity 71–80
see also information exchange

self-assessment 132
self-censorship 167
self-discipline 4
see also discipline
self-reflexivity, *see* reflexivity
side-stepping 92, 150, 151, 152
social control 1, 4–6, 9, 16n4,
20, 24, 29, 31–3, 38, 57–9, 62,
80, 127, 143–4, 146, 168,
177–8, 188
in the private economy 140

quality control 26
social order 2, 36
social pragmatics 45, 62, 188–9
social problems 5, 34
social subject
dispersed social subject 14, 80
unified/essentialist social
subject 80, 86n5
socio-economic interests 2, 33,
55, 58–9, 63, 82, 117, 147,
172, 173, 174
sociolinguistics 12
speech acts 13, 45, 47, 59n3, 66,
71, 84, 86n4, 90
surveillance *see* power (in the
modern state)

unequal encounter 61
user-friendly documents 8–9, 22,
27, 32, 146, 183